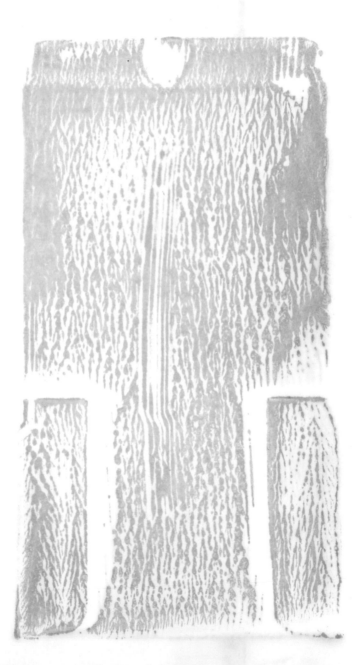

THERMOCHEMICAL KINETICS

THERMOCHEMICAL KINETICS

Methods for the Estimation of
Thermochemical Data and Rate Parameters

SIDNEY W. BENSON

Chairman, Department of Thermochemistry
and Chemical Kinetics
Stanford Research Institute
Menlo Park, California

JOHN WILEY & SONS, INC., NEW YORK · LONDON · SYDNEY

Library of Congress Catalog Card Number: 68-21177
GB 471 06780 6
Printed in the United States of America

*This book is dedicated to Natasha, Nicky, Jeannette,
and our furry but faithful friend Tara Lee*

Preface

Over the last decade a number of relatively facile methods for the rapid and quantitative estimation of both thermochemical data and kinetic parameters for gas phase reactions have been developed in my laboratories. They have now reached the stage in which they provide a very useful tool for the critical analysis of relatively complex chemical reaction systems. This book is a systematic presentation of these methods with examples of their application. It is assumed that the reader is familiar with the elementary application of thermodynamics to chemical equilibria (ideal gases) and that he is also familiar with the basic ideas of chemical kinetics.

Chapter I reviews some of the relations between kinetic and thermochemical parameters, whereas in Chapter 2 methods are outlined for estimating entropies, heats of formation, and molar heat capacities of gas phase molecules and radicals over the range 300–1500°K. This includes some fairly complex organic structures, such as polycyclic rings. Chapter 3 explores systematically the current data on gas phase reactions and shows how their Arrhenius parameters can be fitted, with the aid of some simple rules, into the framework of transition state theory. Examples are given of the methods of estimation of activation energies and A-factors for some of these reactions. Chapter 4 discusses the applications of the methods to complex reaction systems, including chain pyrolyses, telomerizations, and the oxidation of organic compounds. Useful thermochemical data are contained in the appendix.

The close relation between thermochemical properties and kinetic parameters which is involved in the theory and methods discussed in the present volume has inspired the somewhat unusual title "Thermochemical Kinetics."

I have omitted the very important areas of condensed phase reactions because the methods for their treatment have not reached the same stage of advancement as they have for the gas phase reactions. This is by no means a necessary condition, and I hope that this book will provide the incentive for some hardy souls to extend the gas phase methods to condensed phases. All current indications are favorable in the outcome.

Much of the material in this book has formed the basis for the Kinetic Workshops, held during the last two summers at Stanford University. I am indebted to members of the Workshop, as well as to my own students and colleagues for interesting and helpful discussions on many of the reactions discussed here. In particular, I should like to thank Dr. David M. Golden, Dr. Gilbert Haugen, Dr. Frank Cruickshank, Professor Alan S. Rodgers, Dr. Robert Shaw, Dr. G. Neil Spokes, and Professor H. E. O'Neal for their friendly suggestions and criticisms. I also wish to express my appreciation to Mrs. Elaine Adkins for her unflagging efforts in typing and copying the seemingly endless versions of the manuscript.

Sidney W. Benson

Menlo Park, California
March 1968

Contents

x   Contents

I

Thermodynamic Equilibria and Rates of Reaction

1.1 THERMODYNAMICS AND KINETICS

The second law of thermodynamics tells us that every closed, isolated system will approach an "equilibrium" state in which its properties are independent of time. If we know the enthalpies, entropies, and equations of state of the chemical species involved, we can predict with accuracy the chemical composition of this final equilibrium state. However, thermodynamics is unable to say anything about the time required to attain equilibrium, or about the behavior, or about the composition of the system during the period of change. These latter problems are the province of chemical kinetics, which is directly concerned with the description of chemical systems the properties of which are varying with time.

At first glance there appears to be very little in the way of a close relation between kinetics and thermodynamics. This turns out, however, not to be a correct conclusion. As we try to show in the present book, thermodynamics, or more explicitly, the thermochemical properties of substances, place a strong quantitative constraint on the kinetic parameters that are used to describe time-varying systems. The reason for this is that a "true" state of equilibrium is a dynamic state in which, on the molecular level, chemical changes are still occurring. The apparent macroscopic constancy of the composition and properties of the system arises from the fact that at equilibrium, for any given species M_j, its rate of production is precisely equal to its rate of destruction. Hence $d(M_j)/dt = 0$.

Note that for each independent, stoichiometric chemical equation that we can write for a system, all species in the equation are related to each other

1

by the stoichiometric coefficients. If, for example, one such equation is

$$aA + bB + \cdots \underset{-1}{\overset{1}{\rightleftharpoons}} pP + qQ + \cdots, \tag{1.1}$$

$$\frac{1}{p}\left[\frac{d(P)}{dt}\right] = \frac{1}{q}\left[\frac{d(Q)}{dt}\right] = \cdots = -\frac{1}{a}\left[\frac{d(A)}{dt}\right] = -\frac{1}{b}\left[\frac{d(B)}{dt}\right] \equiv R_1. \tag{1.2}$$

In this book we use the definition of R as a generalized, specific, molar rate of reaction for (1.1).

The stoichiometric relation between reactants and products means that there is one and only one independent kinetic equation per stoichiometric equation, which is needed to specify the equilibrium state. For simplicity, we can describe this by the statement $R = 0$. During the approach to equilibrium $R \neq 0$.

In general R will be some function of the external variables, such as volume, temperature, electric, magnetic, or gravitational fields, etc., and also of the chemical composition of the system. Hence the statement that at equilibrium, $R_1(V, T, A, B, P, Q,$ etc.$) = 0$ implies a relation between these quantities. However, thermodynamics gives us another relation between these quantities in the form of the equilibrium constant K_1. This in turn must imply a quantitative relation between the equilibrium constant K_1 and the rate parameters that appear in the equation $R_1 = 0$. In the exceptional case that the rate law describing (1.1) takes on a very simple mass law form in terms of forward and reverse specific rate constants k_1 and k_{-1} the relation becomes

$$K_1 = \frac{k_1}{k_{-1}}. \tag{1.3}$$

This tells us that, of the three quantities k_1, k_{-1}, and K_1, only two are independent. A detailed knowledge of any two of them completely specifies the third, via (1.3). In general, equilibrium data are more readily available than kinetic data; so we make most frequent use of this last equation to relate forward and reverse rate constants where only one is known.

1.2   IDEAL GAS PHASE REACTIONS

The concept of a molecule takes on a relatively unambiguous meaning only in the case of a dilute gas where individual molecules spend long periods of time isolated from each other relative to the time that they spend in a state of collision. The collision state itself needs more precise definition, and we describe it for a pair of molecules j and k at that state in which the energy of their interaction $|E_{jk}| \geq kT$.

The definition stated above is, of course, a completely arbitrary, but extremely useful, one, with some surprising consequences. The most obvious is that at absolute zero all molecules in a system are in a constant state of collision, and the concept of an individual molecule may either not be useful or need redefinition. Another consequence is that two ions at room temperature ($T \sim 300°K$) in a gas phase must be looked on as being in a state of collision at a distance of 550 Å because their coulombic interaction $E_{jk} = \epsilon^2/r_{jk} = RT = 600$ cal/mole when $r_{jk} = 550$ Å.

For the reasons given above we restrict our discussion to dilute, neutral gases in which molecular concepts take direct, simple application, and thermodynamic and kinetic parameters can be expressed in terms of simple molecular parameters. Experience shows that reactions in condensed phases between nonpolar or only slightly polar molecules do not differ greatly from gas phase reactions. However, ionic reactions in solvents of high dielectric constant have no parallel to gas phase reactions and are not considered.

1.3 DETAILED BALANCING

Quantum mechanics via the uncertainty principle places limits on our ability to describe a molecule precisely. In general a maximal description comprises a set of quantum numbers describing the electronic, translational, rotational, and internal vibrational states of the species. We may, if we wish, consider every such set of numbers as describing a distinct chemical entity.

In a dilute gas at equilibrium molecular collisions will tend to exchange energy between collision partners and hence produce changes in the quantum numbers of any given molecule. Such processes may be looked on as the simplest of chemical acts.

The principle of detailed balancing asserts that at equilibrium, the specific rate of every elementary collision process is exactly equal to the specific rate of its inverse, or reverse, process. The specific rate of an elementary collision process must be proportional to the number of collisions, which in turn is proportional to the product of the concentrations of colliding species. The coefficient of proportionality we call the specific reaction rate constant. Thus if we consider N_2 molecules in their ground ($v = 0$) vibrational state and consider the process of collisional excitation, we can describe it by the equation

$$N_2^{(0)} + M \underset{-1}{\overset{1}{\rightleftarrows}} N_2^{(1)} + M \tag{1.4}$$

where M represents any collision partner. At equilibrium

$$R_1 = \frac{d(N_2^{(1)})}{dt} = \frac{-d(N_2^{(0)})}{dt} = 0 = k_1(M)(N_2^{(0)}) - k_{-1}(M)(N_2^{(1)}), \tag{1.5}$$

or

$$\frac{(N_2^{(1)})}{(N_2^{(0)})} = \frac{k_1}{k_{-1}}. \tag{1.6}$$

However, this ratio is also given by the equilibrium relation

$$\frac{(N_2^{(1)})_{\text{eq.}}}{(N_2^{(0)})_{\text{eq.}}} = K_1 = e^{-h\nu/kT} \tag{1.7}$$

where ν is the vibrational frequency of N_2. Hence

$$\frac{k_1}{k_{-1}} = K_1. \tag{1.8}$$

If the system contains many different gases M_i, each capable of transferring energy to N_2, we can write a similar set of kinetic equations for each one separately with the final result

$$\frac{k_1}{k_{-1}} = \frac{k_1'}{k_{-1}'} = \frac{k_1''}{k_{-1}''} = \cdots = K_1 \tag{1.9}$$

where k_1' and k_{-1}' refer to molecule M_1, etc.

If the process we are considering involves more of a chemical act, such as atom abstraction, we have a similar result. For example

$$H + Cl_2 \underset{-1}{\overset{1}{\rightleftarrows}} HCl + Cl \tag{1.10}$$

$$\frac{k_1}{k_{-1}} = K_1 = \frac{(HCl)_{\text{eq.}}(Cl)_{\text{eq.}}}{(Cl_2)_{\text{eq.}}(H)_{\text{eq.}}} \tag{1.11}$$

Although the results above appear satisfactory for equilibrium systems, we may question whether they still hold for a system not at equilibrium, specifically, for systems undergoing chemical reaction.

Note that the typical chemical rate constant, even for so elementary an act as vibrational excitation, is not a simple molecular constant but instead an average over all the equilibrium population of translational, rotational, and vibrational states of the colliding pair. It can readily be conceived that during the course of a chemical reaction, the populations of the various quantum states are different from that prevailing at true equilibrium. In such a situation the chemical rate constants may well change during the course of the reaction and thus be different from the equilibrium rate constants. What then happens to detailed balancing and to such relations as (1.8) and (1.9)?

One simple effect arises in chemical reactions that are appreciably endothermic or exothermic. An exothermic reaction liberates heat, which must escape from the reaction system by conduction and/or convection to the walls of the vessels, which themselves are in a thermostat. Because conduction and convection are measurably slow processes in gases, we will find that an exothermic reaction in a gas will give rise to a temperature increase in the reacting gas, which in turn will increase the reaction rate constant. Endothermic reactions similarly give rise to cooling effects.

The answers to difficulties raised by the foregoing are as follows. In most chemical systems, perturbations of the population of molecules among energy states are generally small and negligible. Under these conditions the specific reaction rate constants are the same as those at equilibrium, and the relation $K_1 = k_1/k_{-1}$ holds.[1]

In systems where the perturbations of the population are not small or negligible, the observed rate constants are different from the ones measured at equilibrium. Nevertheless the principle of detailed balancing applies to each elementary act. Thus if k_1' is the nonequilibrium, specific rate constant for elementary process 1 in a perturbed population and k_{-1}' is its inverse process,

$$\frac{k_1'}{k_{-1}'} = K_1 \qquad (1.12)$$

still holds with K_1 the true equilibrium constant.

Consider strong departures from equilibrium that occur in the dissociation of diatomic or small molecules. In such systems the nonequilibrium, perturbed rate constants still must yield the equilibrium ratio for forward and inverse processes. This is especially the case in complex chemical reactions, which may take place via the production of a series of unstable free radicals or atoms. Despite the appearance of such entities and the complex rate laws they give rise to, the inverse rate constants can still be deduced via the equilibrium relationship.

As an example, the rate law for the simple overall reaction of $H_2 + Br_2 \rightleftarrows 2HBr$ is given by

$$\frac{-d(Br_2)}{dt} = \frac{k_1(H_2)(Br_2)^{1/2}}{1 + k_2[(HBr)/(Br_2)]} . \qquad (1.13)$$

At higher temperatures, where the reverse reaction is important, the rate law of the reaction of H_2 and Br_2 must be of such a form that the rate $d(Br_2)/dt$ reduces to zero at equilibrium. This requires that we write, for the reverse reaction,[2]

$$\frac{-d(HBr)}{dt} = \frac{2k_{-1}(HBr)^2/(Br_2)^{1/2}}{1 + k_2[(HBr)/(Br_2)]} \qquad (1.14)$$

[1] Perturbations produced by temperature gradients must be treated explicitly by adding to the kinetic equations, the equations for heat conduction and convection. Similar perturbations in composition may occur and must also be treated by additional equations for diffusion of species.

[2] This is a "strong," not an absolute, requirement which rests on kinetic justification. For more details, see S. W. Benson, *Foundations of Chemical Kinetics*, McGraw-Hill, New York, 1960, Section IV.3.

with

$$K_1 = \frac{k_1}{k_{-1}} = \frac{(HBr)^2_{eq.}}{(H_2)_{eq.}(Br_2)_{eq.}}. \tag{1.15}$$

Under conditions where both forward and reverse reactions are appreciable, the correct rate law is

$$\frac{-d(Br_2)}{dt} = \frac{1}{2}\frac{d(HBr)}{dt} = R_1 = \frac{k_1(H_2)(Br_2)^{1/2}}{1 + k_2[(HBr)/(Br_2)]}\left\{1 - \frac{(HBr)^2}{K_1(H_2)(Br_2)}\right\}. \tag{1.16}$$

Catalysts may be looked upon as substances which perturb the populations of chemical intermediates. Rate constants in the presence of catalysts may, of course, be markedly changed from their "normal" values. Despite this, the ratios of forward and reverse processes must still yield the true equilibrium constant. This result is comprised in the familiar rule, "A catalyst may speed up the approach to equilibrium but cannot change the equilibrium point."

1.4   THERMOCHEMICAL QUANTITIES

In dilute gases the measured equilibrium constant K_1 is related to the standard free energy change ΔG_1° of a stoichiometric reaction by the relation

$$\Delta G_1^\circ = -RT \ln K_1$$
$$= -2.303RT \log K_1$$
$$= -\theta \log K_1 \tag{1.17}$$

where 2.303 reflects the change from natural base to decadic logarithms and $\theta = 2.303RT = 4.576T/1000$ kcal/mole is a computationally convenient way to measure temperature.[3]

By definition,

$$\Delta G_1^\circ \equiv \Delta H_1^\circ - T\,\Delta S_1^\circ \tag{1.18}$$

where ΔH_1° is the standard enthalpy change in the reaction and ΔS_1° is the standard entropy change, both at the reaction temperature. Now because ΔC_p°, the molar heat capacity change in a gas reaction, is generally small, ΔH_1° and ΔS_1° may be assumed constant over any small range in temperature ($\Delta T \leq 100°K$), whereupon (1.17) yields the familiar van't Hoff relation for the variation of equilibrium constant with temperature:

$$2.303 \log K_1 = \frac{-\Delta H_1^\circ}{RT} + \frac{\Delta S_1^\circ}{R} \tag{1.19}$$

with ΔH_1° and ΔS_1° considered constant.

[3] At $1000°K$, $\theta \sim 4.6$ kcal/mole and at $500°K$, $\theta \sim 2.3$ kcal/mole. For every 4.6 kcal/mole change in ΔG_1°, K_1 changes by a factor of 10 at $1000°K$ and a factor of $10^2 = 100$ at $500°K$.

One of the most precise methods for obtaining ΔG_1° is by the direct measurement of K_1. If we can measure the equilibrium concentration of reactants and products, K_1 can be obtained directly, and the error in ΔG_1° is simply related to the error in the measure of K_1. If K_1 is measured to $\pm 10\%$, the resultant error in ΔG_1° is $\pm 0.1(RT)$, or at $500°K$, ± 0.10 kcal/mole. The alternative method for obtaining ΔG_1° from known values of ΔH_1° and ΔS_1° is generally subject to uncertainties at least tenfold larger, for ΔH_1° is seldom known or measurable to better than ± 0.5 kcal/mole; likewise ΔS_1° is not usually known to better than ± 1 gibbs/mole.

The most reliable method for obtaining ΔH_1° and ΔS_1° is from the van't Hoff relation. From (1.19) we can eliminate ΔS_1° by taking values of K_1 at two different temperatures T_1 and T_2. Then we find, on solving for ΔH_1°,

$$-\Delta H_1^\circ = R\,\frac{T_1 T_2}{\Delta T_{12}}\ln\frac{K_{1(1)}}{K_{1(2)}}$$

$$= R\,\frac{T_m^2}{\Delta T}\ln\frac{K_{1(1)}}{K_{1(2)}} \tag{1.20}$$

where $T_m{}^2 = (T_1 T_2)$ and $\Delta T = \Delta T_{12} = T_2 - T_1$. If we can measure K_1 over a sufficiently long temperature interval so that it changes by at least a factor of e (~ 2.72), independent errors of $\pm 10\%$ in K_1 at each end of this interval will yield ΔH_1° with an uncertainty of about $\sqrt{2} \times 0.10 \times RT_m \times (T_m/\Delta T)$ where T_m is the mean temperature in the range ΔT. At $T_m = 500°K$ with $\Delta T \sim 100°K$, this becomes ± 0.70 kcal/mole. Precision of $\pm 3\%$ in K_1 will reduce this uncertainty proportionately to ± 0.2 kcal/mole.

Such precision as that achieved in the measurements above will yield average values of ΔH_1° and consequently ΔS_1° over the temperature range. It is not possible to measure changes in ΔH_1° and ΔS_1° in this range or equivalently $\langle \Delta C_p^\circ \rangle$ over the range to better than ± 7 gibbs/mole ($\pm 10\%$ in K_1) or ± 2 gibbs/mole ($\pm 3\%$ in K_1). The related uncertainties in ΔS_1° become the vector sums of the uncertainties in ΔG_1° and ΔH_1° or at $500°K$, ± 1.4 gibbs/mole ($\pm 10\%$ in K_1) and ± 0.44 gibbs/mole ($\pm 3\%$ in K_1) respectively.

Frequently it is possible to estimate ΔS_1° to an uncertainty of better than ± 1 gibbs/mole. Under these conditions a single measurement of K_1 to within a precision of even $\pm 20\%$ (± 0.2 kcal at $500°K$) yields values of ΔH_1° with an uncertainty of only ± 0.55 kcal/mole, which is considerably better than that obtained from the van't Hoff relation. This method is referred to as the "third law method" and is of great utility because of the readiness with which ΔS_1° values can be frequently estimated.

As we see in Chapter 2 it is generally the case that ΔC_p° can be estimated to within ± 1 gibbs/mole over the temperature range 300 to $1500°K$. This makes it possible to extrapolate ΔG_1°, ΔS_1°, and ΔH_1° values from any given temperature to any other temperature within this range with relatively little additional uncertainty.

1.5   STANDARD STATES

The thermochemical quantities K, ΔG°, ΔH_f°, S°, and C_p° are generally tabulated for standard states of 1 atmosphere and ideal gas. We frequently want to transform these to standard states expressed in concentration units, generally 1 mole/liter (1 M). For a stoichiometric reaction

$$aA + bB + \cdots \rightleftarrows pP + qQ + \cdots \tag{1.21}$$

the relation between equilibrium constants is

$$K_p = K_c(RT)^{\Delta n} \tag{1.22}$$

with K_p in pressure units, K_c in concentration units, and where Δn is the mole change in the reaction as written

$$\Delta n = (p + q + \cdots) - (a + b + \cdots). \tag{1.23}$$

The relation given above comes from the ideal gas law, which relates pressure (P) and concentration (c)

$$P = cRT. \tag{1.24}$$

For reactions in which the mole change of gases is not zero ($\Delta n \neq 0$) this transformation introduces additional corrections into the effective heat of reaction and entropy change.

By definition, the heat of reaction is given by

$$\Delta H_p^\circ = RT^2\left(\frac{\partial \ln K_p}{\partial T}\right)_{\text{eq.}}, \tag{1.25}$$

and from (1.22) this becomes

$$\Delta H_p^\circ = RT^2\left(\frac{\partial \ln K_c}{\partial T}\right)_{\text{eq.}} + \Delta nRT = \Delta H_c^\circ + \Delta nRT. \tag{1.26}$$

Thus for an increase in gas moles $\Delta n > 0$, $\Delta H_p^\circ > \Delta H_c^\circ$, whereas the converse is true for $\Delta n < 0$.

If we now represent K_c in the van't Hoff form

$$-RT \ln K_c = \Delta H_c^\circ - T \Delta S_c^\circ, \tag{1.27}$$

the solution for ΔS_c°, using (1.26), (1.22), and (1.17) gives[4]

$$\Delta S_c^\circ = R \ln K_c + \frac{\Delta H_c^\circ}{T}$$

$$= R \ln K_p - \Delta n R \ln (RT) + \frac{\Delta H_p^\circ}{T} - R \Delta n$$

$$= \Delta S_p^\circ - R \Delta n - \Delta n R \ln (RT). \tag{1.28}$$

Note that ΔH_c° (1.26) corresponds to our usual definition of ΔE_c°, the change in internal energy for the reaction, and (1.17) involves the change from Gibbs to Helmholtz free energy functions $[\Delta G^\circ = \Delta A^\circ + \Delta(PV)]$. However, ΔS_c° and ΔS_p° differ from the expected correction by a term $R \Delta n$, which comes uniquely from the mole change in the reaction and could not be deduced from the entropy changes in standard states alone. This has been a frequent source of confusion in the literature.

EXAMPLE

In the reaction $N_2O_4 \rightleftarrows 2NO_2$, $\Delta H_{300}^\circ = 13.9$ kcal/mole and $\Delta S_{300}^\circ = 42.3$ gibbs/mole. Write the equilibrium constant K_c in van't Hoff form and calculate its value at 400°K. From the preceding, with $\Delta n = 1$,

$$\Delta H_c = \Delta H_p - RT \qquad\qquad = 13.3 \text{ kcal/mole,}$$
$$\Delta S_c = \Delta S_p - R - R \ln (RT) = 33.9 \text{ gibbs/mole.}$$

Hence

$$2.303 \log K_c = -\frac{6650}{T} + 16.95.$$

EXAMPLE

The equilibrium constant for the formation of N_2O_5 from NO_2 and O_2 via

$$\tfrac{1}{2}O_2 + 2NO_2 \rightleftarrows N_2O_5$$

is expressed in van't Hoff form (1 mole/liter: standard state) as

$$\log K_c = \frac{2670}{T} - 9.55.$$

Calculate ΔH_p° and ΔS_p° from this expression. In this case $\Delta n = -1.5$. Hence

$$\Delta S_p^\circ = \Delta S_c^\circ + R \Delta n + \Delta n \ln (RT) = -43.7 - 1.5 (2 + \ln RT);$$
$$\Delta H_p^\circ = \Delta H_c^\circ + \Delta n (RT) \qquad\qquad = -12.2 + 1.5 RT.$$

Picking $T = 300°$K as a mean temperature, these become

$$\Delta S_p^\circ = -56.3 \text{ gibbs/mole;}$$
$$\Delta H_p^\circ = -13.1 \text{ kcal/mole.}$$

[4] In the logarithmic term R should be expressed in liter-atm. units, i.e., 0.082 liter-atm/mole-°K.

1.6   ARRHENIUS PARAMETERS

The great majority of chemical reaction rate constants lend themselves readily to expression in Arrhenius form:

$$k = Ae^{-E/RT} = A \times 10^{-E/\theta} \tag{1.29}$$

where again $\theta = 2.303RT$ kcal/mole. Experimentally it is found that A and E are constant over a small temperature range ($\sim 100°$K). Even over very large temperature ranges ($500°$K) it is found that A and E do not change very much with temperature.

By virtue of the equilibrium relation between forward and reverse rate constants we can make a very direct relation between Arrhenius parameters and thermochemical quantities. For the reaction stoichiometry

$$aA + bB + \cdots \underset{-1}{\overset{1}{\rightleftarrows}} pP + qQ + \cdots \tag{1.30}$$

$$K = \frac{k_1}{k_{-1}} = \frac{A_1 e^{-E_1/RT}}{A_{-1} e^{-E_{-1}/RT}} = \left(\frac{A_1}{A_{-1}}\right) e^{-(E_1 - E_{-1})/RT}. \tag{1.31}$$

Hence because $K_1 = e^{\Delta S_1^\circ/R - \Delta H_1^\circ/RT}$, we can write

$$R \ln \left(\frac{A_1}{A_{-1}}\right) = 2.303R \log \left(\frac{A_1}{A_{-1}}\right) = \Delta S_1^\circ \tag{1.32}$$

and

$$\Delta H_1^\circ = E_1 - E_{-1}. \tag{1.33}$$

When there is no mole change in the reaction, ΔS_1° and ΔH_1° are both unaffected by changes in standard states. Because the forward and reverse rates have the same order, the Arrhenius parameters are all changed by identical amounts. When $\Delta n \neq 0$, the Arrhenius parameters for forward and reverse reactions are changed by different amounts.

The activation energy of a chemical reaction rate is defined by the relation

$$E \equiv RT^2 \left(\frac{\partial \ln k}{\partial T}\right). \tag{1.34}$$

When E is a constant, or nearly constant over a small temperature range, the direct integration of (1.34) leads to the Arrhenius equation (1.29) with A the constant of integration. By its definition, E will have the same units as RT, kcal/mole. The A factor will have the same units as k.

For a reaction of the mth overall order, the specific rate is given by $k(C)^m$ where (C) is the concentration of active species. Hence k will have dimensions of time^{-1} × concentration$^{(1-m)}$ because the specific rate will have dimensions of moles/liter-sec. This will then also be the dimensions of A.

For a first-order reaction, A has dimensions of time^{-1} and is independent of standard states or units used to measure concentrations. For an mth-order reaction, however, A will depend on the units used to measure concentration, be it in moles/liter or partial pressures.

The ideal gas relationship $(P = cRT)$ between concentration and pressure units for expression of k leads to the following for an mth-order rate constant:

$$k_c = k_p(RT)^{m-1}. \tag{1.35}$$

Hence for the Arrhenius parameters,

$$E_c \equiv RT^2\left(\frac{\partial \ln k_c}{\partial T}\right)$$

$$= RT^2\left(\frac{\partial \ln k_p}{\partial T}\right) + (m-1)RT$$

$$= E_p + (m-1)RT; \tag{1.36}$$

$$A_c = k_c e^{E_c/RT}$$

$$= k_p(RT)^{m-1}e^{[E_p+(m-1)RT]/RT}$$

$$= A_p(RT)^{m-1}e^{(m-1)}. \tag{1.37}$$

It is more usual to measure rates in concentration units, so that, inverting the relations above, we have

$$E_p = E_c - (m-1)RT;$$
$$\ln A_p = \ln A_c - (m-1)\ln(RT) - (m-1). \tag{1.38}$$

Note the formal relations between the transformations of Arrhenius parameters and the corresponding thermochemical quantities [(1.26) and (1.28)].

EXAMPLE

The reaction $2NO + Cl_2 \rightarrow 2NOCl$ is found to be given by a third-order rate law with a specific reaction rate constant k the Arrhenius parameters of which are given by

$$\log k = \frac{-803}{T} + 3.66.$$

The units of A are liter^2/mole^2-sec^{-1}. Calculate the parameters in units of torr^{-2}-sec^{-1}. Use 400°K as the mean reaction temperature. We first note that $(m-1) = 2$.
From the preceding

$$E_p = E_c - 2RT = 3.7 - 1.6$$
$$= 2.1 \text{ kcal/mole};$$
$$A_p = A_c(760RT)^{-2}e^{-2} \text{ torr}^{-2}\text{-sec}^{-1}$$
$$= 10^{3.66}(10^{-8.66})$$
$$= 10^{-5.00} \text{ torr}^{-2}\text{-sec}^{-1}.$$

EXAMPLE

The early stages of the reaction of $H_2 + Br_2 \rightarrow 2HBr$ are described by a $\frac{3}{2}$ order rate; $R = k(H_2)(Br_2)^{1/2}$ with k, in atmosphere units, given by

$$\log k = -41.6/\theta + 11.36.$$

Calculate at 700°K the Arrhenius parameters in molar units. In this case $(m - 1) = \frac{1}{2}$, and we have

$$A_c = A_p(eRT)^{+1/2} = 10^{12.50} \text{ (liter/mole)}^{1/2} \text{sec}^{-1};$$

$$E_c = E_p + \tfrac{1}{2}RT = 42.3 \text{ kcal/mole}.$$

1.7 MODIFIED ARRHENIUS EQUATION

Although the bulk of gas phase rate constants are expressible in simple Arrhenius form, a small group of them are not. This occurs in the case of termolecular recombinations of atoms or of atoms with diatomic molecules:

$$O + O + M \rightarrow O_2 + M;$$

$$O + NO + M \rightarrow NO_2 + M.$$

In the experimental cases given above, we may find it necessary to express the rate constants in the form of a modified Arrhenius equation in which we introduce a simple temperature variation for the A factor. The equation takes the form

$$k = A'T^n e^{-E'/RT} \tag{1.39}$$

where A', E', and n are the new parameters. Such a form can be readily derived from the general definition of activation energy (1.34):

$$E \equiv RT^2 \left(\frac{\partial \ln k}{\partial T} \right).$$

If we set $E = E' + CT$ where E' and C are constants, this equation can be integrated directly to yield

$$\ln k = -\frac{E'}{RT} + \frac{C}{R} \ln T + \text{constant}. \tag{1.40}$$

Setting the constant of integration equal to A' and $n = C/R$, we can immediately obtain (1.39). We note that the constant C has the dimensions of a molar heat capacity, and it can be identified with an average molar heat capacity of activation, averaged over the range for which (1.39) is presumed valid. Although n tends to be small for gas phase reactions and on the order of unity, it can become very large for ionic reactions in solution (for example, as high as 20).

One consequence of this modified Arrhenius equation discussed above is that the A factor and activation energy are now both explicitly dependent on temperature. These must be included in any transformations between pressure and concentration units and in making relationships to thermochemical data.

When data is measured and cast in the form of the Arrhenius equation, the relation between the parameters are as follows:

$$A = A'(eT_m)^n;$$
$$E = E' + nRT_m. \tag{1.41}$$

1.8   FREE ENERGY OF ACTIVATION

The relation between equilibrium constants and forward and reverse rate constants $K_1 = k_1/k_{-1}$ permits us to make a formal division of rate constants into parts. K_1 can be written as

$$K_1 = e^{-\Delta G_1^\circ / RT} = 10^{-\Delta G_1^\circ / \theta} \tag{1.42}$$

where ΔG^0 is the standard Gibbs free energy change in the stoichiometric reaction 1. We can proceed to write any rate constant k_1 in the form

$$k_1 = \nu_1 e^{-G_1^* / RT} = \nu_1 10^{-G_1^* / \theta} \tag{1.43}$$

where G_1^* can be called a free energy of activation for reaction 1, and ν_1 can be called a frequency factor for the reaction. For the reverse reaction we can write

$$k_{-1} = \nu_{-1} e^{-G_{-1}^* / RT}, \tag{1.44}$$

and if we choose to equate $\Delta G_1^\circ = G_1^* - G_{-1}^*$, we see that $\nu_1 = \nu_{-1}$.

If we consider G_1^* and G_{-1}^* as thermochemical quantities, we can label ν_1 and ν_{-1} as kinetic quantities. In Chapter 3 we show how the transition state theory leads to such a partition of rate constants into a product of a kinetic quantity[5] and a thermodynamic quantity. Here it is sufficient to note that any kinetic quantities identified in this manner must be the same for forward and inverse processes. We may also note that rate laws, even for very complex processes, can always be written as a product of a kinetic expression (involving rate constants and concentrations) and a thermodynamic expression usually of the form

$$1 - \frac{(P)^p(Q)^q \cdots}{K_1(A)^a(B)^b \cdots} \tag{1.45}$$

---

[5] These are the quantities which involve dimensions of time.

where K_1 is the equilibrium constant for the overall reaction

$$aA + bB + \cdots \underset{1}{\overset{}{\rightleftarrows}} pP + qQ + \cdots.$$

It is this thermodynamic factor which makes the net rate go to zero at equilibrium.[6]

One consequence of this discussion above is that any parameter that does not affect the equilibrium constant but that does affect the kinetic behavior of the system must have an identical effect on both forward and reverse rate constants. This is true, for example, of catalysts, which must speed up the reverse as well as the forward rates by precisely equal factors.

1.9   NEGATIVE ACTIVATION ENERGIES

The general experience is that raising the temperature of a reaction leads to an increase in the specific rate constants describing the reaction. Occasionally this is not true. Thus the termolecular reaction $2NO + O_2 \rightarrow 2NO_2$ slows down as we raise the temperature, and the same is true for the reaction $O + O_2 + M \rightarrow O_3 + M$.

Now the activation energies for forward and reverse reactions are related to the enthalpy change by

$$\Delta H_1 = E_1 - E_{-1}. \tag{1.46}$$

Hence a negative activation energy for one of the steps, let us say E_{-1}, implies that $E_1 < \Delta H_1$. In the ozone dissociation, for example, ΔH_1 is the bond dissociation energy for O_3. The significance of this is that the activation energy for O_3 decomposition is less than the bond dissociation energy! How are we to understand this paradoxical result? Does it mean that an O_3 molecule can be decomposed by an energy less than that required to break the $O-O_2$ bond in O_3?

The answers to the questions raised above are provided by a closer look at what is meant by activation energy. As we have noted earlier, the rate constant for a chemical reaction is not a simple molecular quantity. It is instead an average of the individual reaction rate constants over the population of all the different quantum states of the system. Following a derivation given by Tolman,[7] we can write the rate constant for a reaction as

$$k = \frac{\sum p_j e^{-E_j/RT} k_j}{\sum p_j e^{-E_j/RT}} \tag{1.47}$$

where p_j is the degeneracy of the jth quantum state of the molecule with energy E_j, and k_j is the spontaneous, first-order rate constant with which molecules in the jth state with energy E_j will decompose. Then, from the

[6] See the rate law for the $H_2 + Br_2$ reaction on pg. 6.
[7] Richard C. Tolman, *Statistical Mechanics*, N.Y. Chem. Cat. Co., New York, 1928.

definition of activation energy,

$$E \equiv RT^2 \left(\frac{\partial \ln k}{\partial T} \right)$$

$$= \frac{RT^2 \sum k_j p_j (E_j/RT^2) e^{-E_j/RT}}{\sum k_j p_j e^{-E_j/RT}} - \frac{RT^2 \sum p_j (E_j/RT^2) e^{-E_j/RT}}{\sum p_j e^{-E_j/RT}} \qquad (1.48)$$

$$= \frac{\sum E_j k_j p_j e^{-E_j/RT}}{\sum k_j p_j e^{-E_j/RT}} - \frac{\sum p_j E_j e^{-E_j/RT}}{\sum p_j e^{-E_j/RT}}, \qquad (1.49)$$

or

$$E = \langle E \rangle_{\text{reacting}} - \langle E \rangle_{\text{nonreacting}}. \qquad (1.50)$$

The second term on the right-hand side of (1.49) can be recognized as the definition of the average energy of the molecules in the system, whereas the first term can be identified as the average energy of the reacting molecules. Hence we find the simple result that the experimental activation energy is the difference between these two quantities.

A reacting molecule at any temperature T has a certain amount of internal thermal energy (such as vibrational). If it should react by breaking spontaneously into fragments, these fragments at their instant of formation also have a certain amount of internal thermal energy. If these two amounts of energy are equal, the activation energy for the reaction at temperature T is precisely the same as the value at absolute zero. If, to the contrary, the fragments have less energy than the nonreacting molecules, the activation energy is less than its value at absolute zero, and we have a simple explanation for our paradox. Another way of stating it is that the fragments are being formed "cold," that is, with less than the average thermal energy they have when they come to thermal equilibrium in the reaction flask. In terms of the reverse reaction of recombination, this implies that the rate of recombination is higher for fragments with less than average thermal energy. As we raise the temperature we decrease this population, and the effective rate of recombination decreases with it.

Such effects as those described above can become very pronounced at extremely high temperatures where RT is very large. Thus at 5000°K, the activation energy for NO_2 decomposition into $NO + O$ can be as much as $3RT$ or 30 kcal lower than the bond dissociation energy of 72 kcal. This leads to an apparent activation energy for dissociation of only 42 kcal/mole.

1.10   REACTION-COORDINATE-ENERGY DIAGRAM

Relations such as that just encountered in systems with negative activation energies are best visualized in terms of what are called reaction-coordinate-energy diagrams. During the course of an elementary chemical reaction requiring activation energy, a molecule is raised from a low-energy state and a normal

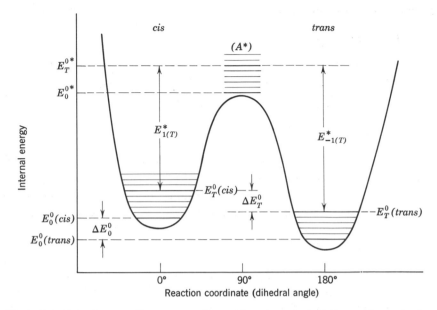

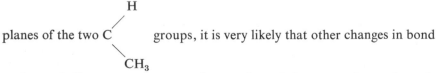

Figure 1.1   Reaction coordinate energy diagram for a hypothetical cis-trans isomerization. A number of authors have chosen to draw what they call "free-energy" diagrams rather than energy diagrams. These can be very misleading since the free energy involves entropy, which is not a property of individual molecules, but rather a property of a population. In particular, molecules from a population whose average energy is below the barrier height may decompose, whereas this is not true of molecules whose individual internal energy is below the energy barrier.

geometry to a high-energy state in which large changes in molecular geometry are possible. One or more of these changes in geometry can correspond to the conversion to products. This behavior is illustrated in Figure 1.1 for a hypothetical case of unimolecular isomerization of *cis*- to *trans*-butene-2.

The ordinate represents the total energy of a single molecule as a function of its "reaction coordinate," which is plotted along the abscissa. The solid line corresponds to the potential energy of the molecules at different values of the "reaction coordinate." The light shaded lines are drawn to suggest different vibrational levels of the cis and trans forms. Although the reaction coordinate in this case can be thought of simply as the angle between the

planes of the two $C \overset{\diagup H}{\underset{\diagdown CH_3}{}}$ groups, it is very likely that other changes in bond

angles and distances accompany the rotation of these two planes through the energy barrier at 90°. E_T^0 (cis) represents the energy of the average cis molecule at temperature T, E_T° (trans) the energy of the average trans molecule, and $E_T^{\circ*}$ the energy of the average reacting molecule (A^*).

The heat of reaction at absolute zero is indicated on the drawing by ΔE_0°; it is drawn between the zero vibrational levels. At any finite temperature T, the average molecules will be somewhere above these zero-vibrational levels, as is indicated by the solid line at E_T° (cis) and at E_T° (trans). Similarly the average reacting molecule at temperature T°K will not be precisely at the top of the energy barrier but will be slightly above it, as is indicated by the solid line above the barrier at $E_T^{\circ*}$. E_1^* and E_{-1}^* are, respectively, the activation energies for the cis-trans and trans-cis reaction paths at temperature T.

2

Methods for the Estimation of Thermochemical Data

2.1 SOME THERMODYNAMIC RELATIONS

When a chemical reaction proceeds in the gas phase to a state of dynamic equilibrium, that state is completely described by the specification of temperature T, pressure P, and chemical composition. From P and the chemical composition we can calculate the equilibrium constant K_P and the *standard Gibbs free energy change* ($\Delta G°$) for the process of transforming reactants to products at temperature T. Below we consider all species as ideal gases.

If the stoichiometry of the reaction above is

$$aA + bB \rightleftarrows rR + qQ, \tag{2.1}$$

$$K_P = \frac{(R)^r (Q)^q}{(A)^a (B)^b} \tag{2.2}$$

and

$$\Delta G_T° = -RT \ln K_P$$
$$= r \Delta G_{fT}°(R) + q \Delta G_{fT}°(Q) - a \Delta G_{fT}°(A) - b \Delta G_{fT}°(B) \tag{2.3}$$

where, in (2.2), the concentrations of each species has been expressed in units of atmospheres. Quantities, such as $\Delta G_{fT}°(R)$, etc. (2.3), represent the standard Gibbs free energies of formation of 1 mole of R at the temperature T and pressure of 1 atm from the elements in their standard states at T and 1 atm pressure.

The units of K_p then are $(atm)^{\Delta n}$ where

$$\Delta n = r + q - a - b \tag{2.4}$$

is the mole change in the reaction.[1] By definition

$$\Delta G_T^\circ = \Delta H_T^\circ - T \Delta S_T^\circ \tag{2.5}$$

where ΔH_T°. The standard enthalpy change for the reaction is related to the standard heats of formation ΔH_{fT}° by

$$\Delta H_T^\circ = r \, \Delta H_{fT}^\circ(R) + q \, \Delta H_{fT}^\circ(Q) - a \, \Delta H_{fT}^\circ(A) - b \, \Delta H_f^\circ(B), \tag{2.6}$$

and $\Delta S_T{}^0$, the standard entropy change in the reaction, is related to the standard absolute entropies of the species by

$$\Delta S_T^\circ = r S_T^\circ(R) + q S_T^\circ(Q) - a S_T^\circ(A) - b S_T^\circ(B). \tag{2.7}$$

If we know the standard entropies and the standard heats of formation at the temperature T of all reactants and products, we can calculate ΔH_T° and ΔS_T° for the reaction and from these the equilibrium constant.

Entropies and heats of formation thus constitute our basic thermochemical data. Their variation with temperature is given by the thermodynamic relations

$$\left[\frac{\partial(\Delta H^\circ)}{\partial T}\right]_p = \Delta C_p^\circ \qquad \left[\frac{\partial(\Delta S^\circ)}{\partial T}\right]_p = \frac{\Delta C_p^\circ}{T} \tag{2.8}$$

where ΔC_p° is the change in standard molar heat capacity for the reaction and is given by

$$\Delta C_p^\circ = r C_p^\circ(R) + q C_p^\circ(Q) - a C_p^\circ(A) - b C_p^\circ(B). \tag{2.9}$$

In (2.9) $C_p^\circ(R)$, etc. are the standard molar heat capacities of the reactants and products and are functions of temperature but not of pressure for ideal gases.

In order to calculate ΔH_T° or ΔS_T°, given the values of $\Delta H_{T_0}^\circ$ and $\Delta S_{T_0}^\circ$, we need to know the functional dependence of ΔC_p° on temperature over the range from T to T_0. Integration of (2.8) then gives the relations

$$\Delta H_T^\circ = \Delta H_{T_0}^\circ + \int_{T_0}^{T} (\Delta C_p^\circ) \, dT;$$

$$\Delta S_T^\circ = \Delta S_{T_0}^\circ + \int_{T_0}^{T} \left(\frac{\Delta C_p^\circ}{T}\right) dT. \tag{2.10}$$

We see later that, although values of C_p° for individual species may be large and may change grossly over temperature intervals of $500°K$, ΔC_p° for reactions tend to be very small and change very little over such intervals.

---

[1] Note that this depends on our convention for writing stoichiometric equations. In general we follow the common usage of taking the smallest set of integers.

Because of this we can, with little error, take an average value $\Delta C_{pT_m}^\circ$ over the interval $(T - T_0)$ and reduce (2.10) to

$$\Delta H_T^\circ = \Delta H_{T_0}^\circ + \Delta C_{pT_m}^\circ (T - T_0);$$

$$\Delta S_T^\circ = \Delta S_{T_0}^\circ + \Delta C_{pT_m}^\circ \ln \frac{T}{T_0} \tag{2.11}$$

$$= \Delta S_{T_0}^\circ + 2.303 \, \Delta C_{pT_m}^\circ \log \frac{T}{T_0}.$$

2.2 SOURCES OF DATA

With roughly 100 elements in the periodic table, there are 100 atomic species, 200 possible univalent ions (positive and negative), 5050 diatomic molecules, about 10^6 triatomic molecules, and $\sim 10^{2n}$ n-atomic molecules. It is clearly a hopeless task to expect to have tabulated, experimental thermochemical data on all polyatomic species or even restricted subclasses of these. Fortunately, it is possible, with the techniques of statistical thermodynamics, to calculate with good precision the standard entropies and heat capacities of molecules if we know their geometrical structures and vibrational frequencies. For large numbers of simple molecules these data are available, and very accurate values of C_p° and S° over large ranges of temperature have been tabulated. This is not the case for heats of formation, and ΔH_f° values must be measured experimentally for each particular compound. However, many of the more common, simpler molecules have already been measured, and, for the more complex species, a well-documented body of empirical data exists for estimating their values from the former. Also, for many of the more complex species for which structural information is not available, good empirical rules are available for estimating geometrical structure and vibrational frequencies with adequate precision to allow the calculation of S° and C_p° with good accuracy.

However, even the calculations of S° and C_p° described above are not trivial or rapid, and we make use of them only in exceptional cases. An extremely rapid and nearly as accurate method of estimation of thermochemical data is to be found in the "Additivity Rules," which we shall now discuss.

2.3 ADDITIVITY RULES FOR MOLECULAR PROPERTIES

Chemists and physicists have known for some time that most molecular properties of larger molecules can be considered, roughly, as being made up of additive contributions from the individual atoms or bonds in the molecule. The physical basis of such an empirical finding appears to reside in the fact that the forces between atoms in the same or different molecules are very "short range"; that is, they are appreciable only over distances of the order of 1 to 3 Å. Because of this, the individual atoms in a typically substituted hydrocarbon, such as isopropyl chloride, $CH_3CHClCH_3$, seem to contribute nearly constant amounts to such molecular properties as refractive index, ultraviolet and infrared absorption spectra, magnetic susceptibility, and also entropy, molar heat capacity, and even heat of formation.

About a decade ago, Benson and Buss[2] showed that it was possible to make a hierarchial system of such additivity laws in which the simplest- or "zeroth-" order law would be the law of additivity of atom properties. In an atom additivity scheme, one assigns partial values for the property in question to each atom in the molecule. The molecular property, thereby, is the sum of all the atom contributions. For an exceptional property, such as molecular weight, such a law is precise. However, there is an obvious limitation on such a law: In any chemical reaction, since there is a conservation of atoms, an atom additivity law would predict that any molecular property would be similarly conserved; that is, it is the same for reactants as for products. This is certainly not the case for entropy and enthalpy in most chemical reactions, although it is roughly correct in many cases where there is no change in mole number. However, even here, too many obvious exceptions exist, such as $H_2 + F_2 \rightarrow 2HF + 128$ kcal, $N_2 + O_2 \rightarrow 2NO - 43$ kcal, $H_2 + Cl_2 \rightarrow 2HCl + 44$ kcal, etc.

2.4   ADDITIVITY OF BOND PROPERTIES

The next higher- or first-order approximation in additivity schemes is the additivity of bond properties. Table 2.1 shows a listing of such bond contributions to C_p°, S°, and ΔH_f° of ideal gases at 25°C.

To illustrate the use of the Table 2.1, let us calculate C_p° and S° for some compounds.[3]   (For convenience, we shall insert subscript T only when $T \neq 25°C$.)

EXAMPLES

1. $C_p^\circ(CHCl_3) = C_p^\circ(C{-}H) + 3C_p^\circ(C{-}Cl)$
      $= 1.74 + 3 \times 4.64 = 15.66$ gibbs/mole;
   $C_p^\circ(\text{obs.}) = 15.7$ gibbs/mole;
   $S^\circ(CHCl_3) = S^\circ(C{-}H) + 3S^\circ(C{-}Cl) - R \ln 3$ [4]
      $= 12.90 + 3 \times 19.70 - 2.2 = 69.8$ gibbs/mole;
   $S^\circ(\text{obs.}) = 70.9$ gibbs/mole.

[2] S. W. Benson and J. H. Buss, *J. Chem. Phys.*, **29**, 546 (1958).
[3] For original references to thermochemical data, see the footnote in Appendix.
[4] $R \ln 3$ is a symmetry correction, $\sigma = 3$ being the symmetry number of $CHCl_3$, arising from the threefold axis. See Section 2.11 for further discussion.

Table 2.1 Partial Bond Contributions for the Estimation of C_p°, S°, and ΔH_f° of Gas-phase Species at 25°C, 1 atm[a]

Bond	C_p°	S°	ΔH_f°	Bond	C_p°	S°	ΔH_f°
C—H	1.74	12.90	−3.83	S—S	5.4	11.6	—
C—D	2.06	13.60	−4.73	C_d—C^b	2.6	−14.3	6.7
C—C	1.98	−16.40	2.73	C_d—H	2.6	13.8	3.2
C—F	3.34	16.90	—	C_d—F	4.6	18.6	—
C—Cl	4.64	19.70	−7.4	C_d—Cl	5.7	21.2	−0.7
C—Br	5.14	22.65	2.2	C_d—Br	6.3	24.1	9.7
C—I	5.54	24.65	14.1	C_d—I	6.7	26.1	21.7
C—O	2.7	−4.0	−12.0	>CO—H[c]	4.2	26.8	−13.9
O—H	2.7	24.0	−27.0	>CO—C	3.7	−0.6	−14.4
O—D	3.1	24.8	−27.9	>CO—O	2.2	9.8	−50.5
O—O	4.9	9.1	21.5	>CO—F	5.7	31.6	—
O—Cl	5.5	32.5	9.1	>CO—Cl	7.2	35.2	−27.0
C—N	2.1	−12.8	9.3	ϕ-H[d]	3.0	11.7	3.25
N—H	2.3	17.7	−2.6	ϕ-C[d]	4.5	−17.4	7.25
C—S	3.4	−1.5	6.7	(NO_2)—O[d]	—	43.1	−3.0
S—H	3.2	27.0	−0.8	(NO)—O[d]	—	35.5	+9.0

[a] See Sec. 2.11 and 2.12 for corrections to entropy for symmetry and electronic contributions. C_p°, and S_0° estimated from the rule of additivity of bond contributions, are good to about ±1 cal/mole-°K, but they may be poorer for heavily branched compounds. The values of ΔH_f° are usually within ±2 kcal/mole but may be poorer for heavily branched species. Peroxide values are not certain by much larger amounts. All substances are in ideal gas state.

[b] C_d represents the vinyl group carbon atom. The vinyl group is here considered a tetravalent unit.

[c] >CO— represents the bond to carbonyl carbon, the latter being considered a bivalent unit.

[d] NO and NO_2 are here considered as univalent, terminal groups, but the phenyl group $\phi(C_6H_5)$ is considered as a hexavalent unit.

2. $C_p^\circ(2,3\text{-dimethylpentane}) = 6C_p^\circ(\text{C—C}) + 16C_p^\circ(\text{C—H})$

$$= 6 \times 1.98 + 16 \times 1.74 = 39.8 \text{ gibbs/mole};$$

$$C_p^\circ(\text{obs.}) = 39.7 \text{ (estimate only)};$$

$$S^\circ(2,3\text{-dimethylpentane}) = 6S^\circ(\text{C—C}) + 16S^\circ(\text{C—H}) - 4R \ln 3 + R \ln 2 \text{ [5]}$$

$$= -98.40 + 206.40 - 8.8 + 1.4$$

$$= 100.6 \text{ gibbs/mole};$$

$$S^\circ(\text{obs.}) = 99.0.$$

[5] We subtract $4R \ln 3$ for the internal symmetry of four CH_3 groups and add $R \ln 2$ for the entropy of mixing of two optical isomers.

3. $\Delta H_f^\circ(\text{benzyl iodide}) = 5\,\Delta H_f^\circ(\Phi\text{—H}) + \Delta H_f^\circ(\Phi\text{—C})$
$$+ 2\,\Delta H_f^\circ(\text{C—H}) + \Delta H_f^\circ(\text{C—I})$$
$$= 16.25 + 7.25 - 7.66 + 14.2$$
$$= +30.0\ \text{kcal/mole};$$

$\Delta H_f\ (\text{obs.}) = 30.4\ \text{kcal/mole}.$

4. $\Delta H_f^\circ(\text{2-chlorobutadiene 1,3}) = 5\,\Delta H_f^\circ(C_d\text{—H}) + \Delta H_f^\circ(C_d\text{—C}) + \Delta H_f^\circ(C_d\text{—Cl})$
$$= 16.0 + 6.7 - 0.7 = +22.0\ \text{kcal/mole};$$

$\Delta H_f^\circ(\text{obs.}) = (\text{not known})$

5. $\Delta H_f^\circ(\text{ethyl acetate}) = 8\,\Delta H_f^\circ(\text{C—H}) + \Delta H_f^\circ(>\!\text{CO—C}) + \Delta H_f^\circ(>\!\text{CO—O})$
$$+ \Delta H_f^\circ(\text{C—O}) + \Delta H_f^\circ(\text{C—C})$$
$$= -30.64 - 14.4 - 50.5 - 12.0 + 2.73$$
$$= -104.8\ \text{kcal/mole};$$

$\Delta H_f^\circ(\text{obs.}) = 103.4\ \text{kcal/mole}.$

We find that the law of bond additivity reproduces C_p and S° values to within ± 1 gibbs/mole (cu) on the average, but the law is poorer for very heavily branched compounds. Values of ΔH_f° are generally estimated to within ± 2 kcal/mole but again are subject to larger errors in heavily branched compounds and in compounds containing very electronegative groups such as NO_2 and F.

It is clear that bond additivity rules will give the same properties for isomeric species such as *n*-butene and isobutene, *cis*- and *trans*-olefins, etc., and so cannot be employed to distinguish differences in properties of isomers. It is generally the case that isomeric differences, which give rise to large steric effects in molecules, cannot be treated by *any* simple additivity scheme but must be treated either by exceptional rules or by individual examination.

2.5 ADDITIVITY OF GROUP PROPERTIES

The next higher- or second-order approximation to additivity behavior is to treat a molecular property as being composed of contributions due to groups. A group is defined as a polyvalent atom (ligancy ≥ 2), in a molecule together with all of its ligands. The nomenclature we follow is to identify first the polyvalent atom and then its ligands. Thus C—$(H)_3(C)$ represents a C atom connected to three H atoms and another C atom, that is, a primary methyl group. Molecules, such as HOH, CH_3Cl, and CH_4, which contain only one such atom (that is, one group), are irreducible entities and cannot be treated by group additivity. The molecules that can be treated are those with two or more polyvalent atoms. Examples of decomposition of molecules into groups are as follows.

1. CH_3—CH_3: Contains two identical groups each with a carbon atom bound to a carbon atom and three H atoms. Note that all unbranched paraffin hydrocarbons contain only two groups, $[C—(C)(H)_3]$ and $[C—(C)_2(H)_2]$. The totality of saturated paraffins are composed of four groups; the preceding two and those for tertiary and quaternary C: $[C—(C)_3(H)]$ and $[C—(C)_4]$.

2. $CH_3CHOHCH_3$: Contains four groups (that is, four polyvalent atoms):

$$2[C—(C)(H)_3] + [C—(C)_2(O)(H)] + [O—(C)(H)].$$

With increased substitution the number of groups increases and this provides a basic limitation on the use of group properties. Thus for non-branched, chlorinated hydrocarbons we need all the groups symbolized by $[C—(C)(H)_n(Cl)_{3-n}]$ and $[C—(C)_2(H)_n(Cl)_{2-n}]$ where $n = 0, 1, 2,$ and/or 3. This is a total of seven groups or five more than are needed for the paraffins. For the branched chlorocarbons only one further group is needed $[C—(C)_3(Cl)]$.

The first six tables in the Appendix list the current available values of group contributions to C_p°, S°, and ΔH_f°. Values of C_p° and S° estimated from these groups are on the average within ± 0.3 gibbs/mole of the measured values, whereas ΔH_f° estimates are within ± 0.5 kcal/mole. For heavily substituted species, deviations in C_p° and S° may go as high as ± 1.5 gibbs/mole, and ΔH_f° may deviate by ± 3 kcal/mole.[6]

The following examples will illustrate the application of group additivity.

EXAMPLE

1.
$$C_p^\circ(i\text{-butane}) = 3[C—(C)(H)_3] + [C—(C)_3(H)]$$
$$= 18.57 + 4.54 = 23.1 \text{ gibbs/mole}$$
$$C_p^\circ(\text{obs.}) = 23.1 \text{ gibbs/mole.}$$

2.
$$S^\circ(\text{pentene-2}) = [C—(C_d)(H)_3] + 2[C_d—(C)(H)] + [C—(C_d)(C)(H)_2]$$
$$+ [C—(C)(H)_3] - 2R \ln 3 \text{ (symmetry of } CH_3)$$
$$= 30.41 + 16.0 + 9.8 + 30.41 - 4.32$$
$$= 82.3 \text{ gibbs/mole (trans isomer)}$$
$$S^\circ(\text{pentene-2})(\text{obs.})_{\text{trans}} = 82.0 \text{ gibbs/mole.}$$

3.
$$S^\circ(sec\text{-butyl alcohol}) = 2[C—(C)(H)_3] + [C—(C)_2(O)(H)] + [O—(H)(C)]$$
$$+ [C—(C)_2(H)_2] + R \ln 2 \quad \text{(for optical isomers)}$$
$$- 2R \ln 3 \quad \text{(for } CH_3 \text{ groups)}$$
$$= 60.8 - 11.0 + 29.1 + 9.4 + 1.4 - 4.4$$
$$= 85.3 \text{ gibbs/mole}$$
$$S^\circ(\text{obs.}) = 85.8 \text{ gibbs/mole.}$$

---

[6] For more detailed comparisons, see the group of papers by Benson et al., in *Chem. Reviews*, in press (1968).

4. $$\Delta H_f^\circ(t\text{-butyl methyl ether}) = 3[\text{C—(C)(H)}_3] + [\text{C—(C)}_3(\text{O})]$$
$$+ [\text{O—(C)}_2] + [\text{C—(O)(H)}_3]$$
$$= -30.2 - 6.6 - 23.0 - 10.1$$
$$= -69.9 \text{ kcal/mole}$$
$$\Delta H_f^\circ(\text{obs.}) = -70 \pm 1 \text{ kcal/mole.}[7]$$

In the Tables A.1 to A.6 are listed two types of corrections for higher order interactions. One of these is a correction for cis-trans isomerization. It is not possible to include such interactions directly into the group properties because they represent the interactions of nonbonded, next-nearest neighbors. In consequence, the group properties have been tabulated for the usually more stable trans isomers and corrections are needed to obtain the less stable *cis*-olefins.

The second correction is for gauche interactions of large groups, that is, anything bigger than H atoms. These again are interactions of next-nearest neighbors, and so they are not directly included in a group scheme. The method of obtaining such interactions is to write out the structure of a given molecule and then to enumerate the gauche configurations of every group with respect to those preceding it that have not been counted. These inter-actions have to do with the rotomeric configurations around the bonds. In the case of linear paraffins, the most stable conformation is one in which all heavy groups are trans to each other. This is illustrated by the three con-formations shown in Figure 2.1 for *n*-butane. The two mirror-image gauche conformations are less stable than the trans by about 0.8 kcal mole.

Figure 2.2 shows three conformations of 2-methyl butane. The two mirror-image gauche conformations each have one gauche methyl interaction, whereas the less stable syn conformation has two gauche methyl interactions.

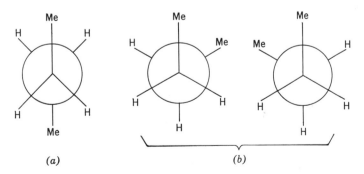

(a) (b)

Figure 2.1   Rotomeric conformations of *n*-butane. (a) trans; (b) gauche (these are mirror images).

[7] Making two oxygen gauche corrections gives $\Delta H_f^\circ = -69.3$ kcal/mole.

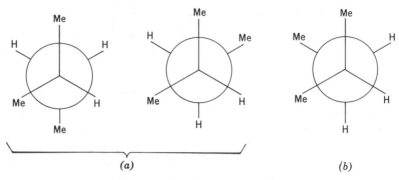

Figure 2.2   Rotometic conformations of 2-methyl butane. (*a*) gauche (mirror images); (*b*) syn.

In 2-methyl pentane there is one gauche methyl interaction, and in 2,3-dimethyl pentane there are three gauche interactions. In ditertiary butyl ether, which appears to have about 10 kcal of "strain" energy, there are four gauche interactions. The value of ΔH_f°, computed from the table without gauche corrections, is -96.7 kcal/mole compared to an observed value of -87.2 ± 0.2 kcal/mole. For methyl, *t*-butyl ether, which has two oxygen gauche corrections, the corrected $\Delta H_f^\circ = -69.3$ kcal/mole, whereas the observed value is -70.0 ± 1.2 kcal/mole.

Although the magnitudes of even more distant interactions are explored later, it is worthy of note that the heat of isomerization of *cis*-ditertiary butyl ethylene to the trans form is -9.3 kcal/mole compared to -1.0 kcal/mole for the *cis*-dimethylethylene (that is, *cis*-butene-2) to trans isomerization. Interactions of such a nature cannot be anticipated from any simple scheme of corrections and in many cases can only be detected by examination of precise structural models.

2.6   NONGROUP INTERACTION, RINGS

The principle of additivity schemes rests on the assumption that whatever the additive unit, atom, bond, group, etc., its "local" properties remain unchanged in a series of homologous compounds. That is, there is no significant interaction with more distant units. Linear molecules such as the normal paraffins, ethers, and their terminally substituted derivatives [e.g., $Cl-(CH_2)_n-O(CH_2)_m-X$] are ideally suited to such an assumption, and hence it is not surprising that these fit additivity rules extremely well, namely to the precision of the experimental data. However, as soon as we introduce structural features into a molecule, which bring more distant units into proximity, we may expect departures from additivity laws. This has already been noted in the preceding section in connection with cis- isomers for olefins and with gauche configurations of highly branched molecules. In order to accommodate such species into an additivity scheme we must add "corrections" for these nongroup interactions.

The extreme example of such higher order interactions is provided by ring compounds. There is no simple, natural way of incorporating ring systems even into a group additivity scheme. We can manage to do so by adding a "correction" for the structure. (The Appendix tables contain lists of such corrections for various ring structures both homo- and heterocyclic.) To evaluate a property for example, for cis-1-methyl,2-ethyl cyclopentane, we would add all the usual contributions for the groups present and then add corrections for the nongroup interactions:

ΔH_f°(cis-1-methyl, 2-ethyl cyclopentane)

$$= 2C—(C)(H)_3 + 4C—(C)_2(H)_2 + 2C—(C)_3(H)$$

$$+ C_5 \text{ ring correction} + \text{cis correction} + \text{gauche correction}$$

$$= -20.16 - 19.80 - 3.80 + 6.4 + 1.0 + 0.8$$

$$= -35.6 \text{ kcal/mole};$$

ΔH_f°(obs.) $= -35.9$ kcal/mole.

2.7 ESTIMATION OF THERMOCHEMICAL DATA AT HIGHER TEMPERATURES

The additivity laws already discussed allow us to obtain ΔH_f°, S°, and C_p° at 298°K. To obtain values at higher temperatures, we need to know C_p° as a function of T. For the hydrocarbons and simply substituted hydrocarbons, such data is available, and Tables A.1 through A.6 in the Appendix list group contributions to C_p° at a series of increasing temperatures. Average values of C_p° for use in equations, such as (2.11), can be quickly estimated from the tables, using linear interpolation between the listed temperatures.

EXAMPLE

Calculate $S_{840}^\circ(n\text{-}C_4H_{10}) - S_{298}^\circ(n\text{-}C_4H_{10})$.

From the Appendix tables $C_{298}^\circ(n\text{-}C_4H_{10}) = 2C_p^\circ[C—(C)(H)_3]$
$$+ 2C_f^\circ[C—(C)_2(H)_2]$$
$$= 23.3 \text{ gibbs/mole.}$$

Interpolating the group values between the nearest listed temperatures of 800°K and 1000°K we estimate

$$C_{p840}^\circ = 49.5 \text{ gibbs/mole.}$$

As an average value over the range, we would then choose $C_{pT_m}^\circ = 36.4$ gibbs/mole, noting that the values tend to increase faster than the average rate at the lower temperatures. From (2.11) we then find

$$S_{840}^\circ - S_{298}^\circ = (C_{pT_m}^\circ)\ln\frac{840}{298} = 37.8 \text{ gibbs/mole}.$$

For comparison the observed value is 37.0 gibbs/mole.

Alternatively, we can estimate and add increments over smaller temperature intervals:

$$S_{840}^\circ - S_{298}^\circ = \langle C_{p400}\rangle \ln\left(\tfrac{500}{300}\right) + \langle C_{p670}\rangle \ln\left(\tfrac{840}{500}\right)$$
$$= 29.6 \times 0.51 + 43.8 \times 0.51 = 37.4 \text{ gibbs/mole}.$$

In considering enthalpy corrections we must note the following problem. Our primary enthalpy data for compounds are standard heats of formation, which means that they refer in turn to the standard states of the elements. If we wish to compute a heat of formation at a higher temperature than $298°K$, we need to obtain ΔC_{pf}° for the change in molar heat capacity in forming the compound from elements in their standard states. For a large number of compounds, tabulations are already available of ΔH_{fT}° over a range of temperatures. If we are using data from such a table, we must never use it with anything but other ΔH_{fT}° data. However, if we use the present tables, in which we have listed group properties only at $298°K$ for ΔH_f°, it is not always necessary to compute ΔH_{fT}° because, for most purposes, we will be using these ΔH_{fT}° to obtain heats of reaction at T, and the C_{pT}° of the elements will cancel. For these latter purposes, it is sufficient to compute a value that will correspond to $\Delta H_{f298}^\circ + (H_T^\circ - H_{298}^\circ)$, the correction term being an absolute enthalpy increment for the compound. Its value is given by an equation like (2.11):

$$H_T^\circ - H_{298}^\circ = \int_{298}^{T} C_p^\circ \, dT = C_{pT_m}^\circ(T - 298). \tag{2.12}$$

To call attention to the ambiguity in such a procedure as that described above, let us label such mixed quantities, "apparent heats of formation." Where actual heats of formation at T are desired, then, ΔC_{pT}° may be calculated using the values, given in Table A-7, of the C_p° of the elements in their standard states.

EXAMPLE

Calculate ΔH_{f840}° (n-butane) $- \Delta H_{f298}^\circ$ and calculate also the enthalpy increment $(H_{840}^\circ - H_{298}^\circ)$ for n-butane.

From the preceding example we note that $C_{pT_m}^\circ$ (n-C_4H_{10}) over this temperature interval is 36.4 gibbs/mole, so that from (2.12) above, we find

$$H_{840}^\circ - H_{298}^\circ = 36.4(840 - 298) = 2.0 \text{ kcal/mole}.$$

The equation for the formation of n-butane is

$$4C(s) + 5H_2(g) \rightleftarrows n\text{-}C_4H_{10}(g).$$

Hence $\Delta C_{pf}^{\circ} = C_p^{\circ}(n\text{-butane}) - 4C_p^{\circ}[C(s)] - 5C_p^{\circ}[H_2(g)]$. Using C_p° already calculated at 298°K, and Table A-7 for the corresponding values for the elements we find that

$$\Delta C_{pf298}^{\circ} = -19.2 \quad \text{and} \quad \Delta C_{pf840}^{\circ} = -5.2 \text{ gibbs/mole}$$

with $\Delta C_{pfm}^{\circ} = -12.2$ gibbs/mole being a reasonable value in this range. Hence from (2.11)

$$\Delta H_{f840}^{\circ}(n\text{-butane}) - \Delta H_{f298}^{\circ}(n\text{-butane}) = -12.2(840 - 298)$$
$$= -6.6 \text{ kcal/mole.}$$

The "observed" value from the API tables is -6.5 kcal/mole.

Note that ΔC_{pf}° can be very large and either positive or negative in value. In consequence calculations of ΔH_{fT}° may require rather sizable corrections. However, it should also be noted that a large amount of the magnitude of ΔC_{pf}° is contributed by Δn, the change in moles of gases. For butane $\Delta n = -4$, and this contributes a constant -8.0 gibbs/mole to ΔC_{pf}°.

Let us now consider a typical problem, the calculation of an equilibrium constant.

EXAMPLE

Calculate K_p for the following reaction at 730°K:

$$(CH_3)_3CCH_2Cl \rightleftarrows (CH_3)_2C{=}CHCH_3 + HCl.$$

PROCEDURE

We first calculate ΔH_f°, S°, and ΔC_p° at 298° for each of the compounds except HCl, which is listed separately, and from this compute ΔH_{298}° and ΔS_{298}°. We then compute ΔC_p° at 298° and at 730°K and estimate $\Delta C_{pT_m}^{\circ}$, which we use to calculate ΔH_{730}° and ΔS_{730}° and finally ΔG_{730} and $K_{p(730)}$.

1. $\Delta H_f^{\circ}[(CH_3)_3CCH_2Cl] = 3 \Delta H_f^{\circ}[C{-}(C)(H)_3] + \Delta H_f^{\circ}[C{-}(C)_4]$
    $$+ \Delta H_f^{\circ}[C{-}(C)(H)_2(Cl)]$$
    $$= -30.24 + 0.50 - 16.2 + (\text{two gauche corrections}$$
    $$= +0.8 \text{ each})$$
    $$= -44.3 \text{ kcal/mole};$$

   $\Delta H_f^{\circ}(2\text{-methyl butene-2}) = 3 \Delta H_f^{\circ}[C{-}(C_d)(H)_3] + \Delta H_f^{\circ}[C_d{-}(C)_2]$
    $$+ \Delta H_f^{\circ}[C_d{-}(H)(C)] + 1 \text{ cis correction}$$
    $$= -30.24 + 10.63 + 6.1 + 1.0 = -12.5 \text{ kcal/mole,}$$

and $\Delta H_f^{\circ}(HCl) = -22.1$ kcal/mole (from Table A-8). Thus $\Delta H_{298}^{\circ} = +9.7$ kcal/mole.

2. Using the same decomposition of neopentyl chloride and 2-methyl butene-2 into groups, we find for S°

$$S^{\circ}[(CH_3)_3CCH_2Cl] = 91.23 - 35.10 + 37.8 - 4R \ln 3 \ (t\text{-butyl symmetry})$$
$$= 85.2 \text{ gibbs/mole};$$
$$S^{\circ}(\text{olefin}) = 91.2 - 12.7 + 8.0 - 3R \ln 3 \ (\text{symmetry}) + 1.0 \text{ cis correction}$$
$$= 81.0 \text{ gibbs/mole.}$$

Therefore, with $S^{\circ}(HCl) = 44.6$, we find $\Delta S_{298}^{\circ} = 40.4$ gibbs/mole.

3. By the same technique we use in B, we find $\Delta C^\circ_{p298} = 7.0 + 26.9 - 31.9 = +2.0$ gibbs/mole. At $730°K$, assuming $C^\circ_p(HCl) \approx 7.0$ gibbs/mole, we find from the tables that $\Delta C^\circ_{p730} \sim 7.0 + 49.7 - 59.9 = -3.2$ gibbs/mole. Hence we can take ΔC°_{pm} as -0.6 gibbs/mole.

4. Using (2.11), we now calculate

$$\Delta H^\circ_{730} = \Delta H^\circ_{730} - 0.6 \times (730 - 298) = 9.4 \text{ kcal/mole};$$

$$\Delta S^\circ_{730} = \Delta S^\circ_{730} - 0.6 \times 2.3 \times \log\left(\tfrac{730}{298}\right) = 39.9 \text{ gibbs/mole}.$$

Hence $\Delta G^\circ_{730} = \Delta H^\circ_{730} - 730\,\Delta S^\circ_{730} = -19.7$ kcal/mole,

$$\log K_p = \frac{-\Delta G^\circ_{730}}{4.576 T} = 5.91,$$

and

$$K_{p(730)} = 8.1 \times 10^5 \text{ atm.}$$

2.8　STRUCTURAL METHODS OF ESTIMATING C°_p

Lacking values for bonds or groups to estimate C°_p, we can make very good estimates by assigning vibrational frequencies to the molecule and thereby obtain the vibrational contribution to C°_p. This is usually the only difficult part of the calculation. From the methods of statistical mechanics we know that C°_p of an ideal gas can be broken down as follows:

$$C^\circ_p = C^\circ_p(\text{translation}) + C^\circ_p(\text{rotation}) + C^\circ_p(\text{vibration})$$
$$+ C^\circ_p(\text{electronic}) + R. \tag{2.13}$$

Where quantum effects are not important $C^\circ_p(\text{translation}) = \tfrac{3}{2}R$, but $C^\circ_p(\text{rotation}) = R$ for linear molecules or $\tfrac{3}{2}R$ for nonlinear molecules. $C^\circ_p(\text{electronic})$ is usually zero except for a handful of odd-electron species or species such as O_2, and even then it is small. C°_p then becomes

1. Linear molecules:

$$C^\circ_p = \tfrac{7}{2}R + C^\circ_p(\text{vibration}) + C^\circ_p(\text{elec.}). \tag{2.14}$$

2. Nonlinear molecules:

$$C^\circ_p = \tfrac{8}{2}R + C^\circ_p(\text{vibration}) + C^\circ_p(\text{elec.}). \tag{2.15}$$

For small molecules containing H and D atoms and only one other heavy atom we can usually neglect $C^\circ_p(\text{vibration})$ at $298°K$, as well as $C^\circ_p(\text{elec.})$, and we find from (2.14) and (2.15) that species such as HCl, DBr, etc. have C°_{p298} of about 7 cal/mole-°K, whereas for H_2O, NH_3, NO_3, CH_4, etc. 8 cal/mole °K is usually within 10% of the observed C°_{p298} (see Tables A.9, A.10, A.11).

For larger molecules the vibrational frequencies can be assigned on a very simple empirical basis. First let us note that in a molecule containing N

atoms, there are $(3N - 5)$ fundamental frequencies for linear molecules and $(3N - 6)$ for nonlinear ones. These frequencies can be further subdivided into three classes: stretching frequencies, bending (or deformation) frequencies, and hindered internal rotations. Because N atoms in a molecule must be connected by at least $(N - 1)$ bonds there will be $(N - 1)$ stretching modes, each corresponding to the stretching of a characteristic bond and the remaining $(2N - 4)$ or $(2N - 5)$ frequencies belong to the class of deformations plus hindered rotations. In simple rings N atoms will be connected by N bonds, so that they have one more stretching mode than a noncyclic system.

Hindered (or free) internal rotations can only occur around single bonds, and their number is given by the number of single bonds connecting polyvalent atoms. Thus a saturated, substituted paraffin $C_nH_{2n+2-m}X_m$ where X is a univalent atoms will have $(n - 1)$ single bonds connecting the n carbon atoms and $(n - 1)$ internal rotations. If rings exist, of course, as in cyclohexane and benzene, internal rotations are not possible, so ring compounds must be treated as special cases.

One further distinction is worth making, namely the separation of frequencies into those involving H and D atoms and all of the rest. The reason for this is that H and D atom frequencies are generally very high because of the low mass of H (or D) and at low temperatures contribute very little to C_p°. This separation can be effected by treating the molecule as if it were composed only of heavy atoms. If it has, for example, P heavy atoms then it has $(3P - 6)$ or $(3P - 5)$ related frequencies of which $(P - 1)$ are stretches and $(2P - 5)$ or $(2P - 4)$ are deformations.

Table 2.2 shows a decomposition of vibrational frequencies for a few selected molecules. In Table A.13 (Appendix) are shown some characteristic bending and stretching frequencies, which are probably accurate to $\pm 10\%$. Table A.15 in the Appendix lists the contributions of a typical harmonic oscillator to C_p° at different temperature. Figure 2.3 shows the same data in graphic form. The values are tabulated in terms of the dimensionless ratio $x = ch\tilde{\nu}/kT = 1.44\tilde{\nu}/T$ with $\tilde{\nu}$ in cm^{-1}, T in °K, k the Boltzmann constant, h Planck's constant, and c the velocity of light.

2.9 VIBRATIONAL CONTRIBUTIONS TO C_p°

From statistical mechanics we find that an internal harmonic mode of oscillation of a molecule with frequency $\tilde{\nu}$ (cm^{-1}) contributes to vibrational heat capacity, the term C_{vib}, with

$$\frac{C_{\text{vib}}}{R} = \frac{x^2 e^x}{(e^x - 1)^2} \tag{2.16}$$

Table 2.2 Classification of Vibrational Frequencies of Some Selected Molecules

Molecules	Number of Atoms N	Total Number of Frequencies	Numbers of Stretching Modes	Number of Bending Modes
C_2H_6	8	18	$7\begin{Bmatrix}6\ C\!-\!H\\1\ C\!-\!C\end{Bmatrix}$	$11\begin{Bmatrix}1\ \text{Int. Rot. (all H)}\\10\ \text{Def.} \quad \text{(all H)}\end{Bmatrix}$
Isopropyl chloride	11	27	$10\begin{Bmatrix}7\ C\!-\!H\\1\ C\!-\!Cl\\2\ C\!-\!C\end{Bmatrix}$	$17\begin{Bmatrix}2\ \text{Int. Rot. (all H)}\\15\ \text{Def.}\begin{Bmatrix}12\text{-H}\\3\ \text{heavy}\end{Bmatrix}\end{Bmatrix}$
Methyl cyclohexane	21	57	$21\begin{Bmatrix}14\ C\!-\!H\\7\ C\!-\!C\end{Bmatrix}$	$36\begin{Bmatrix}1\ \text{Int. Rot. (all H)}\\35\ \text{Def.}\begin{Bmatrix}27\text{-H}\\8\text{-heavy}\end{Bmatrix}\end{Bmatrix}$

Isopropyl chloride structure:

```
  H   H  H
  |   |  |
H—C—C—C—H
  |   |  |
  H  Cl  H
```

Methyl cyclohexane structure (C_7H_{14}):

```
        H H     H
         \     /
    H H   C   C   H
     \   / \ / \ /
  H—C—C   C   C—H (C7H14)
     /   \     / \
  H—C—H   H   H H
     |
  H—C—H
     |
     H
```

Heptene-2

CH_3—CH=CH—CH$_2$—CH$_2$—CH$_2$—CH$_2$—CH$_3$
(C_7H_{14})

21   57 $20\begin{cases}14\ \text{C—H}\\6\ \text{C—C}\end{cases}$ $37\begin{cases}5\ \text{Int. Rot.}\begin{cases}2\text{-H}\\3\text{-heavy}\end{cases}\\32\ \text{Def.}\begin{cases}26\text{-H}\\6\text{-heavy}\end{cases}\end{cases}$

Methyl methacrylate

($C_5H_8O_2$)

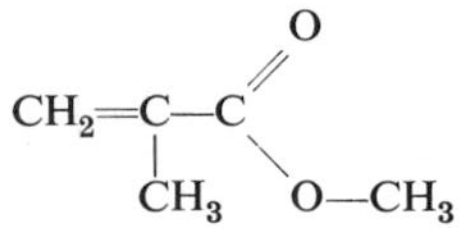

15   39 $14\begin{cases}8\ \text{C—H}\\3\ \text{C—C}\\3\ \text{C—O}\end{cases}$ $25\begin{cases}4\ \text{Int. Rot.}\begin{cases}2\text{-H}\\2\text{-heavy}\end{cases}\\32\ \text{Def.}\begin{cases}14\text{-H}\\7\text{-heavy}\end{cases}\end{cases}$

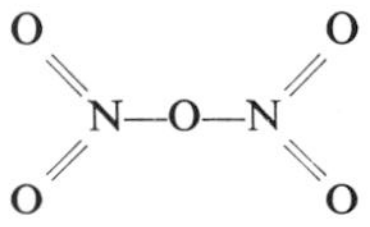

(N_2O_5)

7   15 $6\{6\ \text{N—O}\}$ $9\begin{cases}2\ \text{Int. Rot. (all heavy)}\\7\ \text{Def. (all heavy)}\end{cases}$

33

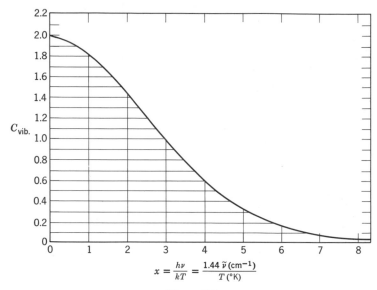

$$x = \frac{h\nu}{kT} = \frac{1.44\,\tilde{\nu}\,(\text{cm}^{-1})}{T\,(^\circ\text{K})}$$

Figure 2.3

where $x = h\tilde{\nu}c/kT$. To orient ourselves let us note that C_{vib}/R goes monotonically from zero at $x \gg 1$ to 1 at $x = 0$. Some typical values taken from Figure 2.3 are 0.06 for $x = 6$, 0.30 for $x = 4$, 0.71 for $x = 2$, and 0.90 for $x = 1.0$. At 300°K the quantity kT/hc is approximately 210 cm^{-1} so that $x \sim 15$ for H stretching modes ($\tilde{\nu} \sim 3000$ cm^{-1}), and $x \sim 6$ for H deformations ($\tilde{\nu} \sim 1300$ cm^{-1}). We see that both of these types of vibrations will contribute very little to C_p° at 300°K. An error of $\pm 10\%$ in $\tilde{\nu}$ will contribute an error of about ± 0.04 gibbs/mole to C_p° when x is in the range $1 \leq x \leq 4$, although outside these limits C_p° is much less sensitive to x.

At 300°K only frequencies in the neighborhood of 200 to 1000 cm^{-1} are in a region where appreciable errors in C_p° arise from even a $\pm 20\%$ error in $\tilde{\nu}$. At 600°K only $\tilde{\nu}$ values from 400 to 2000 cm^{-1} have this sensitivity. Above 1500°K almost all except H stretching frequencies are nearly fully excited and contribute close to their maximum of R to C_p°.

Hindered internal rotations have more complex contributions C_{ir} to C_p°. They vary from zero at very low temperatures where V_0, the height of the energy barrier to rotation, is very large compared to RT and reach a maximum contribution, which can approach or slightly exceed R, for very heavy rotors with large moments of inertia. This occurs at intermediate, or even low, temperatures. C_{ir} then decreases to $R/2$ for a free internal rotation at very high T. Molecules with practically free internal rotation are nitromethane (CH_3NO_2) and toluene (C_6H_5—CH_3). Table A.16 gives the contribution to C_p° per rotor as a function of V_0/RT and Q_f, the partition function for the free rotor.

From statistical mechanics we can write

$$Q_f = \frac{\pi^{1/2}}{\sigma} \left(\frac{8\pi^2 I_r kT}{h^2} \right)^{1/2}$$

$$= \frac{2.8}{\sigma} \times 10^{19} (I_r'T)^{1/2} = \frac{3.6}{\sigma} \left[I_r \left(\frac{T}{100} \right) \right]^{1/2} \qquad (2.17)$$

where I_r is the reduced moment of inertia in cgs units, σ is its internal symmetry number, and I_r has masses in amu and distances in angstroms.

For symmetrical coaxial rotors, as in ethane, I_r can be calculated directly from the formula

$$\frac{1}{I_r} = \frac{1}{I_1} + \frac{1}{I_2} \qquad (2.18)$$

where I_1 and I_2 are the moments of inertia of each top about its symmetry axis. In C_2H_6 where $I_1 = I_2$

$$I_r = \frac{I_1}{2} = \tfrac{3}{2} m_H r_{C-H}^2 \sin^2 (180 - \theta) = 2.66 \times 10^{-40} \text{ g cm}^2/\text{molecule}$$

where $\theta = 109°$ is the H—C—C angle in C_2H_6 and $r_{C-H} = 1.09$ Å.

For light tops attached to a heavy molecule I_r can be taken as the moment of the top directly. For asymmetric tops, which are more nearly the rule, fairly complex treatments have been made. For our purposes, however, we can approximate Q_f by treating them as though they were symmetrical. Barriers V_0 can be taken as 3.5 kcal for rotations about bonds bearing three substituents on each atom in the bond, 2.2 kcal for bonds bearing only two substituents on one of the atoms, and 1.1 kcal, if there is only one substituent on one of the atoms. Thus, C_2H_6, C_2H_5Cl, and CF_3CH_3 will be assigned

barriers of 3.5 kcal, CH_3NH_2, CH_3—CH=CH$_2$, NH_2—NH$_2$; CH_3—C$\overset{\displaystyle O}{\underset{\displaystyle H}{\diagup\diagdown}}$

will be assigned 2.2 kcal; and CH_3OH and H_2O_2, 1.1 kcal.

EXAMPLE

Calculate the contribution to C_p° of the hindered rotation in CH_3CHCl_2 at 300°K and 500°K. Because the $CHCl_2$ end is so heavy, we can treat this molecule as having a CH_3 group with $I_r = 5.3 \times 10^{-40}$ g cm^2. We then find from (2.17) that $Q_{500} = 4.7$; $Q_{300} = 3.6$, and with $V_0 = 3.5$ kcal, we see from Table A. 16 that C_{p300}°(int. rot.) = 2.1 and C_{p500}°(int. rot.) = 2.1 gibbs/mole.

EXAMPLE

Calculate $C_p^\circ(500°K)$ of CH_3CHCl_2, using average frequencies. $C_2H_4Cl_2$ has eight atoms, including four heavy atoms. It will have $3 \times 8 - 6 = 18$ frequencies, as follows:

	Average Frequency (cm^{-1})	x	C_p°(vib.)
7 stretches: 4C—H	3100	8.9	0.1
1C—C	1000	2.9	1.0
2C—Cl	650	1.87	3.0
11 Deformations 1 Int. Rot.			
($V = 3.5$ kcal):	—		2.1
2C—C—Cl bends	400	1.15	3.6
1Cl—C—Cl bend	280	0.81	1.9
2H—C—H bends	1450	4.2	1.1
$5\begin{cases} \text{H—C—C} \\ \text{H—C—Cl} \end{cases}$ bends	1150	3.3	4.3
			17.1 gibbs/mole

The average frequencies are assigned from Table A. 16 and x calculated at 500°K. The C_p°(vib.) contributions are then taken from Table A. 15. The total value of C_{p500}°(vib.) thus calculated is 17.1 gibbs/mole. Adding 7.9 gibbs/mole for other contributions, we find $C_{p500}^\circ(C_2H_4Cl)_2 = 25.0$ compared to 24.8 gibbs/mole from group additivity values (also from other measurements).

2.10 ELECTRONIC CONTRIBUTIONS TO C_p°

Radicals or molecules like NO, NO_2, or ClO_2 have odd numbers of electrons and in consequence may have low-lying electronic states. A few radicals, such as CH_2 and CF_2, are believed to have excited electronic states only a few kcal/mole above their ground states. Our information about such low-lying electronic states is very limited, but fortunately not too many species have such states.

Low-lying states can contribute significantly to the entropy of the species, but they contribute very little to C_p°. This can be illustrated by choosing a species with only one electronic state at an energy E_e above the ground state and a statistical weight (degeneracy) relative to the ground state g_e. Then, by the methods of statistical mechanics, we can show that it contributes to C_p° the amount C_p°(elec.) given by

$$\frac{C_p^\circ(\text{elec.})}{R} = \frac{g_e x^2 e^{-x}}{(1 + g_e e^{-x})^2} \tag{2.19}$$

where $x = E_e/RT$. C_p°(elec.)/R has a maximum at a value of x between 2 (for $g_e \ll 1$) and $\sim \ln g_e$ (for $g_e \gg 1$). At $g_e = 1$ the maximum occurs at

$x = 2.3$ with $(C_p^\circ/R)_{max} \sim 0.41$. When g_e is small the maximum is proportionately smaller, and C_p°/R never becomes appreciable. However, for $g_e \gg 1$, $(C_p^\circ(\text{elec.})/R)_{max}$ is approximately 2.3 $\log g_e/4$ or less than 0.6 if $g_e = 10$, which would be unusually high.

Because $C_p^\circ(\text{elec.})$ is zero both at very low and at very high temperatures, we see that it never gets much beyond about 1 gibbs/mole at temperatures of the order of $E_e/2R$, and thus we will usually make what amounts to a small error in neglecting it.

2.11 SYMMETRY NUMBERS AND ISOMERS

From a statistical point of view, the molar entropy of a compound is given by $R \ln W$ where W is the number of distinguishable configurations that the compound can have. These configurations must be compatible with certain imposed constraints, such as the chosen standard molar volume and temperature, and must be suitably weighted by the Boltzmann energy distribution $e^{-E_i/RT}$ where E_i is the energy of the ith configuration.

The so-called "translational entropy" of an ideal gas represents the contribution to $R \ln W$ of the various configurations achieved by different assignments of 1 mole (N_A) of particles within the standard volume of 24.6 liters at 25°C.

Gibbs was the first to point out that any permutation of the identical molecules would lead to an indistinguishable configuration of the gas. Because, for N_A molecules in a box, there are $N_A!$ permutations, he corrected this simple calculation of W, defined above, by dividing it by $N_A!$. This is the origin of the famous "entropy of mixing" paradox. There is no such correction for distinguishable molecules.

The rotational entropy of an ideal gas arises from the contributions to $R \ln W$ of the various configurations achieved by changing the orientation of the molecular axis of a polyatomic molecule in space. For molecules made up of nonidentical atoms, such as H—O—Cl or N—N—O, this poses no problem. However, if the molecule contains identical atoms, we must correct for those indistinguishable configurations, which merely correspond to having permuted the positions of identical atoms. In principle this correction could be as large as $(n_a! \, n_b! \cdots)$ where n_a and n_b, etc. are the number of indistinguishable atoms of type a, b, etc. in the molecule. In practice this is hardly ever the case because the rigidity of the molecule rules out certain permutations.

For homonuclear diatomic molecules such as H_2, O_2 we have two identical atoms that can be permuted by a simple 180° rotation. Hence we get the full correction of 2!. In a molecule such as O_3, only the two end O atoms are identical, so the correction is again 2! = 2. However, in the hypothetical cyclic molecule O—O—O, where all O atoms are identical, we would have the full correction of $3! = 6$. In CH_4 with four identical H atoms, we might expect a maximum correction of $4! = 24$. However, not all permutations of the four atoms can be arrived at by simple rotations. In particular, half of the permutations that would correspond to an inversion of the molecule through the central C atom are not possible and so the correction is $4!/2 = 12$. A flabby CH_4 molecule that could invert rapidly would require the full correction.

The correction to the rotational entropy due to these features of indistinguishable atoms is spoken of as a symmetry correction and is made by subtracting $R \ln \sigma$ from the rotational entropy. σ is the symmetry number and is defined as the total number of *independent* permutations of identical atoms (or groups) in a molecule that can be arrived at by simple rigid rotations of the entire molecule. Some typical symmetry numbers are $H_2O(2)$; $SO_2(2)$; SO_3 planar (6); NH_3 nonplanar (3); $CH_4(12)$; $SF_6(24)$; benzene, $C_6H_6(12)$; cyclopropane, $C_3H_6(6)$; cyclobutane, nonplanar (4); $C_2H_4(4)$; $H_2O_2(2)$; cyclobutadiene, planar (8).

A simple method of estimating σ is to multiply the symmetries of each of the independent symmetry axes. Thus CH_4 $\sigma = 12$ can be looked upon as having four independent threefold symmetry axes. Each one goes through a different C—H axis and involves rotation of the remaining CH_3 group about this axis. Hence $\sigma = 4 \times 3 = 12$. SF_6 has six-fourfold axes. Hence $\sigma = 6 \times 4 = 24$. The triangular bi-pyramid, PF_5, with two apical and three equatorial F atoms has one threefold and one twofold axis. Hence $\sigma = 3 \times 2 = 6$. Benzene has six twofold axes. Hence $\sigma = 6 \times 2 = 12$.

For molecules with hindered internal rotation, such as ethane, there is a contribution to the external rotation of six due a twofold axis and a threefold symmetry axis. In addition, the internal rotation of the CH_3 group has a threefold axis. We shall combine these and represent the overall $\sigma = \sigma_{ext.} \times \sigma_{int.} = 18$. On the same basis all the normal alkanes have $\sigma = 18$, due to an external twofold axis, and $\sigma = 9$ for the two terminal CH_3 groups. For neopentane, C_5H_{12}, $\sigma_{ext.} = 12$, as it does in CH_4, whereas $\sigma_{int.} = 3^4$ for the four methyl groups. Hence $\sigma = 12 \times 3^4 = 972$, an extremely large correction.

For readers who are familiar with point groups and their symmetry designations, Table 2.3 summarizes the symmetry numbers of molecules belonging to the different groups.

A different type of correction accompanies isomeric species. Let us suppose that we have two isomeric forms of a molecule that have the same ΔH_f°, but are physically distinguishable. Thus, they can be optical isomers, rotational conformers, etc. If we have an equilibrium mixture of such species, we must add a term to S° of $R \ln 2$ gibbs/mole to represent the entropy of mixing of these species. If there are n such species, *all of the same*

Table 2.3   Symmetry Numbers for Various Point Groups

Point Group	σ	Point Group	σ	Point Group	σ
C_1, C_i, C_s	1	$D_2, D_{2d}, D_{2h} \equiv V$	4	$C_{\infty v}$	1
C_2, C_{2v}, C_{2h}	2	D_3, D_{3d}, D_{3h}	6	$D_{\infty h}$	2
C_3, C_{3v}, C_{2h}	3	D_4, D_{4d}, D_{4h}	8	T, T_d	12
C_4, C_{4v}, C_{4h}	4	D_6, D_{6d}, D_{6h}	12	O_h	24
C_6, C_{6v}, C_{6h}	6	S_6	3		

Taken from G. Herzberg, *Molecular Spectra and Molecular Structure*, Van Nostrand, Princeton, N.J., 1945. C_j indicates a j-fold axis of symmetry. D_j denotes a molecule of the class C_j with a j-fold axis and J-twofold axes at right angles to the C_j axis and at equal angles to each other. T denotes tetrahedral symmetry, and O, octahedral symmetry.

energy content, the correction is $R \ln n$ given by the formula for 1 mole of mixture:

$$\Delta S_{\text{mixing}} = -R \sum_i n_i \ln (n_i)$$

where n_i is the equilibrium mole fraction of the ith form. When they all have the same energy so that $n_i = 1/n$, this becomes the familiar $R \ln n$.

When we calculate entropies for such species as *sec*-butyl iodide, we shall add $R \ln 2$ to the estimate from the group tables to correct for such optical isomerism. Similarly, species such as ROOH and H_2O_2, in which the O—H and O—R bonds are nearly at right angles, exist in right- and left-hand forms and have a higher entropy by ($R \ln 2$). This is also true of 1,3- disubstituted allenes.

EXAMPLE

Estimate the entropy of dimethyl peroxide from groups

$$S^\circ = 2S^\circ[\underline{C}\text{—O(H)}_3] + 2S^\circ[\text{O—(C)(O)}] - R \ln \sigma + R \ln 2$$
$$= 60.82 + 18.8 - 5.8 + 1.4 = 75.2 \text{ gibbs/mole.}$$

2.12   ESTIMATIONS OF C°_{pT} FROM MODEL COMPOUNDS

We have noted that it is possible to estimate C°_{pT} from structural considerations. However, the calculation is time consuming, and more often we can do just as well by making comparisons with known compounds or compounds for which group values are available. The same is true for ΔH°_{f298} and for S°_{298}. Let us consider some examples.

Suppose we wish to estimate S°_{298} of a compound such as $CH_3CH{=}NH$ for which no data exist. We start by taking the simplest molecule having a similar mass and structure with known properties. In this case, this would be $CH_3CH{=}CH_2$ for which $S^\circ_{298} = 63.8$ gibbs/mole.

We now consider the corrections we need to apply. These can be classified as follows.

1. Translational (depends on total mass)
2. Rotational (depends on moments of inertia)
3. Vibrational (depends on frequencies)
4. Symmetry including optical centers
5. Internal rotations.

$S°$(trans.) varies as $\frac{3}{2}R \ln M$ where M is the molecular weight. If we change M to M', $S°$(trans.) changes by an amount $\frac{3}{2}R \ln (M'/M)$. If $M'/M = 1.10$, this becomes an increase of $\sim0.15R = 0.3$ gibbs/mole. In the example above $(M'/M) = 43/42$ and $\Delta S°$(trans.) $\simeq 0.08$ gibbs/mole, which is negligible.

$S°$(rot.) varies as $\frac{1}{2}R \ln (I_A I_B I_C)$ where I_A, I_B, and I_C are the three principal moments of inertia of the molecule. $\Delta S°$(rot.) becomes $\frac{1}{2}R \ln (I'_A I'_B I'_C / I_A I_B I_C)$. Each I varies as $\Sigma m_i r_i^2$ where m is the mass of the heavier atoms and r_i the cartesian projection (xy, yz, zx) of their distances from the center of gravity. Unless we have grossly changed m_i or r_i, in going from our model compound, $\Delta S°_{(rot.)}$ will be very small. Note that a doubling of one principal moment of inertia increases $S°_{(rot.)}$ by $\frac{1}{2}R \ln 2$ or only 0.7 gibbs/mole. In the case chosen, the change in $S_{(rot.)}$ is negligible.

In changing from a $=CH_2$ group to $=NH$, we have lost one atom and hence three internal vibrations. These are a C—H stretch and two C—C—H bends. From Table A.13 we estimate these at 3100 and 1100 cm^{-1}, respectively. At 298°, $x = ch\tilde{\nu}/kT$ becomes 14.5 and 5.3, and from Table A.17 in the Appendix, we estimate a loss of 0.06 gibbs/mole from the loss of the H atom.

In the case above, there is no change in symmetry or in internal rotations, so that the estimated value of $S°_{298}$ (CH_3—CH=NH) is 63.8 gibbs/mole with an estimated uncertainty of not more than ±0.5.

By the method described above we are not surprised that $S°_{298}$ (CH_3—CO—CH_3) is 70.5, and that for structurally similar isobutene it is 70.6 gibbs/mole.

We can make a further comparison of $S°_{298}$ (CH_3CHO) = 63.2 and $S°_{298}$ ($CH_3CH=CH_2$) = 63.8 gibbs/mole. From comparing $S°_{298}$ (CH_3CH_2OH) = 67.3 with $S°_{298}$ ($CH_3CH_2CH_3$) = 64.6, we note a symmetry difference of $R \ln (18/3) = 3.6$, favoring the alcohol and giving a difference of only 0.9 gibbs/mole in the symmetry corrected (intrinsic) entropies.[8] Once again, there are no other major corrections. Small corrections for the change in hindered rotation barriers and number of hydrogen atoms approximately cancel.

In Table 2.4 we list values of $C°_p$ and $S°$ for structurally similar molecules over the range 300°K to 1000°K. They are arranged in various groupings to

[8] $S°_{(int.)} = S°_{(obs.)} + R \ln (\sigma/n)$.

point out the effect of adding H atoms to a heavy skeleton or of adding internal rotations. Because translational and rotational contributions to C_p° above $300°K$ are constant, they have been subtracted and the values in parenthesis give the residues due to internal degrees of freedom.

Table 2.4   Some Examples of Structural Similarities in C_p° and S°

Molecule (σ total)		C_p° (C_{vib}) [c]			S° [d]		
		$300°K$	$600°K$	$1000°K$	$300°K$	$600°K$	$1000°K$
A. N≡N	(2)	7.0 (0.1)	7.2 (0.3)	7.8 (0.9)	45.8	50.7	54.5
C≡O	(1)	7.0 (0.1)	7.3 (0.4)	7.9 (1.0)	47.3	52.2	56.0
H—C≡N	(1)	8.6 (1.7)	10.6 (3.7)	12.2 (5.3)	48.3	54.9	60.7
H—C≡C—H	(2)	10.6 (3.7)	13.9 (7.0)	16.3 (9.4)	48.0	56.6	64.3
B. O=C=O	(2)	8.9 (2.0)	11.3 (4.4)	13.0 (6.1)	51.1	58.1	64.3
O=N≡N	(1)	9.3 (2.4)	11.6 (4.7)	13.1 (6.2)	52.6	59.8	66.1
C. H$_2$C=O	(2)	8.5 (0.6)	11.5 (3.6)	14.8 (6.9)	52.3	59.1	65.8
H$_2$C=CH$_2$	(4)	10.3 (2.4)	16.9 (9.0)	22.4 (14.5)	52.4	61.7	71.8
H$_3$C—C≡CH	(3)	14.6 (6.7)	21.8 (13.9)	27.7 (19.8)	59.4	71.9	84.5
HO—OH	(2)[a]	10.3 (2.4)	13.3 (5.4)	15.0 (7.1)	55.7	57.9	61.9
D. O—N=O	(2)[b]	8.9 (1.0)	11.0 (3.1)	12.5 (4.6)	57.4	64.2	70.2
O$_3$	(2)	9.4 (1.5)	11.9 (4.0)	13.2 (5.3)	57.1	64.5	71.0
F—O—F	(2)	10.4 (2.5)	12.5 (4.6)	13.3 (5.4)	59.2	67.2	73.8
F—CH$_2$—F	(2)	10.3 (2.4)	15.7 (7.8)	20.0 (12.1)	59.0	67.9	77.0
E. O—Cl—O	(2)[c]	10.9 (3.0)	12.7 (4.8)	13.4 (5.5)	63.7	71.9	78.7
O=S—O	(2)	9.5 (1.6)	11.7 (3.8)	13.0 (5.1)	59.4	66.7	73.0
CH$_3$—S—CH$_3$	(18)	17.8 (9.9)	27.0 (19.1)	35.2 (27.3)	68.4	83.7	99.6

[a] H$_2$O$_2$ exists in a skew form with optically active isomers. Hence S° includes a term $R \ln 2$ due to entropy of mixing.
[b] S° includes a term $R \ln 2$ due to electron spin.
[c] Values in parentheses are $C_p^{\circ} - C_p^{\circ}(\text{trans.}) - C_p^{\circ}(\text{rot.}) - R$.
[d] These are absolute entropies. To obtain intrinsic entropies, add $R \ln (\sigma/n_i g_e)$ where g_e is the electronic degeneracy.

In Group A we note that C_p° ($298°K$) increases by about 2 eu per H atom added for the linear molecules, which is about the increase obtained on extending the linear molecule by one heavy atom (Group B). In contrast to this we note C_p° only gains 1 eu per H atom in going from CH$_2$O to C$_2$H$_4$. Comparing C_{p298}° of CO$_2$ and CH$_3$CCH, we note an increase in the internal contributions of 1.2 eu per H atom. We find about the same increment in comparing ClO$_2$ with (CH$_3$)$_2$S.

In comparing entropies, we should correct $S°$ by symmetry, electronic spin, and optical isomers. We do this by adding to the listed $S°$, $R \ln \sigma$, subtracting $R \ln g_e$ and subtracting $R \ln n_i$. The symmetry number σ includes, for convenience, internal symmetry arising from hindered rotors, as in $(CH_3)_2S$. The electronic degeneracy g_e is usually equal to $2j + 1$ where j is the total electronic angular momentum. For polyatomic molecules, it is generally taken as $2S + 1$ where S is the total spin. The quantity n_i is the total number of energetically equivalent optical isomers. We call these corrected values the intrinsic entropies or $S°_{int.}$.

For CH_2O at $298°K$, $S°_{int.} = 53.7$ eu, and for C_2H_4, $S°_{int.} = 55.2$ eu. For H_2O_2, $S°_{int.} = 55.7$ eu, and for NO_2, $S°_{int.} = 57.4$ eu. For O_3, $S°_{int.} = 58.5$ eu, and for CH_2F_2, $S°_{int.} = 60.4$ eu. Comparing $S°_{int.}((CH_3)_2S)$ of 74.2 eu. with $S°_{int.}(ClO_2) = 63.7$ eu, we see that the internal rotations and vibrations associated with the CH_3 groups contribute about 5.3 eu per CH_3. Most of this arises directly from the internal rotations. From Table A.18 we can obtain 5.8 eu per CH_3 group at $300°K$.

Free Radicals

Except for a few stable free radicals such as NO, NO_2, ClO_2, and NF_2 there are very few direct thermochemical data on free radicals. The best values for heats of formation are almost invariably deduced from kinetic measurements of bond dissociation energies, whereas entropies and heat capacities are only calculable from statistical formulas. Because of this, there are large gaps in our knowledge of the thermochemical data on free radicals. Heats of formation usually are uncertain to about ± 1 kcal/mole in the best cases and can be considerably worse. However, there is every indication that the laws of group additivity apply to radicals, so that we can deduce $\Delta H_f°$ for all of the paraffin radicals from our knowledge of $\Delta H_f°$ for $CH_3\dot{C}H_2$; $(CH_3)_2\dot{C}H$ and $(CH_3)_3\dot{C}$.[9]

The estimation of the entropies of radicals can be deduced by group additivities from the properties of the simple radicals, but these latter must be calculated from assumed structures and frequency assignments. Although there is good ground for believing that substituted methyl radicals are planar, and consequently have a higher symmetry number than a nonplanar radical,

---

[9] This is not strictly true because there is no stable compound corresponding to the hypothetical formula $\dot{C}H_2—\dot{C}H_2$ if, by analogy with the substituted $X—CH_2—CH_2—X$, we treat the odd electron as though it were the same as a substituents X. A true group treatment would require values for all of the groups $\dot{C}—(C)(H)_2$, $\dot{C}—(C)_2(H)$, $\dot{C}—(C)_3$, $C—(\dot{C})(H)_3$, $C—(\dot{C})(C)(H)_2$, $C—(\dot{C})(C)_2(H)$, and $C—(\dot{C})(C)_3$. However, the assumption that the groups $C—(\dot{C})(C)_2(H)$ etc. have the same partial heat of formation as the corresponding nonradical, paraffin groups $C—(C)_3(H)$ seems to be valid within the limits of present data, and so we shall employ it.

this is still a gross uncertainty in our estimates. In similar fashion, we usually assume only spin degeneracy and assign an entropy of $R \ln 2$ to odd electron radicals, such as $\dot{C}H_3$, $CH_3\dot{C}O$, and $\dot{C}H_2$—CH=CH_2. The existence of low-lying electronic states is always a source of uncertainty in our estimates of S° and C_p°. Still larger uncertainties are related to the assignment of barriers to internal rotation in complex radicals such as t-butyl, $(CH_3)_3\dot{C}$, and allyl, $\dot{C}H_2$—CH=CH_2.

With the warnings we give above in mind, we can assign values to C_p° and S° for radicals by analogy with related compounds. Thus we will assume that $\dot{C}H_3$ radical has the same value of C_{p298}° as CH_4 and NH_3, both of which are 8.5 eu. The expected uncertainty here can only arise from low-lying electronic states and is clearly small. The value of S_{298}° ($\dot{C}H_3$), using spin = $\frac{1}{2}$, $g_e = 2$ and $\sigma = 6$, can be assigned as 46.0 by analogy with S_{298}° (NH_3) = 46.0, $\sigma_{NH_3} = 3$. Further comparisons can be made with S_{298}° (CH_4) = 44.5, $\sigma_{CH_4} = 12$; S_{298}° (H_2O) = 45.1, $\sigma_{H_2O} = 2$. A lower limit of 45.7 can be fixed by correcting the translational entropy of NH_3 from $M = 17$ to $M = 15$.

For the more complex $CH_3\dot{C}H_2$ radical ($\sigma = 6$), the comparison we give in Table 2.5 can be made. It is unlikely that the assigned S° intrinsic ($\dot{C}_2H_5$) is in error by more than ± 1.0 eu. (Note: We have assumed a zero internal barrier to rotation.)

Conjugated radicals offer more of a problem because they have stiffer structures. Thus the conjugated allyl radical $\dot{C}H_2$—CH=CH_2 is estimated to have a stabilization energy due to conjugation of about 12 kcal/mole. This would represent a barrier to rotation of the CH_2 group, which can be compared to a barrier of about 2 kcal/mole for the CH_3 group in the model compound CH_3—CH=CH_2. Again the analogies with similar compounds given in Table 2.6 provide a quick basis for assigning a value of about 3 eu to this loss in free CH_3 rotation.

Comparing the intrinsic entropies of C_3H_6 and C_3H_8, we note a difference of 4.2 eu, whereas CH_3OCH_3 is only 0.9 less than C_3H_8. Correcting for the mass difference, we can assign about 0.2 eu (Table A.17) to the vibrational modes due to two H atoms, and the remaining 4.0 eu to the internal rotation, and thus arrive at S° (allyl) = 63.0 eu, after we subtract an additional 0.1 eu for the loss of one H atom and add 1.0 eu for a 13 kcal barrier internal rotation of one conjugated $\dot{C}H_2$ group (Table A.20).

Table 2.5

Species	CH_3CH_3	CH_3NH_2	CH_3OH	CH_2=CH_2	$CH_3\dot{C}H_2$
σ, spin	18, 0	3, 0	3, 0	4, 0	6, $\frac{1}{2}$
S_{298}°	54.9	57.7	57.3	52.5	58.1
S_{298}° (*intrinsic*)	60.6	59.9	59.5	55.3	60.3

Table 2.6

Species	$CH_3CH_2CH_3$	CH_3NHCH_3	CH_3OCH_3
σ, spin	18, 0	9, 0	18, 0
S°_{298}	64.6	65.3	63.7
S°_{298} (*intrinsic*)	70.3	69.7	69.4

Species	$CH_3{-}CH{=}CH_2$	$\dot{C}H_2{-}CH{=}CH_2$	$CH_2{=}C{=}CH_2$
σ, spin	3, 0	2, $\frac{1}{2}$	4, 0
S°_{298}	63.9	63.0	58.3
S°_{298} (*intrinsic*)	66.1	63.0	61.1

Where structural analogues are not readily available, values of S° and C°_p for radicals $R\cdot$ can be estimated from their molecular hydrogenated parents RH. We do this by making corrections for the various degrees of freedom lost or altered significantly when we remove the H atom.

The ethyl radical provides a useful example. Starting with the parent C_2H_6, for which S° and C°_p are available over a broad range, we can arrive at the corrections at 300°K given in Table 2.7. These give $S^{\circ}_{p300}(C_2H_5\cdot) = S^{\circ}_{300}(C_2H_6) + 4.9$ eu = 59.8 gibbs/mole and $C^{\circ}_{p300}(C_2H_5\cdot) = 11.2$ gibbs/mole. Note that the barrier of 0 kcal in $C_2H_5\cdot$ is assigned on the basis of a sixfold symmetry axis for internal rotation, and experience shows that barriers to rotation for sixfold axis are negligible.

Vibration assignments made above are taken from Table A.13, and the corresponding S° and C°_p from Tables A.17 and A.15, respectively. The barrier corrections to S° and C°_p are taken from Tables A.20 and A.16, respectively.

Table 2.7

	ΔS°	ΔC°_p
Translation	Negligible	None
Rotation	Negligible	None
Vibration		
One C—H stretch (3100 cm^{-1})	0	0
Two H$_2$—C bends (1450 cm^{-1})	0	−0.2
Hindered Rotation		
Barrier change from	+1.3	−1.3
3 kcal → 0 kcal		
Symmetry and spin	+3.6	None
Totals	+4.9 eu	−1.5 eu

Most of the C_p° and S° values for the radicals listed in Table A.12 have been arrived at in the manner described above, as have the data on biradicals we use in Chapter 3. Note that $S_{300}^\circ(C_2H_5)$, derived in this manner, is significantly higher than the value assigned on the basis of structural analogy.

2.13   VIBRATIONAL CONTRIBUTIONS TO ENTROPY

Vibrational contributions to S° are very easily estimated from the methods of statistical mechanics, and they are given by the following formula for a simple harmonic oscillator with frequency $\tilde{\nu}$ (cm^{-1}):

$$\frac{S^\circ}{R} = \ln Q_v + \frac{\partial \ln Q_v}{\partial \ln T} \tag{2.20}$$

where Q_v is the vibrational partition function (omitting zero point energy);

$$Q_v = (1 - e^{-x})^{-1}; \qquad x = ch\frac{\tilde{\nu}}{kT}. \tag{2.21}$$

Hence, on substitution,

$$\frac{S^\circ}{R} = -\ln(1 - e^{-x}) + \frac{x}{e^x - 1}. \tag{2.22}$$

Values of S°/R are shown plotted in Figure 2.4 as a function of x, and, for easier use, S° is tabulated in Table A.17 for different frequencies and temperatures. In the limit that $x \le 1$, these equations reduce to

$$Q_v = \frac{1}{x}\left(1 + \frac{x}{2} + \frac{x^2}{12} +\right) \approx \frac{1}{2} + \frac{1}{x}; \tag{2.23}$$

$$\frac{S^\circ}{R} = -\ln\left[x\left(1 - \frac{x}{2}\right)\right] + \left(1 + \frac{x}{2} + \frac{x^2}{6} +\right)^{-1}$$

$$= 1 - \ln x + \frac{x}{2} + \frac{5x^2}{24} + \frac{x^3}{24}$$

$$\approx 1 - \ln x + \frac{x}{2}. \tag{2.24}$$

Even when $x = 1$, the error in the approximate formulae given [(2.23) and (2.24)] amount to an error of less than 5% in Q_v and 0.4 gibbs/mole in S°.

Tables A.17 and A.13 together make it possible to estimate vibrational entropies for molecules or radicals over the temperature range 300°K to 1500°K with great facility because interpolations can easily be made from them.

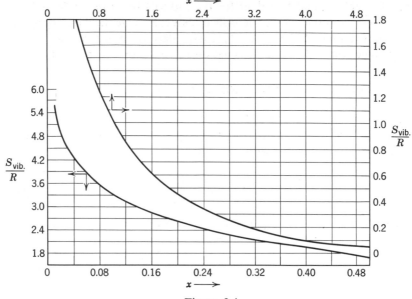

Figure 2.4

EXAMPLE

Calculate the absolute vibrational entropy of CH_3Br at 750°K. With five atoms, we have $15 - 6 = 9$ internal frequencies, of which four are stretches and five are deformations. We assign them as listed in Table 2.8 from Table A.13.   This can be compared with the more precise estimate from known frequencies of 5.3 gibbs/mole.

Table 2.8

	Frequency	$S_v^\circ(750°K)$[a]
Three C—H stretches	3100	0.2
One C—Br stretch	560	2.0
Two H—C—H bend	1450	0.8
Three H—C—Br bends	1150	2.4
Total S_v°		5.4 gibbs/mole

[a] From Table A.17.

When internal rotations are involved, we use (2.17) to calculate Q, the partition function for a free rotor and then, using the rules suggested in Section 2.9, assign a barrier to rotation.   From these assignments we use Table A.18 to find the free rotor entropy and then Table A.19 to assign corrections.

EXAMPLE

Estimate the entropy contribution due to the hindered rotation in C_2H_6 at 800°K. From Table A.18, we see that the entropy of a free CH_3 rotating against a heavy group is 6.8 gibbs/mole at 800°K. However, in C_2H_6, the reduced moment of inertia I_r is just one-half this value, and because $S_f^\circ \propto \frac{1}{2} R \ln I_r$, this introduces a correction of $-\frac{1}{2}R \ln 2 = 0.7$ gibbs/mole for a value of 6.1 gibbs/mole. The barrier $V = 3.0$ kcal, and $V/RT = 1.8$. From Table A.18, Q_f, the partition function at 800°K, becomes

$$Q_f(800) = \frac{1}{\sigma} \frac{Q_f'(600°K)}{(2)^{1/2}} \times \left(\frac{800}{600}\right)^{1/2} = \frac{1}{3} \times \frac{15.6}{1.41} \times 1.16 = 4.2.$$

The factor of $2^{1/2}$ corrects for the reduced moment. From Table A.19, we now find the correction of $S_f^\circ = -0.3$, so that the final value is 5.8 gibbs/mole. Note that, although we have used the symmetry to make the correction to S_f°, the value of 5.8 does not contain it because of our usual method of making internal and external symmetry corrections at the same time. If we were to make it now, the value would become 3.6 gibbs/mole.

EXAMPLE

Estimate the entropy to hindered rotation in 1,2-dibromoethane at 500°K. This is an unsymmetrical top with two different rotomeric forms, gauche and trans, each of which would have different moments of inertia and different barriers. We neglect such differences, as well as the fact that the tops are not coaxial, and calculate the reduced moment of the —CH_2Br top as though it were a symmetrical top about the C—C axis.

To a first approximation, we can neglect the two H atoms relative to the heavy Br atom,

$$I(CH_2Br) \sim m_{Br} r_{C-Br}^2 \sin^2 (70.5°)$$
$$= 81 \times (1.9)^2 \times 0.95 = 290 \text{ amu-Å}^2$$
$$I_r = \frac{1}{2}I(CH_2Br) = 145.$$

This yield $Q_f(500°K) = 92$ from (2.17) because $\sigma = 1$. From Table A.18, we find $S_f^\circ = 9.8$ gibbs/mole, and using a 4.0 kcal barrier (adding 0.5 kcal per bulky group), $V/RT = 4.0$; from Table A.19 the correction becomes 1.1 gibbs/mole, so that the net entropy $S_{hr}^\circ(500°K) = 8.7$ gibbs/mole.

2.14 STRAIN ENERGY AND RESONANCE ENERGY

The term "strain energy" is frequently used in speaking of highly branched or cyclic compounds. Such a term can only have meaning relative to some reference state, which is arbitrarily assigned zero strain. Because unbranched hydrocarbons and their derivatives fit the additivity laws for ΔH_f° so well, they are taken as the "unstrained" standards. On this basis we can assign a strain energy E_s to a compound as the difference between its observed ΔH_f°

and its value estimated from the group additivity relations using the group values which have been, of course, derived from the unstrained standards.

Thus E_s for the alicyclic rings $(CH_2)_m$ is given by

$$E_s[(CH_2)_m] = \Delta H_f^\circ[(CH_2)_m] - m\,\Delta H_f^\circ[C—(C)_2(H)_2]. \qquad (2.25)$$

The principle described above permits us to calculate strains in cyclic olefins, aromatics, heterocyclic compounds and polycyclic compounds. Table 2.9 illustrates these calculations.

Table 2.9   Strain Energies in Some Compounds[a]

Compound	ΔH_f° (obs.) (kcal/mole)	ΔH_f° (calc.) (kcal/mole)	E_s (kcal/mole)
Cyclopropane	12.7	−14.9	27.6
Ethylene oxide	−12.5	−40.1	27.6
Cyclopentane	−18.5	−24.8	6.3
Cyclopentene	+7.9	+2.5	5.4
Cyclopentadiene-1,3	32.0	26.0[b] (29.6)	6.0 (2.4)
Cyclohexane	−29.5	−29.7	0.2
Bicycloheptane (2,2,1)	−8.0 ± 3	−27.7	20.0 ± 3
Benzene	19.8	42.3[b] (52.8)	−22.5 (−33.0)

[a] Note that the nongroup interaction corrections in Table A.1 correct for these strains.
[b] These values are derived from group values based on butadiene. However, butadiene has a conjugation energy of 3.6 kcal based on butene-1. The values in parentheses correct for this conjugation energy and are based on trans olefins.

It will be noticed that the strain energy in benzene relative to butene-1 is negative (!), that is, −33.0 kcal/mole. This is very close to the stabilization or resonance energy of 36 0 kcal/mole of benzene computed from the heat of hydrogenation and referenced to cyclohexene. If we correct for the resonance energy, we calculate a strain energy of 3.0 kcal/mole in benzene. However, if we examine this separation in some detail, we shall find that there is no way of truly identifying strain and resonance energies separately in benzene.

We may speak of "resonance energy" or "stabilization energy" or more generally "interaction energy" as the deviation of the observed ΔH_f° of a compound from that obtained from additivity rules based on groups whose own interaction energy is arbitrarily defined as zero. Because there is no absolute energy, all such concepts, such as that of potential energy, must always invoke some standard and quite arbitrary zero.

Once again the remarkable fit of the unbranched paraffins to the group additivity rule provides a basis for measuring interaction energy. A simple example is provided by butadiene, $CH_2{=}CH—CH{=}CH_2$, which is made up of four groups: $2[C_d\text{---}(H)_2] + 2[C_d\text{---}(C_d)(H)]$. The $C_d\text{---}(C_d)(H)$ group we find from the tables has a ΔH_f° of $+7.0$ kcal/mole. This can be compared with related group $C_d\text{---}(C)(H)$, which has $\Delta H_f^\circ = +8.8$ kcal/mole. Twice the difference between those of $2 \times 1.8 = 3.6$ kcal represents the difference in interaction of a double bond with an adjacent saturated group and with another double bond. This is frequently called a resonance energy of two conjugated double bonds. For purely empirical purposes, it is better referred to as a double-bond interaction energy.

If we compare our definitions of "strain" and "interaction" energies, we note that there is no way of separating the two. In effect the difference between an observed and a calculated ΔH_f° gives only a single result, and it is a combination of all the effects we can identify. Only if we have some independent basis for separating strain and resonance can such identification be made.

For benzene, if we consider the hypothetical molecule made of alternate single and double bonds, we can calculate a net stabilization of the real benzene of 33.0 kcal. This value would be based on unconjugated trans olefins, and if we corrected by 3×1 kcal/mole to allow for three *cis* olefins in the hypothetical benzene, we arrive at the frequently quoted 36 kcal. However, we have no way of really setting the strain equal to zero because we have no independent reference point for the strain energy.

It is only because we have no reason to expect "resonance" interaction in cyclopentane that we assign all of the difference in ΔH_f° to strain, although again it is only because we do not expect any strain in our hypothetical alternately bonded benzene that we assign all of the difference in ΔH_f° to resonance.

It is also well to note another difficulty with the present definitions of strain and resonance or interaction energies. We see in our tables that normally we expect a strain energy of about 0.8 kcal/mole for each gauche configuration of large groups. On this basis, we should expect a net strain energy of 4.8 kcal/mole in the "chair" form of cyclohexane because it has six such gauche interactions. The fact that the uncorrected strain energy is only 0.2 kcal/mole can then be interpreted to indicate that cyclohexane actually must have a compensating interaction or configuration energy of 4.6 kcal/mole! This is, however, an artifact arising from excess thermal energy. The CH_2 groups in a normal paraffins have a significantly greater group heat capacity than the CH_2 groups in a ring. If we calculate C_p° for "unstrained" cyclohexane from our tables, we find it is 32.7 eu compared with the observed value of 22 eu. This difference in C_p° contributes, at $298°K$, an excess thermal energy of slightly more than 2 kcal to normal CH_2 groups compared to the C_6-cyclic CH_2.

To make more significant comparisons of strain and interaction energies we should compare ΔH_f° at $0°K$. In addition the residual zero point energies should also be subtracted, so that we are comparing only the net potential or "chemical" energy of the two states. Such comparisons are not always possible, for they require a knowledge of all of the vibrational frequencies and rotational barriers of the two states of the system.

2.15 PI-BOND ENERGIES

There is one additional energy which it is useful to define in discussing radicals. This is the "pi-bond energy," which is associated with multiple bonding. If we consider the very simplest example of C_2H_6, we observe that in the process of removing two H atoms to form C_2H_4, the bond dissociation energies[10] are not equal. The first bond dissociation energy in 98 kcal/mole, corresponding to the heat of reaction at 298°K for

$$CH_3CH_3 \rightarrow CH_3\dot{C}H_2 + \dot{H} - 98 \text{ kcal.} \qquad (2.26)$$

The second bond dissociation is 38.5 kcal/mole, corresponding to ΔH_f° for

$$CH_3\dot{C}H_2 \rightarrow CH_2{=}CH_2 + \dot{H} - 38.5 \text{ kcal.} \qquad (2.27)$$

If group additivity were obeyed, we would expect that these two bond dissociation energies would be equal. We explain the fact that they are not equal by noting that, in removing the second H atom, we have also formed a double bond. It is useful to define E_π°, the strength of this multiple or "pi bond," as the difference in bond dissociation energies of the two H atoms.

$$E_\pi^\circ = DH^\circ(C_2H_5{-}H) - DH^\circ(C_2H_4{-}H) = 59.5 \text{ kcal.} \qquad (2.28)$$

For unsymmetrical compounds, such as propylene, we can define the pi-bond energy as the difference in bond strengths of the same C—H bond, when the other C—H bond is intact or broken. Diagrammatically

$$
\begin{array}{ccc}
 & CH_3H\dot{C}CH_3 + H & \\
 & \nearrow^{1} \qquad \searrow^{2} & \\
CH_3{-}CH_2{-}CH_3 & & CH_3CH{=}CH_2 + 2H. \\
 & \searrow_{1'} \qquad \nearrow_{2'} & \\
 & CH_3CH_2{-}\dot{C}H_2 + H &
\end{array}
$$

By Hess' law, $DH_1 + DH_2 = DH_1' + DH_2'$, so that $E_\pi(\text{propylene}) = DH_1 - DH_2' = DH_1' - DH_2$.

[10] We are using the conventional definition of bond dissociation energy DH°, namely the standard enthalpy change for the reaction in which the designated bond is broken

E_π° corresponds to the energy required to "break" the multiple bond in a double or triple bonded compound to form the corresponding biradical. There is no reason to expect that these biradicals correspond to metastable or observable species or to known spectroscopic states. There are no potential energy minima associated with such biradicals, which would be the criterion for stability. They are in this sense, better labelled, "hypothetical" biradicals in the same sense that a "noninteracting" butadiene whose properties we can derive from butene-1 is a hypothetical, not a real species. Symbolically, we can write pi-bond energies for the following processes:

$$E_\pi^\circ(C_2H_4) + CH_2{=}CH_2 \rightleftarrows \dot{C}H_2{-}\dot{C}H_2;$$

$$E_\pi^\circ(HCN) + HC{\equiv}N \rightleftarrows H\dot{C}{=}\dot{N}.$$

For olefins we expect that the pi-bond energies will correspond to the minimum activation energies required to covert cis to trans species, and in the few cases where data are available this has turned out to be true.

It should be noted that the energy required to break $CH_2{=}CH_2$ into $2\ddot{C}H_2$ radicals is precisely the sum of $E_\pi^\circ(C_2H_4) + DH^\circ(\dot{C}H_2{-}\dot{C}H_2)$ However, there is no independent method whereby $DH^\circ(\dot{C}H_2{-}\dot{C}H_2)$ can be measured, and in fact when $\Delta H_f^\circ(\ddot{C}H_2)$ is available, this relation can be used to calculate $DH^\circ(\dot{C}H_2{-}\dot{C}H_2)$. Using $\Delta H_f^\circ(\ddot{C}H_2) = 89$ and $\Delta H_f^\circ(C_2H_4) = 12.5$ kcal/mole, we note that $DH^\circ(CH_2{=}CH_2) = 165.5$ kcal/mole, so that, with $E_\pi^\circ(C_2H_4) = 59.5$, we deduce $DH^\circ(\dot{C}H_2{-}\dot{C}H_2) = 106$ kcal/mole. Although this seems rather high compared to $DH^\circ(CH_3{-}CH_3) = 88$ kcal/mole, it is in line with C—C single bond dissociation energies connecting C atoms in sp^2 hybridization states. Thus in butadiene-1,3, $DH^\circ(C_2H_3{-}C_2H_3) = 103$ kcal, in biphenyl $DH^\circ(\Phi{-}\Phi) = 116$ kcal/mole, and in the radical $\dot{C}H_2CH_3$, $DH^\circ(CH_2{-}CH_3) = 97$ kcal/mole.

It should be further noted that we may expect the ground state of the $\dot{C}H_2{-}\dot{C}H_2$ biradical to be flat by analogy with the planar structures observed for butadiene, acrolein biacetyl, glyoxal, etc., which also have (sp^2) C atoms joined by a single bond. We can estimate from the stabilization energy of butadiene that it requires 3.6 kcal to bend the two $\dot{C}H_2$ groups to the perpendicular conformation.

2.16 ENTROPIES OF RING COMPOUNDS

Although there are a reasonable number of enthalpy data on ring compounds, entropy data are, on the whole, sparse. Thus we shall be forced, in many instances, to estimate entropies and molar heat capacities for ring compounds either from frequency assignments or from model compounds.

Table 2.10   Comparisons of the Entropies of Some Ring Compounds with Open Chain Compounds

Ring (σ)		$S_{int.}^{\circ}$[a]	Open Chain Compound (σ)		$S_{int.}^{\circ}$[a]	$\Delta S_{int./rot.}^{\circ}$[b]	Residual[c] Ring Entropy
C_2H_4	(4)	55.3	C_2H_6	(18)	60.7	5.4	
$CH_3CH=CH_2$	(3)	66.1	C_3H_8	(18)	70.3	4.2	
Trans-butene-2	(18)	76.7	n-C_4H_{10}	(18)	79.7	3.0	
C_3H_6	(6)	60.4	C_3H_8	(18)	70.3	4.9	0
$\overline{CH_2CH_2O}$	(2)	59.5	C_2H_5OH	(3)	69.7	5.1	
			CH_3OCH_3	(18)	69.5	5.0	
$\overline{CH_2CH_2NH}$	(1)		$C_2H_5NH_2$	(3)	(69.9)		
			$(CH_3)_2NH$	(9)	69.8		
$\overline{CH_2CH_2S}$	(2)	62.5	$(CH_3)_2S$	(18)	74.1	5.8	
			C_2H_5SH	(3)	73.0	5.3	
C_4H_8	(8)	67.6	n-C_4H_{10}	(18)	79.7	4.0	2.7
C_5H_{10}	(10)	74.6	n-C_5H_{12}	(18)	89.1	3.6	5.2
C_6H_{12}	(6)	74.9	n-C_6H_{14}	(18)	98.5	4.7	1.0
C_7H_{14}	(14)	81.8	n-C_7H_{16}	(18)	107.9	4.4	3.0
C_8H_{16}	(16)	91.9	n-C_8H_{18}	(18)	117.3	3.6	9.1

[a] $S_{int.}^{\circ} = S^{\circ} + R \ln \sigma$ (gibbs/mole).

[b] $\Delta S_{int./rot.}^{\circ} = [S_{int. (open chain)}^{\circ} - S_{int. (ring)}^{\circ}]/(n - 1)$ where n is the number of atoms in the ring.

[c] Defined with reference to cyclopropane as $(n - 1)[4.9 - \Delta S_{int./rot.}^{\circ}]$.

This is particularly true for the case of polycyclic ring systems where almost no C_p° or S° data exist.

As a starting point, let us compare some simple ring systems with the corresponding open chain compounds. In Table 2.10, we compare the intrinsic entropies $S_{int.}^{\circ}$[11] of a number of ring compounds and open chain compounds. The last column in the table lists the ratio of the entropy difference to the number of hindered rotations in the open chain that have been "frozen" in ring formation. This entropy decrement is about 4.7 ± 0.3 gibbs/mole for all but the C_4, C_5, and C_8 rings. It is smaller for these latter, in agreement with the observation that these rings have an unusually low frequency-puckering mode called a pseudorotation, which is responsible for an excess entropy in these systems.

[11] $S_{int.}^{\circ} = S_{(obs.)}^{\circ} + R \ln (\sigma/n)$.

As a reference point, the "two-membered rings" (that is, simple olefins) have been included. We note that they show a rapid change in entropy loss on going from ethylene to *trans*-butene-2. This arises from the sharp drop in torsion frequency going from C_2H_4 to *trans*-C_4H_8—2, which itself begins to approach the frequency equivalent to a hindered rotation. Thus, in tetramethylethylene, the reduced mass of the torsion has become so large that the double bond torsion has a frequency of only about 200 cm^{-1} and a corresponding entropy at 300°K of 2.2 gibb/mole.

Table A.20 in the Appendix lists the torsion frequencies for some substituted olefins.

We can now use these entropy decrements in ring formation to estimate ring entropies, starting with open chain compounds.

EXAMPLE

Estimate the entropy of spiropentane at 300°K.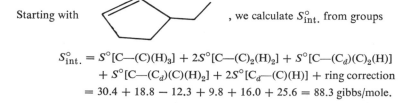

Let us start with the model compound, ethyl cyclopropane, the entropy of which we can estimate from groups as

$$S^\circ_{int.} \left(\triangle\diagup \right) = 3S^\circ[C—(C)_2(H)_2] + S^\circ[C—(C)_3)(H)]$$

$$+ S^\circ[C—(C)(II)_3] + S^\circ(\triangle) \text{ correction}$$
$$= 28.3 - 12.1 + 30.4 + 32.1 = 78.7.$$

Using the entropy decrement in closing to a three-membered ring, of $-2 \times 4.9 = -9.8$ gibbs/mole, this becomes 68.9, and correcting for symmetry ($\sigma = 4$), we find $S^\circ = 66.1$ gibb/mole compared to an observed value of 67.5. Alternatively, starting with

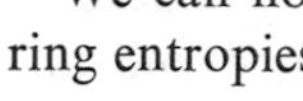

, we obtain 64.1 gibbs/mole.

EXAMPLE

Estimate the entropy of (2,1,2)bicycloheptene-1 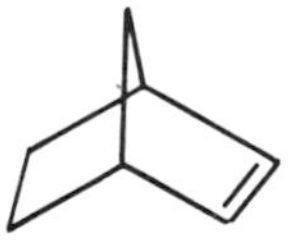 at 300°K. We do this by two independent paths, one starting with ethylcyclopentene, the other with methylcyclohexene.

Starting with , we calculate $S^\circ_{int.}$ from groups

$$S^\circ_{int.} = S^\circ[C—(C)(H)_3] + 2S^\circ[C—(C)_2(H)_2] + S^\circ[C—(C_d)(C)_2(H)]$$
$$+ S^\circ[C—(C_d)(C)(H)_2] + 2S^\circ[C_d—(C)(H)] + \text{ring correction}$$
$$= 30.4 + 18.8 - 12.3 + 9.8 + 16.0 + 25.6 = 88.3 \text{ gibbs/mole.}$$

After closing the new ring, we lose two rotations characteristic of a "tight" (that is, non-puckering) C_5 ring. We use the value of -2×4.9 for this ring decrement to give a value for the bicyclic ring of 78.5 gibbs/mole.

Starting with ⬡—CH_3, we calculate from groups the value of $S_{int.}^{\circ} = 82.8$ gibbs/mole. Note that this has precisely the same groups as the isomeric C_5 ring and differs only in the ring correction. After closing the second ring by forming the bridge CH_2, we lose one rotation, or -4.9 gibbs/mole, to yield $S_{int.}^{\circ}$ of 77.9 gibbs/mole, in excellent agreement with the preceding value.

Some idea of the extra entropy of the C_4 and C_5 rings can be obtained by comparing the intrinsic entropy changes observed by inserting a double bond. This should "tighten" these rings and eliminate the low frequency "pucker."

Table 2.11 compares the intrinsic entropies of some saturated and un-

Table 2.11　Intrinsic Entropies of Some Saturated and Unsaturated Rings

Ring (σ)		$S_{int.}^{\circ}$ [a]	Ring $(H_2)_{(\sigma)}$		$S_{int.}^{\circ}$ [a]	$\Delta S_{int.}^{\circ}$
C_3H_6	(6)	60.4	C_3H_4	(2)	59.3	-1.1
C_4H_8	(8)	67.6	C_4H_6	(2)	64.4	-3.2
C_5H_{10}	(10)	74.6	C_5H_8	(2)	69.2	-5.4
C_6H_{12}	(6)	74.9	C_6H_{10}	(2)	74.3	-0.6
C_6H_{10}	(2)	74.3	[benzene][a]	(12)	69.3	-5.0

[a] Here we have lost $2H_2$.

saturated rings. We see that, whereas there is a very small loss in entropy in dehydrogenating the C_3 and C_6 rings, there is an appreciable loss in doing the same for the C_4 and C_5 rings. In the change from cyclohexene to benzene, we introduce two more double bonds, and it is quite likely that most of the overall loss of 5.0 gibbs/mole comes from the last step in forming benzene.

Values of C_p° for polycyclic rings can be estimated in similar fashion.

3

Arrhenius Parameters for Gas Phase Reactions

3.1 ELEMENTARY PROCESSES IN GAS REACTIONS

We adopt the point of view in this book that in a dilute gas there are only two types of simple kinetic processes. The first of these is a process undergone by an energetically activated chemical species when it is completely isolated from other gas phase species; this is called a unimolecular process. It may correspond to an internal rearrangement of atoms, the breaking of a bond, the rotation of a group, as in cis-trans isomerization, or very simply the internal redistribution of energy.

The second process is bimolecular and requires the collision of two chemical species. The combination of these two chemical species will be referred to as a collision complex. By virtue of our first definition, it follows that the subsequent chemical fate of the collision complex corresponds to a unimolecular process. Thus bimolecular chemical reactions are composite acts consisting of the formation of a collision complex followed by a unimolecular kinetic process.

Although we may consider a termolecular process as the joint, "simultaneous" collision of three species to form a termolecular collision complex, there is something very difficult to define about such an event, and it is much more satisfying to picture the formation of a termolecular collision complex as proceeding in two bimolecular stages. The mechanism of formation of a termolecular complex ABC can be written as

$$A + B \leftrightarrows [AB] + C$$
$$A + C \leftrightarrows [AC] + B \leftrightarrows [ABC] \to \text{products} \qquad (3.1)$$
$$B + C \leftrightarrows [BC] + A$$

where brackets signify collision complexes.

3.2   TRANSITION STATE THEORY OF RATE PROCESSES

The simplest and most universal chemical rate process is a unimolecular reaction. However, in order for a unimolecular reaction to occur, the reacting molecule must accumulate sufficient internal energy to break the necessary bonds or undergo the internal rearrangement. This activation energy must be accumulated in a sequence of a typical or "lucky" collision, with average molecules in the gas or with the vessel walls. The typical collision, of course, corresponds to one in which the energy-rich molecule loses part of its energy to its energy poor partner.

If we observe an energy-rich, polyatomic molecule in a gas, we may expect to see, in the (relatively) long intervals between collisions, that the energy will redistribute itself over the various parts of the molecule as the various atoms execute their not quite harmonic vibrations. At STP there is about $10^{-9.3}$ sec between gas collisions, whereas a 600 cm^{-1} vibration will execute $600 \times 3 \times 10^{10} = 1.8 \times 10^{13}$ oscillations/sec or about 10,000 oscillations between successive collisions. As a result, we may expect to see the energized molecule take a great many different configurations. If any one of them corresponds to the localization of enough of the energy to break a bond, to dissociate a fragment, or to rotate a group past a barrier, chemical reaction occurs.

The most useful quantitative model for the reaction described above is provided by the "transition state theory" originally developed by Henry Eyring and his coworkers.[1] It proposes that molecules having the required energy and the conformation corresponding to the internal energy barrier for chemical reaction be considered in "virtual" equilibrium with "normal," unexcited species. The rate of the chemical reaction is then given by the product of the concentration of these transition-state molecules by the rate constant for their passage over the energy barrier. For the simple case of a

---

[1] S. Glasstone, K. J. Laidler, and H. Eyring, *The Theory of Rate Processes*, McGraw-Hill, New York, (1941).

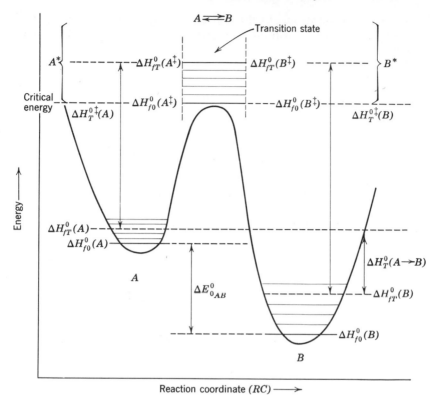

Figure 3.1 Energy-reaction coordinate diagram for an exothermic, unimolecular isomerization. The reaction coordinate is any internal coordinate or combination of internal coordinates that measures uniquely the progress of the reaction. The solid curve gives the potential energy of the molecule corresponding to zero kinetic energy in the reaction coordinate for the appropriate value on the abscissa of the reaction coordinate. For cis-trans isomerization, RC may be the dihedral angle.

unimolecular isomerization, $A \rightarrow B$ we can represent the scheme as

$$A \leftrightarrows A^*$$
$$A^* \leftrightarrows A^{\ddagger} \leftrightarrows B \qquad (3.2)$$

where A^* represents a molecule of A with sufficient internal energy to isomerize, and $A^{\ddagger}$ represents the same A^* molecule in the geometrical conformation corresponding to the top of the barrier or transition state. This is illustrated in the energy-reaction coordinate plot of Figure 3.1.

Note that because, in principle, all reactions are reversible, we must have a totally symmetrical scheme for B and the corresponding transition state $B^{\ddagger}$ must be identical to $A^{\ddagger}$ in every respect except the phase of motion of its atoms. The phase of motion of the atoms of $B^{\ddagger}$ will correspond to change from a B state towards an A state and conversely for the phases of $A^{\ddagger}$. In the simplest case of a cis-trans isomerization, for example $CHD{=}CHD$, we have

The transition state is identified as that state in which the planes of the end methylene groups are at $90°$ to each other. At this point, one direction of rotation corresponds to cis $\rightarrow$ trans, and the opposite rotation corresponds to trans $\rightarrow$ cis.

If $k_A^{\ddagger}$ represents the specific rate constant for the passage over the barrier, the rate of isomerization is given by (neglecting the back reaction)

$$\frac{d(B)}{dt} = -\frac{d(A)}{dt} = k_A^{\ddagger}(A^{\ddagger}). \tag{3.3}$$

For equilibrium of $A^{\ddagger}$ and A with equilibrium constant $K_A^{\ddagger}$, $(A^{\ddagger}) = K_A^{\ddagger}(A)$; hence

$$-\frac{d(A)}{dt} = k_A^{\ddagger} K_A^{\ddagger}(A), \tag{3.4}$$

so that the first-order, isomerization rate constant k_A is given by

$$k_A \equiv -\frac{d(A)}{(A)\, dt} = k_A^{\ddagger} K_A^{\ddagger}. \tag{3.5}$$

If we could look at the equilibrium system $A \rightleftarrows B$, we would see equal numbers of molecules crossing the barrier in each direction. We could consider that motion across the barrier corresponded to a normal coordinate of the composite transition-state species consisting of equal numbers of $A^{\ddagger}$ and $B^{\ddagger}$. The frequency $\nu^{\ddagger}$ associated with a round trip $A^{\ddagger}$ to $B^{\ddagger}$ and back to $A^{\ddagger}$ can be assigned to this normal coordinate, and we note that $k_A^{\ddagger} = k_B^{\ddagger} = 2\nu^{\ddagger}$. Further, the total concentration of transition-state species is $(A^{\ddagger}) + (B^{\ddagger})$, and because $(A^{\ddagger})_{\text{eq.}} = (B^{\ddagger})_{\text{eq.}}$, we could have originally written $(A^{\ddagger}) = \frac{1}{2}K^{\ddagger}(A)$ where $K^{\ddagger} = K_A^{\ddagger} + K_B^{\ddagger}$ is the true "equilibrium constant" for all transition-state species $A^{\ddagger}$ and $B^{\ddagger}$ at the top of the barrier. Hence we can rewrite (3.5)

$$k_A = \nu^{\ddagger} K^{\ddagger}. \tag{3.6}$$

The important assumption made in transition-state theory is that, at compositions far from equilibrium, for example, when back reaction $B \rightarrow A$

is negligible, and $(B^{\ddagger}) \ll (A^{\ddagger})$, the concentration of $A^{\ddagger}$ is the same as it would be if $(B^{\ddagger}) = (A^{\ddagger})$. This further implies that every $(B^{\ddagger})$ that becomes (A^*) is principally deactivated to (A) and contributes negligibly to the net rate of production of $(A^{\ddagger})$. This seems quite reasonable.

If now, we factor out of $K^{\ddagger}$ the internal vibration coordinate that corresponds to passage across the barrier, we have, from statistical mechanics,

$$K^{\ddagger} = K^{\ddagger\prime}(1 - e^{-h\nu^{\ddagger}/kT})^{-1}, \qquad (3.7)$$

and when $h\nu^{\ddagger} \ll kT$ we can expand the exponential, so that

$$K^{\ddagger} \approx K^{\ddagger\prime}\left(\frac{kT}{h\nu^{\ddagger}}\right). \qquad (3.8)$$

Substituting into (3.6) we obtain the transition state result

$$k_A = \left(\frac{kT}{h}\right)K^{\ddagger\prime}. \qquad (3.9)$$

To avoid clumsy notation, we shall omit the prime and write $K^{\ddagger}$, it being understood that the internal coordinate corresponding to motion over the barrier has been factored out.

An additional factor, $\kappa \leq 1$, the transmission coefficient, is usually included in (3.9) and (3.3). It makes allowance for the possibility that a fraction $(1 - \kappa)$ of transition-state complexes $A^{\ddagger}$ may be reflected back towards A^* before completing their passage to B^*. Very little is known about κ. It is a very complex function of the shape of the potential energy surface at the top of the barrier. It is the general practice to set $k = 1$, and for simplicity, we have simply chosen to omit it.

Although we have derived (3.9) for an isomerization, there is no difference in principle for any other type of unimolecular process and therefore it becomes a quite general result. Because bimolecular or termolecular events can be looked upon as involving preëquilibrium formation of "collision" complexes, these can be absorbed into $K^{\ddagger}$, so that (3.9) becomes applicable to processes of any complexity that proceed through a single rate determining step, the transition state barrier.

Thus for the bimolecular reaction

$$A + B \leftrightarrows [AB]^{\ddagger} \rightarrow \text{products}$$

the bimolecular, specific rate constant k_B is given by

$$k_B = \left(\frac{kT}{h}\right)K^{\ddagger}_{AB}$$

where $K^{\ddagger}_{AB}$ is the equilibrium constant for formation of $(AB^{\ddagger})$ from A and B.

The importance of the transition-state result is that all "equilibrium" rate constants can be written as a product of a universal frequency factor (kT/h), which has the value 6.3×10^{12} sec^{-1} at $T = 300°$K and a thermodynamic factor $K^{\ddagger}$, which depends only on the structure and energy of the transition state. The rate is thus independent of the details of the collision process.

Because we can write

$$-RT \ln K^{\ddagger} = \Delta G^{\circ\ddagger} = \Delta H^{\circ\ddagger} - T \Delta S^{\circ\ddagger}, \tag{3.10}$$

we may expect $K^{\ddagger}$ to be susceptible to analysis and correlation by the same additivity laws used for our ordinary thermochemical quantities.

3.3   COLLISION THEORY OF BIMOLECULAR REACTIONS

Historically, bimolecular reactions were interpreted in terms of a collision model derived from the kinetic theory of gases. The model assumed that the rate of a bimolecular reaction between A and B in the gas phase was given by some fraction α of the rate at which A and B collide. The fraction α was further broken down into two factors. First was the Boltzmann factor $e^{-E/RT}$, which represents the fraction of collision pairs $[A \cdots B]$ that have the necessary activation energy E_{AB} localized in the proper internal coordinates so that chemical reaction may take place. The second factor was the steric factor p, which made provision for the possibility that only a fraction $p \leq 1$ of properly energized collisions would have the geometry suitable for reaction.

From the collision point of view the bimolecular rate constant k_{AB} could be written as

$$k_{AB} = p_{AB} Z_{AB} e^{-E_{AB}/RT} \tag{3.11}$$

where Z_{AB} is the frequency of collisions between A and B expressed in some standard concentration units (for example atmospheres or moles/liter).

The kinetic theory of gases gives Z_{AB} as

$$Z_{AB} = \pi \sigma_{AB}^2 \left(\frac{8RT}{\pi \mu_{AB}} \right)^{1/2} \tag{3.12}$$

where σ_{AB} is the distance between the centers of mass of A and B in the collision complex, and $\mu_{AB} = M_A M_B/(M_A + M_B)$ is the reduced molecular weight of the colliding pair.

If all the quantities above are in egs units, Z_{AB} will have units of cc/molecule-sec. To transform to more usual units of liter/mole-sec, we must multiply by $N_{Av}/1000 = 6 \times 10^{20}$, where $N_{Av} = $ Avogardro's number $= 6.02 \times 10^{23}$ molecules/mole.

We can now compare (3.12) with the transition-state formula for a bimolecular reaction

$$k_{AB} = \frac{kT}{h} K_{AB}^{\ddagger} = \frac{kT}{h} \frac{Q_{AB}^{\ddagger}}{Q_A Q_B} e^{-\Delta E_0^{\circ\ddagger}/RT} \tag{3.13}$$

where $Q_{AB}^{\ddagger}$, Q_A, and Q_B are the molecular partition functions for the species $AB^{\ddagger}$, A, and B respectively, and $\Delta E_0^{\circ\ddagger}$ is the energy of formation of the $AB^{\ddagger}$ at $0°K$ from A and B. If we factor each partition function into its translational, rotational, vibrational, and electronic contributions, this last equation becomes

$$k_{AB} = \frac{kT}{h} \left(\frac{Q_{AB}^{\ddagger}}{Q_A \cdot Q_B} \right)_{\text{trans.}} Q_{\text{rot.}\|AB}^{\ddagger}$$

$$\times \left[\frac{Q_{\text{vib.}AB^{\ddagger}} \cdot Q_{\text{rot.}\perp AB^{\ddagger}} \cdot Q_{\text{elec.}AB^{\ddagger}}}{Q_{\text{vib.}A} \cdot Q_{\text{vib.}B} \cdot Q_{\text{rot.}A} \cdot Q_{\text{rot.}B} \cdot Q_{\text{elec.}A} \cdot Q_{\text{elec.}B}} \right] \tag{3.14}$$

$$\times e^{-\Delta E_0^{\circ\ddagger}/RT}.$$

By $Q_{\text{rot.}\|AB}^{\ddagger}$ we mean the apparent rotational partition function for $AB^{\ddagger}$ considered as a hypothetical diatomic molecule of masses M_A and M_B separated by the distance r_{AB}. The quantity $Q_{\text{rot.}\perp AB}^{\ddagger}$ is then the rotational partition function for the remaining degree of rotational freedom around the AB axis. This is an approximate description. More exactly $Q_{\text{rot.}\perp AB}^{\ddagger} = Q_{\text{rot.}AB}^{\ddagger}/Q_{\text{rot.}\|AB}^{\ddagger}$ where $Q_{\text{rot.}AB}^{\ddagger}$ is the total precise rotational partition function for $AB^{\ddagger}$.

If we substitute the proper molecular quantities for the $Q_{\text{trans.}}$ it can be shown that[2]

$$Z_{AB} = \left(\frac{kT}{h} \right) \left(\frac{Q_{AB}^{\ddagger}}{Q_A \cdot Q_B} \right)_{\text{trans.}} [Q_{\text{rot.}\|AB}]. \tag{3.15}$$

Thus if we compare the collision theories, from (3.12), and the transition-state theories, from (3.13), we see that we can make a structural analysis of the steric factor p_{AB} as

$$p_{AB} = \frac{Q_{\text{vib.}AB^{\ddagger}} Q_{\text{rot.}\perp AB^{\ddagger}} Q_{\text{elec.}AB^{\ddagger}} \, e^{-(\Delta E_0^{\circ\ddagger} - E_{AB})/RT}}{Q_{\text{vib.}A} \cdot Q_{\text{vib.}B} \cdot Q_{\text{rot.}A} \cdot Q_{\text{rot.}B} \cdot Q_{\text{elec.}A} \cdot Q_{\text{elec.}B}}. \tag{3.16}$$

From the point of view taken above see that collision theory is a zeroth-order approximation to transition-state theory. In the simple hypothetical case when A and B are atoms all the terms in (3.16) became unity, and $p_{AB} = 1$. This is a somewhat artifical case because there are few chemical reactions

[2] See, for example, S. W. Benson, *Foundations of Chemical Kinetics*, McGraw-Hill, New York, (1960), p. 273.

that two atoms can undergo. Some of these few examples are associative ionization, electronic excitation, and the inverse process of deexcitation:

$$A + B \rightleftarrows A - B^+ + e^-;$$
$$A + B \rightleftarrows A^* + B.$$

$$(3.17)$$

3.4   STRUCTURAL ANALYSIS OF STERIC FACTORS

When A and B are not atoms but are more complex, it is invariably the case that the denominator in (3.16) is larger than the numerator. The reason for this is that in the process of transforming polyatomic A plus polyatomic B into polyatomic $AB^{\ddagger}$ we have changed six external rotations and six translations of A and B into three translations, three rotations, and six internal motions of $AB^{\ddagger}$. One of the latter is, of course, the reaction coordinate.

The factor Z_{AB}, in (3.15), already accounts for the translational partition functions and two of the rotations of $AB^{\ddagger}$. Hence p_{AB} reflects the remaining terms, which include one rotation of $AB^{\ddagger}$ against six rotations for A and B and $(3n - 7)$ internal vibrations in $AB^{\ddagger}$ against $(3n - 12)$ in $A + B$.

The ratio of electronic partition functions is almost always ≤ 1. Because vibrational partition functions are generally in the range of 1 to 10, whereas rotational partition functions are in the range 10 to 100 per rotational degree of freedom, we expect p_{AB} to be in the range 1 to 10^{-5} depending on the complexity of A and B and the "tightness" of the transition state $AB^{\ddagger}$. This latter is of essential importance, for among the $(3n - 7)$ internal vibrations of $AB^{\ddagger}$ we will have one nearly free internal rotation (A against B) about the $A \cdots B$ axis) and up to four rocking modes of A and B with respect to the $A \cdots B$ axis. If these latter are very loose, they can just about cancel the rotational partition functions of A and B, and the result is that p will be very close to unity. This we shall see occurs in the recombination of alkyl radicals, for example $2CH_3 \rightarrow C_2H_6$.

Occasionally we see claims of steric factors in excess of unity. These are rationalized by claiming that the Boltzmann factor $f_B = e^{-E_{AB}/RT}$ in (3.12) is not correct and that one should use instead the factor (for a classical system)[3]

$$f_B = \frac{1}{(S - 1)!} \left(\frac{E_{AB}}{\omega T} \right)^{S-1} e^{-E_{AB}/RT}$$

$$(3.18)$$

to take into account the fact that the activation energy E_{AB} can be distributed among all possible S internal degrees of freedom of the collision complex.

[3] For a quantized system with a geometrical mean vibration frequency $\nu_m = (\nu_1 \cdot \nu_2 \cdot \nu_3 \cdots \nu_s)^{1/s}$ the factor is $f_B \sim \dfrac{1}{(S - 1)!} \left(\dfrac{E_{AB}}{h\nu_m} \right)^{s-1} e^{-E_{AB}/RT}$.

This would be correct if each such distribution has a unit probability of contributing to chemical reaction. However, only those collision complexes that have the proper localization of activation energy in the necessary bonds can react (that is, are in the transition state). All the others will redissociate.[4] Equation (3.18) is thus improper for a bimolecular reaction, and we can take it as a good critique of experimental rate data that when their steric factors exceed unity by any significant amount, they are most likely in error.

Two important exceptions exist to this last rule, and both are apparent rather than real. The first concerns the bimolecular process of energy transfer, indicated by

$$A + M \leftrightarrows A^* + M. \tag{3.19}$$

Here a collision between A and M with energy distributed between the two becomes localized in the internal modes of A^*. In actuality, such a process undoubtedly takes place from the nearby energy states of A just below A^* through a series of "lucky" collisions, and each with a "normal" or even small steric factor.

However, by convention, the overall process described above is usually referred to the ground state of A. Thus at substantial energies E^* in A^* there is a large cumulative degeneracy factor, which reflects the large number of ways of distributing this energy among the S internal degrees of freedom of A. We can see this for the very first step when E^* is small.

Let us assume a molecule A with twelve internal oscillators all of very nearly the same frequency, so that if A has one vibrational quantum, it may exist with equal probability in any of the twelve modes. The degeneracy of the first vibrational state, $A^{(1)}$ is 12, and for the process of collisional excitation of the first and second vibrational levels of A, we can write the hypothetical kinetic mechanism

$$A^{(0)} + M \underset{-1}{\overset{1}{\rightleftarrows}} M + A^{(1)};$$

$$A^{(1)} + M \underset{-2}{\overset{2}{\rightleftarrows}} M + A^{(2)}; \tag{3.20}$$

$$\frac{d(A^{(2)})}{dt} = k_2(M)(A^{(1)}) - k_{-2}(M)(A^{(2)}). \tag{3.21}$$

The degeneracy of the $A^{(2)}$ state is $(S + 1)(S)/2 = 78$, so that $k_2/k_{-2} = (78/12)e^{-h\nu/RT}$ and $k_1/k_{-1} = 12e^{-h\nu/RT}$. If $A^{(1)}$ is at or near equilibrium with $A^{(0)}$ and we are looking at the initial rate of formation of $A^{(2)}$ (that is we

---

[4] S. W. Benson and A. E. Axworthy, Jr., J. Chem. Phys., **21**, 428 (1953).

ignore deactivation of $A^{(2)}$), $(A^{(1)}) = 12(A^{(0)})e^{-E^\circ/RT}$ where $E^\circ = h\nu$ and

$$\frac{d(A^{(2)})}{dt} = 12k_2(M)(A^{(0)})e^{-E^\circ/RT}$$

$$= 78k_{-2}(M)(A^{(0)})e^{-2E^\circ/RT}. \qquad (3.22)$$

We see that even if the steric factor of k_{-2} was 0.1, the apparent steric factor for the overall process would be 7.8 and would exceed unity. It is easy to extrapolate to higher levels and see that if we are dealing with a large number of quanta ($E^* \gg h\nu$), the statistical factor can become very large.

The second process applied to apparently large steric factors is dissociative recombination of ions + electrons:

$$AB^+ + e^- \rightarrow A + B + \text{energy}. \qquad (3.23)$$

Steric factors for these reactions can be as large as 10^5. This is accounted for by the fact that we are using the wrong collision frequency. Electrons, being about 10^4 lighter than most molecules, have 10^2 higher average thermal velocities and thus have 100-fold greater collision rates. The remaining factor of 10^3 comes from the fact that at a 100 Å separation the coulombic interaction of the two ions (E^2/r) is 3.3 kcal, which is much larger than RT (0.6 kcal) at 25°C. Hence ion collisions at low temperatures have a much larger effective diameter than they do for neutral particles. Because this is about twenty to thirty times larger than collision diameters for neutrals, and the collision frequency goes as the square of the effective collision diameter, we find the remaining factor of about 10^3 in the "abnormal" collision cross section.

3.5 UNIMOLECULAR REACTIONS—CATEGORIES

We classify unimolecular reactions into the following categories.

1. Simple fission: involves the breaking of a single bond.
2. Complex fission: involves the breaking of two or more bonds.
3. Isomerization: involves only internal rearrangement of atoms. These may be as simple as a rotation of groups or more usually, a complex reorganization.

Some examples from each of the above categories are:

1. Simple fission:

$$C_2H_5I \rightarrow C_2H_5 + I$$
$$CH_3\!-\!CH_3 \rightarrow 2CH_3$$

2. Complex fission:

$$CH_3—CH—CH_3 \rightarrow CH_3—CH=CH_2 + HI$$
$$\underset{I}{|}$$

$$CH_3—CH—CH_2 \rightarrow CH_3CH=CH_2 + HNO_2$$
$$\underset{H}{|}\quad\underset{NO_2}{|}$$

$$CH_3C\overset{O}{\diagup}\underset{OC_2H_5}{\diagdown} \rightarrow CH_3—C\overset{OH}{\diagup}\underset{O}{\diagdown} + C_2H_4$$

$$\underset{CH_2—CH_2}{\overset{CH_2—CH_2}{|\qquad|}} \rightarrow 2C_2H_4$$

3. Isomerization:

$$\underset{CH_3}{\overset{H}{\diagdown}}C=C\underset{CH_3}{\overset{H}{\diagup}} \quad (cis) \rightarrow \quad \underset{H}{\overset{CH_3}{\diagdown}}C=C\underset{CH_3}{\overset{H}{\diagup}} \quad (trans)$$

$$\overset{CH_2}{\overset{\diagup\diagdown}{CH_2——CH_2}} \rightarrow CH_3—CH=CH_2$$

$$\underset{CH}{\overset{CH_2}{|}}\ \underset{CH}{\overset{CH_2}{|}}\ \underset{CH_2}{\overset{CH}{|}} \rightarrow \underset{CH}{\overset{CH_2}{|}}\ \underset{CH_2}{\overset{CH_2}{|}}\ \underset{CH}{\overset{CH}{|}}$$
$$\underset{CH_3}{|}\qquad\qquad\qquad\qquad\underset{CH_3}{|}$$

The simple fissions appear quite generally to be resolvable into a single elementary, bond-breaking act. In contrast, the more complex fissions involving more than two bonds can be comprised of many consecutive elementary steps. Similarly, simple cis-trans isomerizations appear to go through a single elementary step, whereas the isomerizations involving more than one bond usually may be considered to involve a sequence of resolvable, elementary acts. We consider each of these categories separately.

3.6 SIMPLE FISSION OF ATOMS FROM MOLECULES

For very simple molecules containing fewer than five atoms, the process of simple fission is likely to turn out to be controlled by the rate of accumulation of internal energy by collision and hence become a bimolecular process. This is true for the dissociation of diatomics such as H_2 or I_2 and for the triatomics such as O_3, NO_2, N_2O, and Cl_2O. Tetratomics such as F_2O_2 and NO_2Cl usually decompose bimolecularly but may become intermediate between unimolecular and bimolecular kinetics.

Most molecules with five to eight atoms will be of intermediate molecularity. More complex molecules are generally in the first-order, unimolecular region with a rate controlled by bond fission. However, at sufficiently high temperatures the decompositions of *all* molecules become collision controlled and hence, bimolecular.

For the simple bond fission processes, the transition-state result gives us a facile starting point. Consider the unimolecular, simple fission of AB. We can represent the process by

$$AB \rightleftharpoons AB^\ddagger \rightarrow A + B. \tag{3.24}$$

Then from (3.9) the first-order rate constant for decomposition of AB is given by

$$k_{AB} = \left(\frac{kT}{h}\right) K^\ddagger_{AB}, \tag{3.25}$$

or in thermodynamic language

$$k_{AB} = \frac{kT}{h} e^{\Delta S^\ddagger_{AB}/R} e^{-\Delta H^\ddagger_{AB}/RT}. \tag{3.26}$$

If we use the Arrhenius equation $Ae^{-E/RT}$ for k_{AB} as a point of comparison, we can identify

$$A = \left(\frac{ekT_m}{h}\right) e^{\Delta S^\ddagger_{AB}/R}; \qquad E = \Delta H^\ddagger_{AB} + RT_m \tag{3.27}$$

where T_m is the mean temperature at which the experiments have been carried out.

We note that because (ekT_m/h) will be in the range of $10^{13.5}$ sec^{-1} for most experiments (600°K), A will differ from this usual frequency factor only to the extent that $\Delta S^\ddagger_{AB}$ differs from zero. When, for example, $AB^\ddagger$ is "bigger" and "looser" than AB we may expect $\Delta S^\ddagger_{AB} > 0$ and in consequence an abnormally large A factor. When, in contrast $AB^\ddagger$ is more compact and "stiffer" than AB, we may expect $\Delta S^\ddagger_{AB} < 0$ and an abnormally small A factor. These possibilities are categorized as "loose" or "tight" transition-state complexes, respectively.

We can expect in simple fission reactions, which involve detachment of single atoms from a large molecule, that $\Delta S^\ddagger_{AB}$ will be small except for a statistical factor.   Thus in the reaction $C_2H_6 \rightarrow \dot{C}_2H_5 + H$ any of six equivalent H atoms may become detached, and this leads to a symmetry contribution to $\Delta S_{AB}^{\ddagger}$ of $R \ln 6$.[5]

The other contributions of $\Delta S_{AB}^{\ddagger}$ will come from changes in rotational parameters, vibrational frequencies, or electronic state.   Morse or Lennard-Jones potentials indicate that it is reasonable to use an $A \cdots B^{\ddagger}$ bond distance of about 2.5 times the ground state distance, when the $A \cdots B$ interaction is not strongly coupled to any other interaction in the A or B groups.   Extending one H atom to $2.5 \times 1.09 \, \text{Å} = 2.73 \, \text{Å}$ does not occasion any very important changes in the rotational constants of C_2H_6 because H is so light.   We also do not expect any significant changes in the vibrations or hindered rotation in $C_2H_5^{\ddagger}$, or in the electronic state.   As a result, we anticipate that for the reaction $C_2H_6 \rightarrow \dot{C}_2H_5 + H^{\cdot}$, $\Delta S^{\ddagger} \sim R \ln 6$ and $A_{(300°K)} \sim 1 \times 10^{14} \, \text{sec}^{-1}$.

One additional contribution may be considered, namely, that due to weakened bending modes.   It appears that these are reduced to about one-fifth of their normal value in the transition state.   For the present case, we could assign values of about $220 \, \text{cm}^{-1}$ and $290 \, \text{cm}^{-1}$ for the H—C—C and H—C—H bends.   At 300°K these contribute together about 3.5 eu to ΔS, which would raise A (300°K) to $10^{14.8} \, \text{sec}^{-1}$.

One immediate consequence, which we discuss later, is that we expect, for the reverse reaction, an Arrhenius A factor of from $10^{9.3}$ to $10^{10.1}$ liter-mole-sec, the latter, if we use the loose bending modes.   This is calculated from the overall entropy change in the dissociation.

For a light molecule such as CH_3I, losing a heavy atom I, we expect a significant increase in the moment of inertia in $(CH_3 \cdots I)^{\ddagger}$ of about a factor of 6 and again a significant reduction in the two bending modes.   Here there are no symmetry changes, but we will have lost a low-frequency C—I stretch (reaction coordinate).   Table 3.1 shows a summary of these changes at 600°K.

The changes described above lead to an A factor for the reaction of about $10^{15.2} \, \text{sec}^{-1}$ at 600°K.   With $\Delta S° = 28.4$ gibbs/mole, this leads to an A factor for the recombination of $CH_3 + I$ at 600°K of about $10^{10.9}$ liter/mole-sec.[6]

When internal changes are coupled to the breaking bond, we must explore them in detail.   For example, the reaction $\dot{C}_2H_5 \rightarrow C_2H_4 + H$ involves a considerable change in structure.   We lose a free rotation in the C_2H_5 radical

---

[5] Note that $K^{\ddagger}$ contains this factor, $\sigma_{AB}/\sigma_{AB}^{\ddagger}$, directly.   For more discussion, see S. W. Benson, *J. Am. Chem. Soc.*, **80**, 5151 (1958) and S. W. Benson and W. B. DeMore, *Ann. Rev. Phys. Chem.*, **16**, 433 (1965).

[6] These estimates are based on the assumption that the transition states have the same electron spin as the ground state.

Table 3.1   Entropy Changes in CH₃I Pyrolysis at 600°Kᵃ

$$CH_3I \rightleftarrows (CH_3I)^{\ddagger}$$

Modes	$\Delta S^{\ddagger}$ (gibbs/mole)
Translation	0
Rotation	$+R \ln 6 = 3.6$
Symmetry	0
Spin	0
Internal vibration	Reaction Coordinate
C—I stretch (500 cm⁻¹)	−1.8
2H—C—I bends (1150 cm⁻¹ → 230 cm⁻¹)	+5.6
Total	+7.4

ᵃ We have considered the internal modes of the C—H bonds as inappreciably altered.

as the double bond begins to form. We may picture the transition state as

The contributions to $\Delta S^{\ddagger}$ are tabulated in Table 3.2.

Table 3.2   Contributions to Entropy of Activation at 600°K

$$\text{for } C_2H_5 \rightleftarrows (C_2H_5)^{\ddagger} \rightarrow C_2H_4 + H$$

Modes	$\Delta S^{\ddagger}$ (gibbs/mole)
Translation	0
Rotation	neglect
Symmetryᵃ	$R \ln 6 = 3.6$
Spin	0
Internal	
C—H stretch (3100 cm⁻¹) reaction coordinate	0.0
C—C stretch (1000 cm⁻¹ → 1300 cm⁻¹)	−0.4
H·C—C bend (1150 cm⁻¹ → 800 cm⁻¹)	+0.6
H·C—H bend (1450 cm⁻¹ → 1000 cm⁻¹)	+0.4
CH₂ internal rotation (zero barrier → ½ ethylene torsion 500 cm⁻¹)	−4.1
Total	+0.1

ᵃ A factor of 2 comes from the loss in rotation of the —CH₂ group. It is included here, rather than in the internal rotation correction.

We find $\Delta S^{\ddagger} \sim +0.1$, so that $A_{(600°K)} = 10^{13.6}$ sec^{-1}. For the back reaction[7] this would result in an A factor of about $10^{10.7}$ liter/mole sec.

We may expect similar effects to those described above in other molecules where conjugative or resonance effects are to be expected. Thus, the dissociation of H from propylene leads to a stiff allyl radical and a change of a nearly free rotation of the CH_3 group to a CH_2 semitorsion. A similar effect occurs for toluene when it loses an H atom and forms a stiff benzyl radical.

The loss of a secondary H atom from butene-1 is even more costly because here the formation of the stiff methyl allyl radical CH_3—$\dot{C}H$═CH═$\dot{C}H_2$ involves the freezing of the hindered rotation of two "heavy" groups, [ethyl-vinyl] in butene-1 and at 600°K is about 7 eu. In compensation, however, we get back a semitorsional motion, which we assign at half the frequency of the 300 cm^{-1} associated with butene-2 or 150 cm^{-1}. It contributes about 3.0 eu at 300°K. At 600°K it contributes about 4.0 eu. This appears to be a quite general behavior, which has the result that, no matter what the size of the group, we can assign a loss of about 3.5 $\pm$ 0.5 eu to changes from hindered rotation to semi-pi-bond torsion (see Table A.20). In addition, the terminal CH_2 in butene-1 loosens from a torsion at $\sim$750 cm^{-1} to about half that, or 375 cm^{-1}, which represents a net gain of $+1.3$ eu at 600°K.

There are unfortunately no reliable quantitative data on simple fission of atoms with which to compare the estimates made above. The semiquantitative data that do exist are, however, quite compatible with them.

3.7 SIMPLE FISSION INTO TWO LARGER GROUPS

The fission of a large polyatomic molecule AB into two smaller, but still polyatomic fragments A and B converts six internal modes of A—B into three new translations and three new rotations of the products. These six internal modes correspond to

one A—B bond stretch (reaction coordinate),
one A—B internal rotation,
two rocking modes of A relative to A—B axis,
two rocking modes of B relative to A—B axis.

The fission of AB is expected to give rise to substantial increases in entropy in the transition state and hence to abnormally large A factors. The main reason for this lies in the fact that any appreciable increase in the A—B bond length is expected to weaken considerably the force constants controlling

---

[7] These estimates are based on the assumption that the transition states have the same electron spin as the ground state.

Table 3.3 Arrhenius Parameters for Simple Fission of Molecules into Two Radicals

Reference	Reaction	Log A (sec^{-1})	E (kcal/mole)	T_m (°K)
1.	$C_2H_6 \rightarrow 2CH_3$	17.45	91.7	800
2.		16.0	86.0	850
3.	$C_4H_{10} \rightarrow 2C_2H_5{}^a$	17.4	82	400
4.	$C_2F_6 \rightarrow 2CF_3{}^a$	17.4	88 ± 3	350
5.	$N_2O_5 \rightarrow NO_3 + NO_2$	14.8 ± 1	21 ± 2	330
6.	$CH_3OOCH_3 \rightarrow 2CH_3O$	15.4	36.1	410
7.	$t\text{-BuOO}t\text{-Bu} \rightarrow 2t\text{-BuO}$	15.6	37.4	410
8.	$(CH_3CO)OO(CH_3CO) \rightarrow 2CH_3CO_2$	14.9	31	330
9.	$C_2H_5ONO \rightarrow C_2H_5O + NO$	14.15	37.7	430
10.	$C_2H_5ONO_2 \rightarrow C_2H_5O + NO_2$	16.85	41.2	420
11.	$CH_3N{=}NCH_3 \rightarrow CH_3 + NNCH_3$	17.2	55.5	600
12.	$CF_3N{=}NCF_3 \rightarrow CF_3 + NNCF_3$	16.17	55.2	600
13.	$\Phi\text{-}CH_2CH_3 \rightarrow \Phi\text{-}CH_2 + CH_3$	14.6	70.1	950
14.	$\Phi\text{-}CH_2C_2H_5 \rightarrow \Phi\text{-}CH_2 + C_2H_5$	14.9	68.6	950
15.	$(CH_3)_2NNH_2 \rightarrow (CH_3)_2N + NH_2$	13.22	49.6	850
16.	$C(NO_2)_4 \rightarrow \cdot C(NO_2)_3 + NO_2$	17.5	40.9	470

^{a} Parameters calculated from data on rate of back reaction and overall thermochemistry.
1. C. P. Quinn, *Proc. Roy. Soc.* (London), **A275**, 190 (1963).
2. M. C. Lin and M. H. Back, *Can. J. Chem.*, **44**, 505. 2357 (1966).
3. A. Shepp and K. O. Kutschke, *J. Chem. Phys.*, **26**, 1020 (1957).
4. P. B. Ayscough, *J. Chem. Phys.*, **24**, 944 (1956).
5. R. L. Mills and H. S. Johnston, *J. Am. Chem. Soc.*, **73**, 938 (1951).
6. P. L. Hanst and J. G. Calvert, *J. Phys. Chem.*, **63**, 104 (1959).
7. L. Batt and S. W. Benson, *J. Chem. Phys.*, **36**, 895 (1962).
8. O. J. Walker and G. L. E. Wild, *J. Am. Chem. Soc.*, **1132**, (1937).
9. E. W. R. Steacie and G. T. Shaw, *J. Chem. Phys.*, **2**, 345 (1934).
10. J. B. Levy, *J. Am. Chem. Soc.*, **76**, 3254, 3790 (1954).
11. W. Forst and O. K. Rice, *Can. J. Chem.*, **41**, 562 (1963).
12. E. Leventhal, C. R. Simonds, and C. Steel, *Can. J. Chem.*, **40**, 930 (1962).
13. G. L. Esteban, J. A. Kerr, and A. F. Trotman-Dickenson, *J. Chem. Soc.*, 3873 (1963).
14. J. A. Kerr, R. C. Sekhar, and A. F. Trotman-Dickenson, *J. Chem. Soc.*, 3217 (1963).
15. J. M. Sullivan and A. E. Axworthy, Jr., *J. Phys. Chem.*, **70**, 3366 (1966).

the four rocking modes of A and B groups relative to the A—B axis. It is only in the past decade that reasonably reliable kinetic data have become available for such processes, and what has been most surprising about the data is the very large magnitude of the A factors for these complex fissions. Table 3.3 summarizes some of the data for this category of reaction.

We notice that the A factors for the reactions described above range mainly between 10^{15} to 10^{17} sec^{-1}. They are not all completely comparable because they cover measurements from 330 to 950°K, and this is expected to have a small effect on the A factors. Only the A factor for Me_2NNH_2 of $10^{13.22}$

$\sec^{-1}$ is even close to the once-considered standard, $10^{13} \sec^{-1}$. This latter result is in fact so much below the A factors for the other reactions as to make it quite suspect. It would imply for the recombination of $Me_2N \cdot$ and $\cdot NH_2$ radicals, an A factor of about $2 \times 10^7 \sec^{-1}$, which would be uniquely small in radical recombination studies. Similarly, the A factor reported for the pyrolysis of EtONO is suspiciously low and probably represents a complex quantity, rather than a true rate constant.[8] An A factor of $10^{16} \sec^{-1}$ would be closer to the value calculated from the back reaction rate and the overall ΔS.

Omitting these low values and the measurements involving $\Phi\text{-}\dot{C}H_2$, and with due respect to all of the errors implicit in the measurements of A factors, it is reasonable to represent the remaining group by a mean A factor of $10^{16 \pm 1} \sec^{-1}$. This implies $\Delta S^{\ddagger}$ for these reactions of about 11.5 ± 5 gibbs/mole with about 8 gibbs/mole attributable to the changes in the four rocking frequencies and 3.5 gibbs/mole from increased rotational moment. This would imply an increase in each of the vibrational contributions from these modes of about 2.0 ± 1 gibbs/mole.

For rocking modes involving CH_3, NH_2 or OH groups, the initial frequencies are about 950 cm^{-1} (Table A.13) with a $S_{vib.}$ contribution at $600°K$ (Table A.17) of about 0.75 eu. For these to contribute 2.0 eu each as $\Delta S^{\ddagger}$ at $600°K$ requires a lowering of the rocking frequency to about 300 cm^{-1} in the transition state. This represents a decrease in the rocking force constant f of about a factor of 10, for $\nu \propto f^{1/2}$. It would imply a very low barrier to rocking in the transition state.[9]

Heavier groups, such as C_2H_5 and NO_2, have rocking modes in the lower range of about 400 cm^{-1} (Table A.13), and they contribute at $600°K$ about 2.2 eu to entropy (Figure 2-4). To raise this to 4.2 eu, the frequencies would have to be decreased to about 130 cm^{-1}, or by about the same factor that was required for CH_3 groups.

If these comparisons are made at high, rather than at low, temperatures for example, at $1000°K$ instead of $600°K$, we would find that a change from 950 cm^{-1} to 300 cm^{-1} would contribute 2.3 eu to $\Delta S^{\ddagger}$, instead of the 2.0 eu, whereas a change from 400 cm^{-1} to 130 cm^{-1} is almost precisely parallel. However, there is a somewhat larger effect on the moment of inertia of separating two CH_3 groups versus two heavier t-butyl groups. Because of

[8] The decomposition initially proceeds via EtONO $\underset{2}{\overset{1}{\rightleftarrows}} Et\dot{O} + NO$ and $Et\dot{O} + NO \overset{3}{\rightarrow}$ $CH_3CHO + HNO$, so that the initial rate is approximately given by $-d(Et$ONO$)/dt = k_3K_{1.2}(Et$ONO$)$ with an apparent first-order rate constant $k_3K_{1.2}$, not k_1. If k_3 has an A factor of about 10^8 1/mole-sec, $\Delta S^{\circ}_{1.2}$ would be about 36 eu at $300°K$, in good agreement with a direct estimate of 37.6 eu.

[9] The structural implications of such low frequencies are discussed by S. W. Benson, *Advances in Photochemistry*, Interscience, New York, 1964, Vol. 2, p.1.

this, we expect the A factors for detachment of light groups to be about two- to three-fold larger.

Once again, as in the case of the atom fissions, we note that where the fission is coupled to an internal group, so as to stiffen one or both groups, the A factor is lowered by the resulting change from free rotation to semi-torsion. For a large C_2H_5 group rotating against a phenyl group, we expect a loss of about 5 eu in $\Delta S^{\ddagger}$ at high temperatures, and this is about the amount by which the A factors for ΦCH_2CH_3 and $\Phi CH_2C_2H_5$ are lowered from our standard 10^{16}. On this basis, we predict that for biallyl

$$(CH_2{=}CH{-}CH_2{-}CH_2{-}CH{=}CH_2)$$

splitting into two stiff allyl groups, we would lose about 5 eu, and the A factor would be about 10^{15} sec^{-1}. This would further imply a rate constant of 10^9 l/mole-sec for the recombination of allyl radicals.

Probably the most accurate of the A factors in this group is that for the dissociation of C_2H_6. It can be estimated at $400°K$ from the measured value for the recombination of $2CH_3$ radicals ($10^{10.5}$ liter/mole-sec) and the estimated entropy change for the dissociation ($\Delta S^{\circ}_{400} = 38.6$ gibbs/mole). This gives $A_{400} = 10^{16.9}$ sec^{-1}. Compared to $(ekT/h) = 10^{13.35}$ sec^{-1}, this leads to $\Delta S^{\ddagger} = 16.6$ gibbs/mole. We can assign $+0.7$ of this to the development of free CH_3 rotations in $(C_2H_6)^{\ddagger}$ and another 3.6 to an increased moment of inertia. We are then left with 12.3 or 3.1 gibbs/mole for the loosening of each rocking mode. This requires a reduction of the CH_3 rocking modes (essentially $H{-}C{-}C$ bends) from about 950 to 140 cm^{-1} or a factor of about $\frac{1}{6}$. As we shall see later, this corresponds to substantially free rotation of the methyl groups in the transition state. Note that the factor of $\frac{1}{6}$ is appreciably different from the factor of $\frac{1}{3}$ estimated earlier.

3.8 CIS-TRANS ISOMERIZATIONS

One of the simplest types of unimolecular reaction occurs in geometrical isomerization about a double bond. The transition state seems relatively unambiguous in this reaction and corresponds to two nonbonded methylene groups with their planes at $90°$ to each other. The reaction coordinate is the internal torsional motion about what was originally a double bond. In a theory proposed by Benson, Golden, and Egger[10] it was suggested that because there can be no pi-bond overlap in the transition state, the transition state could be considered to be a biradical. For $CHD{=}CHD$, for example, this would correspond to the hypothetical species $\dot{C}HD{-}\dot{C}HD$. We would expect the $C{-}C$ distance to be about 1.46 Å, as contrasted to 1.34 Å in the ground state. Although electronic triplet and singlet states might be expected to have nearly the same energy, it is likely that only singlet states are

[10] S. W. Benson, D. M. Golden, and K. Egger, *J. Am. Chem. Soc.*, **87**, 468 (1965).

involved. Finally, because of the different groups attached, the transition state will have two optical isomers the entropy of mixing of which contributes a factor of 2 to $K^{\ddagger}$.

The symmetry numbers of the ground and transition states usually cancel each other. The A factor for such reactions can then be written as

$$A_{c-t} \sim 2 \left(\frac{ekT_m}{h}\right) \frac{q^{\ddagger}_{\text{elec.}}}{q_{\text{tors.}}} \tag{3.28}$$

where $q_{\text{elec.}} = 1$, if triplet states are ruled out, and 4 if they participate. $q_{\text{tors.}}$ is the partition function corresponding to the reaction coordinate which is the torsional frequency about the double bond in the ground state. For cis-CHD=CHD, it is about 990 cm^{-1},[11] and at 800°K it contributes a factor of about $\frac{1}{2}$ to A_{c-t}. If we neglect triplet states, this leads to an A factor of 4×10^{13} sec^{-1} for cis-CHD=CHD isomerization, which is in reasonable agreement with the reported value of 10^{13} sec^{-1}.

As soon as we go to heavier substituents on the double bond, the torsion frequencies decrease considerably, to the extent that $kT > h\nu_{\text{tors.}}$ and $q_{\text{tors.}}$ take the classical form

$$\begin{aligned} q_{\text{tors.}} &= (1 - e^{-h\nu_{\text{tors.}}/kT})^{-1} \\ &\approx kT/h\nu_{\text{tors.}} \end{aligned} \tag{3.29}$$

The A factor then becomes

$$A_{c-t} = 2\nu_{\text{tors.}} q^{\ddagger}_{\text{elec.}} \tag{3.30}$$

Note that because of the cancellation of the (kT/h) term, the A factor has become independent of temperature; so $\Delta H^{\ddagger} = E$, and we drop the factor of e in (3.28).

When the groups attached to the double bond can interact with the biradical, we expect to witness a lowering of the activation energy of the reaction by an amount equal to the interaction or "resonance" energy, whereas the A factor will also decrease because of the stiffening of internal rotations accompanying this interaction. For such molecules, the simplified forms of (3.28) and (3.30) must be modified to take into account these changes in $\Delta S^{\ddagger}$.

Table 3.4 lists parameters for some homogeneous gas phase isomerizations together with A factors estimated from the foregoing discussion. With some obvious exceptions, the agreement is reasonably good. One is

$$\text{CH}_3\text{CH}=\text{CHCN}$$

for which no structural basis exists for the abnormally low A factor of 10^{11} sec^{-1}. Comparing it to cis-butene-2 we note that the activation energy is decreased by 11.7 kcal, which would imply a conjugation energy of this amount in the —ĊH—C≡N radical. This seems somewhat high compared

[11] R. L. Arnett and B. L. Crawford, Jr., *J. Chem. Phys.*, **18**, 118 (1950).

to about 7 kcal interaction energy in the $\dot{C}H_2$—$COCH_3$ radical and 12.5 kcal in the allyl radical. If we assume that the absolute value of the rate constant is correct, and increase the A factor to 10^{13} sec^{-1}, it would boost E to 58.1 at 700°K and reduce the resonance energy to 5 kcal, both of which changes seem quite reasonable.

In *cis*-stilbene, the nonplanar, strained ground state has two phenyl hindered rotations with a total S_{ir}° of about 17 eu at 600°K. The torsion

Table 3.4   Arrhenius Parameters for Some Thermal Cis-trans Isomerization

Reference	Reactant	T_m°K	log A (sec^{-1})	E (kcal/mole)	log A (calc.)
1.	*cis*-CDH=CHD	770	13	65	13.6
2.	*cis*-CH$_3$CH=CHCH$_3$	690	13.8	63	13.5
3.	*cis*-CH$_3$CH=CHCN	700	11.0	51.3	13.2
4.	*cis*-CH$_3$CH=CHCOOCH$_3$	660	13.2	57.8	12.8
5.	*cis*-Stilbene	580	12.8	42.8	12.6
6.	*cis*-Methyl cinnamate	610	10.5	41.6	10.9
7.	β-Cyanostyrene (cis)	610	11.6	46.0	12.1
8.	CF$_3$CF=CFCF$_3$ (cis)	650	13.5	56.4	13.1
9.	CHCl=CHCl (cis)	825	12.8	56.0	13.2

1. J. E. Douglas, B. S. Rabinovitch, and F. S. Looney, *J. Chem. Phys.*, **23**, 315 (1955).
2. B. S. Rabinovitch and K. W. Michel, *J. Am. Chem. Soc.*, **81**, 5065 (1959); R. B. Cundall and T. F. Palmer, *Trans. Faraday Soc.*, **57**, 1936 (1961).
3. J. N. Butler and R. D. McAlpine, *Can. J. Chem.*, **41**, 2487 (1963).
4. J. N. Butler and G. J. Small, *Can. J. Chem.*, **41**, 2492 (1963).
5. G. B. Kistiakowsky and W. R. Smith, *J. Am. Chem. Soc.*, **56**, 638 (1934). Note that in the liquid state, log A = 10.4 and E = 36.7 kcal/mole. Data of T. W. T. Taylor and A. R. Murray, *J. Chem. Soc.*, 2078 (1938).
6. G. B. Kistiakowsky and W. R. Smith, *J. Am. Chem. Soc.*, **57**, 269 (1935).
7. G. B. Kistiakowsky and W. R. Smith, *J. Am. Chem. Soc.*, **58**, 2428 (1966).
8. E. W. Schlag and E. W. Kaiser, Jr., *J. Am. Chem. Soc.*, **87**, 1171 (1965).
9. L. D. Hawton, and G. P. Semeluk, *Can. J. Chem.*, **44**, 2143 (1966). This reaction is complicated by heterogeneous effects and radical reactions.

frequency is about 150 cm^{-1}. In the transition state the phenyl rotations have stiffened to about the equivalent of a torsion frequency of about 125 cm^{-1}. At 600°K these could contribute 4.4 eu each for a net loss of 8.8 eu. As we can see from Table 3.4, this gives good agreement between estimated and observed A factors.

Comparison of the experimental activation energies of *cis*-butene-2 and *cis*-stilbene yields a benzyl resonance energy of only 10 kcal, compared to an expected value of about 12.5 kcal. This is only apparent, however, because the pi-bond energies in the two olefins differ by 4 kcal.

The data on the perfluorobutene-2 are interesting because by comparison with butene-2, they imply that the pi-bond energy in the fluorocarbon is about 6 kcal less than in the hydrocarbon.

It is possible to estimate the activation energies for the reactions mentioned above when the pi-bond energies are known. In the case of CHD=CHD, for example, the pi-bond energy at 300°K is 59.5 kcal. If we assume that the ground state of the biradical is planar, in accordance with the observations that sp^2, single-bonded, C-atoms, such as those in butadiene, glyoxol, styrene, etc., form planar structures and that the perpendicular configuration has an activation energy of 3.6 kcal (the conjugation energy in butadiene), we estimate $\Delta H^{\ddagger}_{300} = 63.1$ kcal/mole. At 800°K, using $\langle \Delta C^{\circ}_p \rangle = 1$ gibbs/mole, this becomes 63.6, and $E_{act.} = \Delta H^{\ddagger} + RT = 65.2$ kcal/mole at 800°K, in excellent agreement with the observed value. A similar calculation for butene-2 yields $E_{act.}(700°K) = 62.1$ kcal/mole, whereas for CHCl=CHCl, we estimate (at 800°K), 57.0 kcal/mole, all in excellent agreement with the data. The last value is based on the assumption that the C—H bond strength in CH_2Cl—CH_2Cl is 95.5 kcal/mole. This leads to a pi-bond strength of 49.1 kcal/mole in the olefin.

3.9 COMPLEX FISSIONS—CYCLIC TRANSITION STATES

A number of unimolecular reactions occur in which more than one bond in a molecule is broken. These vary in complexity over quite a range, but all have in common the formation of cyclic transition states. As examples, we may consider the elimination of HX from X-substituted hydrocarbons. These seem to involve four atoms in a ring transition state and are frequently referred to as four-center reactions. The pyrolysis of i-PrI provides an example. The mechanism is

$$CH_3—CH—CH_3 \rightleftharpoons \quad \rightleftharpoons \quad \quad (3.31)$$
$$\qquad\qquad\quad | \\ \qquad\qquad\quad I$$

Nitroalkanes appear to follow a five-center path:

$$CH_3—CH—CH_3 \rightleftharpoons \quad \rightleftharpoons \quad \quad (3.32)$$
$$\qquad\qquad\quad | \\ \qquad\qquad\quad NO_2$$

Alkyl esters pyrolyze by a six-center path:

$$CH_3—C \underset{OCH_2CH_2CH_3}{\overset{O}{<}} \rightleftharpoons \quad \rightleftharpoons$$

$$CH_3—C \underset{O}{\overset{O}{<}} H + \overset{CH—CH_3}{\underset{CH_2}{||}} \quad (3.33)$$

Retrograde (that is, reverse) Diels-Alder reactions have been proposed to follow a concerted six-center path, but there has been considerable controversy as to whether the alternate biradical path is not the correct one. Decomposition of butadiene dimer illustrates the point:

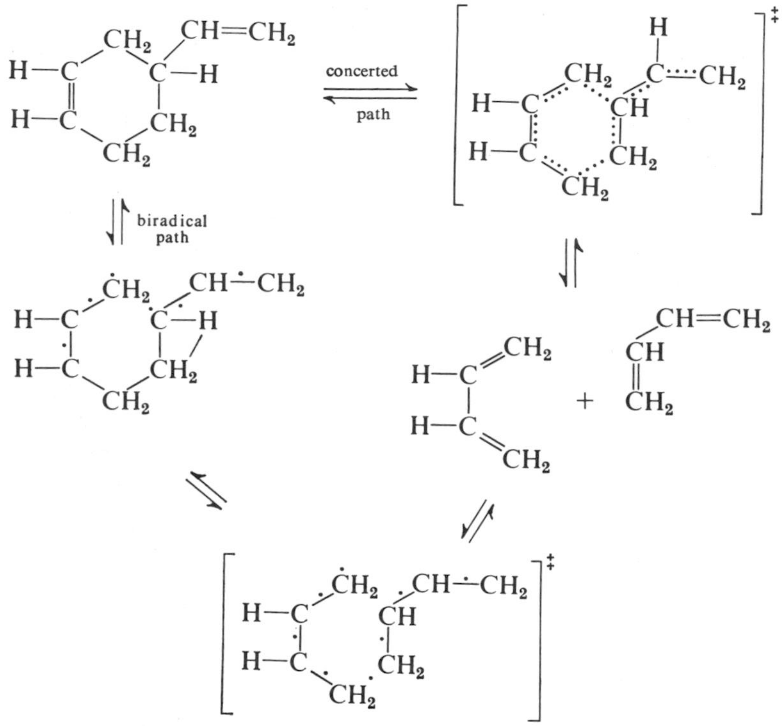

$$(3.34)$$

Note that the biradical path involves the formation of a short-lived biradical intermediate, which may proceed on to fission to final products or recyclize to reactant. Thus there is another transition state between reactant and biradical that has not been drawn.

Depending on the relative rates of ring closure and biradical fission, the overall rate constant for the biradical path may involve either one or both transition states. Again, depending on various factors at present not completely understood, the reaction may follow the concerted path, the biradical path, or both. If the rate of biradical formation should be rate determining, the transition state for this path is about identical with that for the concerted process. We shall return to this reaction. (In Table 3.5 are collected a number of rate constants for these complex four-center fissions.)

The four-center elimination reaction of HX from a substituted RX compound are all endothermic by from 12 to 20 kcal/mole, depending on X, and have activation energies that are very sensitive to structure. We discuss these in more detail later, but for the moment let us consider the A factors and for

Table 3.5 Arrhenius Parameters for Some Four-Center Complex Fissions

Reference	Reaction	T_m (°K)	log A (sec^{-1})	E (kcal/mole)
1.	$CH_3CH_2Cl \rightarrow C_2H_4 + HCl$	720	13.51	56.6
1.	n-PrCl $\rightarrow C_3H_6 + HCl$	720	13.50	55.1
1.	n-BuCl $\rightarrow n$-$C_4H_8 + HCl$	700	13.63	55.2
2.	sec-BuCl $\rightarrow n$-$C_4H_8 + HCl$	630	13.62	49.6
3.	iso-BuCl $\rightarrow i$-$C_4H_8 + HCl$	700	14.0 (12.9)	56.8 (53.3)
4.	t-BuCl $\rightarrow i$-$C_4H_8 + HCl$	780	13.74	44.7
5.	EtBr $\rightarrow C_2H_4 + HBr$	680	13.45	53.9
6.	n-PrBr $\rightarrow C_3H_6 + HBr$	840	13.0	50.7
7.	n-BuBr $\rightarrow i$-$C_4H_8 + HBr$	670	13.2	50.9
8.	sec-BuBr $\rightarrow n$-$C_4H_8 + HBr$	600	13.53	46.5
9.	iso-BuBr $\rightarrow i$-$C_4H_8 + HBr$	530	13.05	50.4
10.	t-BuBr $\rightarrow i$-$C_4H_8 + HBr$	800	13.5	41.5
11.	Cyclohexyl Br $\rightarrow$ cyclohexene $+ HBr$	600	13.52	46.1
12.	Cyclohexyl Cl $\rightarrow$ cyclohexene $+ HCl$	600	13.0	50.0
13.	Cyclopentyl Br $\rightarrow$ cyclopentene $+ HBr$	600	12.84	43.7
10.	t-BuOH $\rightarrow i$-$C_4H_8 + HOH$	1150	13.4	61.6
14.	t-amyl OH $\rightarrow$ 2-methyl butene-1 $+ HOH$	780	13.5	60.0
15.	EtI $\rightarrow C_2H_4 + HI$	630	13.4	50.0
16.	i-PrI $= C_3H_8 + HI$	560	13.0	43.5
17.	t-BuI $\rightarrow i$-$C_4H_8 + HI$	710	13.7	38.1

1. H. Hartman, H. G. Bosche, and H. Heydtmann, *Zeit. Phys. Chem.*, NF **42**, 329 (1964).
2. A. Maccoll and R. H. Stone, *J. Chem. Soc.*, 2756 (1961).
3. K. E. Howlett, *J. Chem. Soc.*, 4487 (1962). Values in parentheses are "best" estimates by O'Neal and Benson (*loc. cit.*).
4. W. Tsang, *J. Chem. Phys.*, **40**, 1171 (1964).
5. P. J. Thomas, *J. Chem. Soc.*, 1192 (1959).
6. A. T. Blades and G. W. Murphy, *J. Am. Chem. Soc.*, **74**, 6219 (1952).
7. A. Maccoll and P. J. Thomas, *J. Chem. Soc.*, 5033 (1957).
8. M. N. Kale, A. Maccoll, and P. J. Thomas, *J. Chem. Soc.*, 3016 (1958).
9. G. P. Harden and A. Maccoll, *J. Chem. Soc.*, 1197 (1959).
10. W. Tsang, *J. Chem. Phys.*, **40**, 1498 (1964).
11. J. S. Green and A. Maccoll, *J. Chem. Soc.*, 2449 (1955).
12. E. S. Swinbourne, *Aus. J. Chem.*, **11**, 314 (1958).
13. M. N. Kale and A. Maccoll, *J. Chem. Soc.*, 5020 (1957).
14. R. F. Schultz and G. B. Kistiakowsky, *J. Am. Chem. Soc.*, **56**, 395 (1934).
15. S. W. Benson and A. N. Bose, *J. Chem. Phys.*, **37**, 2935 (1962).
16. H. Teranishi and S. W. Benson, *J. Chem. Phys.*, **40**, 2946 (1964).
17. W. Tsang, *J. Chem. Phys.*, **41**, 2487 (1964).

simplicity, start with C_2H_5Cl. The transition state involves the formation of a four-atom, cyclic ring, which, in principle, we expect to be fairly tight.

$$
\begin{array}{c}
\overset{H}{\underset{H}{H\!\!\rhd C}}\!\!\!-\!\!\!\overset{H}{\underset{Cl}{C\!\!\lhd H}} \rightleftharpoons
\left[\overset{\;\;\;H\qquad\qquad H}{\underset{\underset{H\;\cdot\;\;Cl}{H\cdot\;\;\;\;\;\cdot H}}{C\;\cdot\;\;\cdot\;C}}\right]^{\ddagger} \rightleftharpoons
\overset{H}{\underset{H}{\;\;\;}}C\!\!=\!\!C\overset{H}{\underset{H}{\;\;\;}} \;+\; H\!\!-\!\!Cl
\end{array}
\qquad (3.35)
$$

The significant contributions to $\Delta S^{\ddagger}$ are a symmetry change of $+R \ln 3$, corresponding to the three equivalent H atoms, which can be eliminated with the Cl, and a loss of about 4 eu at $700°K$, due to the stiffening of the CH_3 internal rotation. These would constitute a net contribution to $\Delta S^{\ddagger}$ of -1.8 eu, so that the A factor should become (3.27) at $700°K$, about $10^{13.2}$ sec^{-1}. Despite some scatter, this seems to be in reasonable accord with the data for EtCl, EtBr and EtI. Symmetry considerations would lead us to expect A factors of $10^{13.5}$ sec^{-1} for i-PrX and $10^{13.7}$ sec^{-1} for t-BuX elimination reactions, all again in reasonable agreement with the data. It is unfortunate that the uncertainty in the measured A factors correspond to factors of about $10^{0.5}$ sec^{-1}, which is the order of the above differences.

A more systematic analysis than that performed above may be made as follows.[12] If we consider the formation of a four-membered ring, the four atoms constituting the ring will have six frequencies associated with them. Of these, four can be taken as stretches, and two as deformations, one in plane and one out of plane. One of the stretches corresponds to the reaction coordinate. When one of the ring atoms is H or D, we can assign two of the stretches and the out-of-plane bend to it. For C_2H_5Cl, the $\Delta S^{\ddagger}$ contributions at $600°K$ are shown in Table 3.6.

In the n-PrX and n-BuX eliminations we lose the internal rotations of an ethyl and a propyl group, respectively. However, these are not entirely lost because they are replaced by low torsional frequencies, about the incipient double bond, of about 350 to 300 cm^{-1}. Thus the net rotational loss in $\Delta S^{\ddagger}$ is probably about the same as for the CH_3 group. However, there are only two reactive H atoms instead of three in EtX, so we may expect the A factor to be about $10^{13.1}$ sec^{-1}, or not very different from the EtX compounds.

The data are consistent with the view submitted above but are not good enough to resolve the rather fine distinction. The same will be true of the iso-butyl-X having only one reactive H atom.

When X is OH, we lose an additional rotation in the transition state and we may expect A factors for t-Bu—OH to be about $10^{13.2}$ sec^{-1}. Again, the data are not good enough to discern such detail.

If the foregoing treatment is correct, we should expect that for the case when R is a cyclic structure, no loss in internal rotation occurs. Thus, for

[12] See H. E. O'Neal and S. W. Benson, *J. Phys. Chem.*, **71**, 2903 (1967) for more detailed discussion of A-factor prediction in concerted reactions.

cyclohexyl-X at high temperatures, the transition state has a symmetry contribution to $\Delta S^{\ddagger}$ of $R \ln 2$ arising from two available H atoms, which is however compensated by the two nearly equivalent ground state structures (axial and equatorial X). Thus we should find $A \sim ekT_m/h$, which is $10^{13.6}$ sec^{-1} at 700°K. From Table 3.5 we note that this is in agreement with the

Table 3.6[a]

	$\Delta S^{\ddagger}$ (gibbs/mole)
Symmetry	$+R \ln 3 = +2.2$
CH$_3$ internal rotation → CH$_2$—C (CH$_3$/H) torsion (400 cm^{-1})	−3.7
C—Cl stretch 650 cm^{-1} → (reaction coordinate)	−1.4
C—C—Cl bend → C—C·Cl bend (400 cm^{-1}) → (280 cm^{-1})	+0.7
H—C—H bend → H—C—C bend (1450 cm^{-1}) → (950 cm^{-1})	+0.6
Total	−1.6

[a] Note that we have neglected the small contributions due to the ring H stretches.

data on cyclohexyl Br. The A factor for cyclopentyl Br, by contrast, seems too low. However, the cyclopentyl rings have abnormally high entropies relative to six-membered rings because of a low-frequency, ring-puckering mode, the pseudo-rotation. Cyclobutane also has such a low-frequency mode. The A factors show very clearly the loss of such a mode in the transition state (see Section 2.16).

Data on the few five-center and larger number of six-center complex fissions are presented in Table 3.7. For purposes of comparison, we have included three isomerization reactions that also go through six-center complexes.

The HONO eliminations involve a transition state in which we have lost one CH$_3$ rotation and one NO$_2$ free rotation. For EtNO$_2$ we expect a symmetry contribution of $R \ln 6$, an internal rotation loss of about -11 eu, -1.0 from the reaction coordinate, yielding a net $\Delta S^{\ddagger} = -8.4$ eu. Hence the A factor of 600°K should be $10^{11.8}$ sec^{-1}, in reasonable accord with the data. For i-PrNO$_2$ the value should be about $10^{12.0}$ sec^{-1}, the extra symmetry contribution being offset somewhat by the increased reduced moment of inertia around the C—N bond. The agreement here is poorer.

The ester pyrolyses involve the stiffening of two large internal rotations about the ether O—C bond and the alkyl C—C bond. The acyl C—O bond

Table 3.7 Arrhenius Parameters for Some Five- and Six-Center Complex Fissions

Reference	Reaction	T_m (°K)	log A (sec^{-1})	E (kcal/mole)
1, 2.	i-PrNO$_2$ → C$_3$H$_6$ + HNO$_2$	570	11.0(11.3)	39.0(40)[a]
2.	EtNO$_2$ → C$_2$H$_4$ + HNO$_2$	650	11.5(11.8)	41.5(43)
3, 4.	CH$_3$COOEt → C$_2$H$_4$ + CH$_3$COOH	820	12.5	47.8
4.	CH$_3$COOiPr → C$_3$H$_6$ + CH$_3$COOH	760	13.0	45.0
5.	CH$_3$COOt-Bu → i-C$_4$H$_8$ + CH$_3$COOH	540	13.3	40.5
6.	C$_2$H$_5$COOt-Bu → i-C$_4$H$_8$ + C$_2$H$_5$COOH	540	12.8	39.2
7.	CH$_3$COOCOCH$_3$ →			
	CH$_2$CO + CH$_3$COOH	600	12.0	34.5
8.	CH$_3$—CH$_2$—O—CH=CH$_2$ →			
	CH$_3$CHO + C$_2$H$_4$	810	11.4	43.8
9.	cis-methylvinylcyclopropane →			
	hexadiene-1,4 (cis)	460	~11.0	31.0
10.	3-Methyl hexadiene-1,5 ⇌ heptadiene-1,5	480	9.8(10.85)	32.5(35.0)[b]
11.	CH$_2$=CH—O—CH$_2$—CH=CH$_2$ →			
	CH$_2$=CH—CH$_2$—CH$_2$CHO	450	11.3	30.6
12.	cis-hexatriene-1,3 → cyclohexadiene-1,3	430	11.8	29.9
13.	s-trioxane → 3CH$_2$O	580	15.0	47.4
14.	Cyclo [—CH(CH$_3$)—O—]$_3$ → 3 CH$_3$CHO	510	15.1	44.2
14.	Cyclo [—CH(nPr)—O—]$_3$ → 3 nPr-CHO	480	14.4	42.0
14.	Cyclo [—CH(iPr)—O—]$_3$ → 3 iPr-CHO	480	14.5	42.0
15.	Cyclohexene → C$_2$H$_4$ + butadiene	860	15.2	66.2
16.	Methyl cyclohexene-3 →			
	C$_3$H$_6$ + butadiene	1020	15.1	66.6
16, 17.	Vinyl cyclohexene-3 → 2-butadiene	1000	15.2 (15.7)	62.0 (61.8)

[a] G. N. Spokes and S. W. Benson, *J. Am. Chem. Soc.*, **89,** 6030 (1967).
[b] Private Comm. H. M. Frey (1968).
1. T. E. Smith and J. G. Calvert, *J. Phys. Chem.*, **63,** 1305 (1959).
2. C. Fréjacques, *Compt. Rend.*, **231,** 1061 (1950).
3. A. T. Blades and P. W. Gilderson, *Can. J. Chem.*, **38,** 1407 (1960).
4. A. T. Blades, *Can. J. Chem.*, **32,** 366 (1954).
5. E. V. Emovan and A. Maccoll, *J. Chem. Soc.*, 335, (1962).
6. E. Warrick and P. Fugassi, *J. Phys. Chem.*, **52,** 1314 (1948).
7. J. Murawski and M. Szwarc, *Trans. Faraday Soc.*, **47,** 269 (1951).
8. A. T. Blades and G. W. Murphy, *J. Am. Chem. Soc.*, **74,** 1039 (1952).
9. R. J. Ellis and H. M. Frey, *J. Chem. Soc.*, 5578 (1964).
10. A. Amano and M. Uchizama, *J. Phys. Chem.*, **69,** 1278 (1965).
11. F. W. Schuler and G. W. Murphy, *J. Am. Chem. Soc.*, **72,** 3155 (1950).
12. K. E. Lewis and H. Steiner, *J. Chem. Soc.*, 3080 (1964).
13. W. Hogg, D. M. McKinnon, and A. F. Trotman-Dickenson, *J. Chem. Soc.*, 1403 (1961).
14. C. C. Coffin, *Can. J. Res.*, **7,** 75 (1932); **9,** 603 (1933); N.A.D. Parlee, **18,** 223 (1940).
15. M. Uchizama, T. Tomioka, and A. Amano, *J. Phys. Chem.*, **68,** 1878 (1964).
16. W. Tsang, *J. Chem. Phys.*, **42,** 1805 (1965).
17. Values in parentheses are estimates from reverse reaction and K_{eq}. by N. E. Duncan and J. E. Janz, *J. Chem.*, **20,** 1944 (1952).

has a large torsion barrier (Table A.19) and a frequency of $\sim$250 cm^{-1}. These are replaced by two low-frequency torsions in the neighborhood of 250 to 400 cm^{-1}. At 700°K the net loss is about 2 eu per rotation or about 6.0 eu. Thus for CH$_3$COOEt we have $+R \ln 3$ from symmetry, -6.0 eu from rotation for a net $\Delta S^{\ddagger} \approx -3.8$ eu. Hence A (700°K) should be about $10^{12.8}$ sec^{-1}, in good accord with the observed $10^{12.5}$ sec^{-1}. The A factors for i-Pr and t-Bu esters should then be higher by factors of 2 and 3, respectively, or $10^{13.1}$ and $10^{13.3}$, in excellent agreement with the data. However, the uncertainties in log A are about ±0.5, which appear when the data for t-Bu acetate and t-Bu propionate is compared. The rate constants have nearly identical values at 550°K, whereas the reported A factors differ by an unaccountable factor of 3. This is a case where group additivity rules can be applied to ground states and transition states and would predict identical values for $\Delta S^{\ddagger}$.

The ethyl vinyl ether pyrolysis is isoelectronic with ethyl formate pyrolysis and the transition states are very similar (see Figure 3.2). The predicted A factor of $10^{11.6}$ sec^{-1} is in good accord with the observed $10^{11.4}$ sec^{-1}.

The lower A factor for the ether, compared with the ester, is due to the nearly free rotation about the vinyl C—O bond in the ether, compared with the stiff acyl C—O torsion in the ester (Table A-19). The ether loses about 4 gibbs/mole more in going to the transition state.

Similarly (CH$_3$CO)$_2$O has an A factor very close to the predicted $10^{12.3}$ sec^{-1}. The very similar transformation of cis-1-methyl, 2-vinyl-cyclopropane involves a loss of only two rotations:

cis
conformation

However, the observed A factor is lower than that for the ether pyrolysis and lower than that anticipated ($10^{11.7}$) from the symmetry contribution of

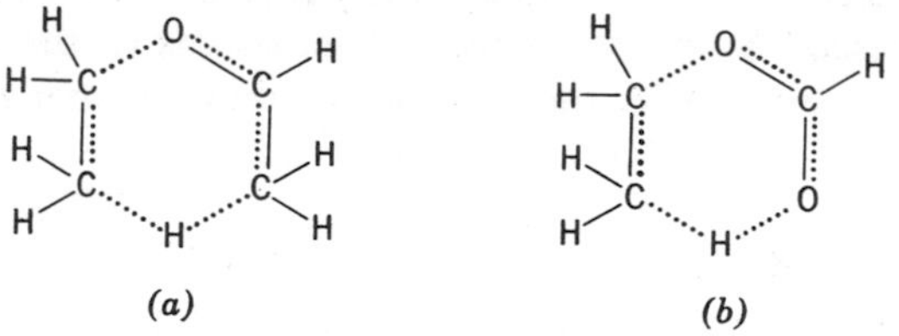

(a)   (b)

Figure 3.2   Two isoelectronic transition states. (a) vinyl ethyl ether pyrolysis; (b) ethyl formate pyrolysis.

$R \ln 3$. This is due in part to the lower temperature, of 450°K, of the reaction, and hence, the lower contribution of the offsetting torsional modes.[13]

In contrast to all of the low A-factor reactions, which have involved the formation of six-membered rings for open chains, the pyrolysis of the symmetrical substituted trioxanes all have A factors about tenfold larger than the expected $10^{13.5}$ sec^{-1}. For these reactions $\Delta S^{\ddagger} \sim 5$ eu, and the transition states must all involve a loosening of the ground state ring structure. This is a quite reasonable result and is predicted directly from the detailed scheme proposed by O'Neal and Benson.[14]

The reverse Diels-Alder reactions of cyclohexenes all have larger A factors than the trioxanes, despite the fact that the overall entropy change for them is smaller than that for the trioxanes. The trioxanes must certainly decompose by a concerted mechanism because the activation energy is so much lower than would be possible for any biradical path. We discuss these reactions later, from the point of view of the biradical intermediate, when we consider the reverse reaction of Diels-Alder additions to butadiene.

3.10   UNIMOLECULAR REACTIONS—BIRADICAL INTERMEDIATES

A large number of unimolecular reactions cannot be rationalized as occurring via a single transition state. Instead we must invoke a fairly complex mechanism involving the formation of one or more intermediate biradicals, of which the best known example is the isomerization of cyclopropane to propylene. Rabinowitch, Schlag, and Wiberg[15] showed that cis-1,2-dideuterocyclopropane underwent geometrical isomerization to the trans form about twelve times faster than the structural isomerization to

[13] It is very surprising that the product is the cis, rather than the expected trans, olefin. This implies that the more crowded cis structure, with the vinyl group over the C_3 ring, is the favored form, and this could account for the low A factor. This is also the favored form for the trans isomerization (see Table 3.7).

[14] S. W. Benson and H. E. O'Neal, loc. cit.

[15] B. S. Rabinovitch, E. Schlag, and K. Wiberg, J. Chem. Phys., 23, 315, 2439 (1955).

propylene. Benson[16] later demonstrated that such a result was kinetically and thermochemically incompatible with a concerted mechanism but made good sense in terms of a short-lived (10^{-10} sec) trimethylene biradical precursor:

$$(3.36)$$

From assignable thermochemical properties of the biradical, it was possible to deduce Arrhenius parameters for each of the Steps 1, 2, and 3 in (3.36) above. The rotation steps take place so rapidly at the relevant temperatures that the biradical reaches rotational equilibrium, once it is formed;[17] that is, $k_r \sim k'_r > (k_2 + k_3)$.

Similar evidence exists for the pyrolysis of cyclobutane compounds. Geometrical isomerization of *cis*-1,2-dimethyl cyclobutane[18] occurs about four times more slowly than the major split into 2-propylene molecules. A minor split into C_2H_4 | butene-2 goes via a biradical, which can live long enough to rotate to produce some *cis*-butene-2 from the trans conformation before it splits to produce the favored *trans*-butene-2. The mechanism is

$$(3.37)$$

Cyclobutene and alkyl cyclobutenes isomerize to butadienes with "normal" A factors of $10^{13.1}$ and an activation energy of 32.5 to 36 kcal/mole. The

[16] S. W. Benson, *J. Chem. Phys.*, **34**, 521 (1961).
[17] This is not the case for "hot" cyclopropane formed by adding CH_2 to C_2H_4. Here the lower A factor for rotation makes rotation and ring closure competitive.
[18] R. Gerberich and W. D. Walters, *J. Am. Chem. Soc.*, **83**, 3935; **84**, 4884 (1961).

hypothetical biradical precursor in this case is indicated in (3.38). The structure of the parent molecule would seem to preclude fully developed allylic resonance in the transition state. The developing pi-electron orbitals in the breaking bond are at right angles to the double bond, so we would not

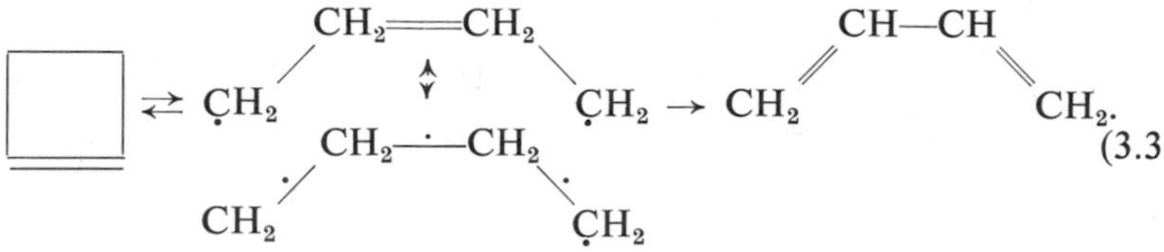

$$\tag{3.38}$$

expect extensive interaction. On this basis we could consider these reactions to proceed in a concerted fashion. The A factors predicted for either path are the same because the transition state must in either case be very rigid. There is only about 3.0 gibbs/mole entropy increase in the overall reaction.

Note, however, that if allylic resonance were even two-thirds developed in the transition state, the biradical path would be energetically possible.

Table 3.8 summarizes some of the kinetic data on these small ring systems, including some heterocyclics. Very striking support for the biradical hypothesis comes from the lowering of both the activation energy and the A factor which is observed when conjugating groups, such as vinyl, carbonyl, or phenyl, are introduced into these systems. We note that the pyrolysis of vinyl cyclopropane produces as the major product, cyclopentene. The biradical mechanism would be

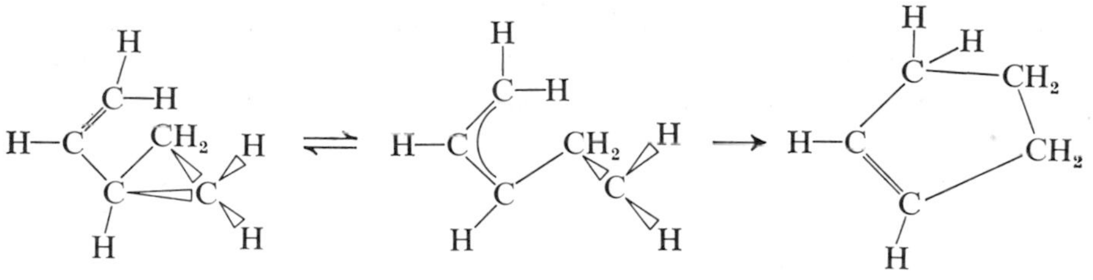

$$\tag{3.39}$$

It should be pointed out that it is only when the vinyl group is in the unfavorable cis position to one of the C—C bonds in the ring that the reaction can occur with full allylic resonance. When the vinyl group is trans to the center of the ring, the geometry of the resulting, stiff allyl radical precludes five-membered ring formation. This is shown in the following diagrams: (See top of page 87.)

The trans form can, however, produce the pentadienes at an appreciably higher activation energy.

Table 3.8 Arrhenius Parameters for the Pyrolysis of Small Ring Compounds

Reference	Reaction	T_m (°K)	log A (sec^{-1})	E (kcal/mole)
1.	$\overline{CH_2—CH_2—CH_2}$ → $CH_3—CH{=}CH_2$	770	15.2	65.0
2.	cis-dideuterocyclopropane → trans	720	16.1 (15.12)	65.1 (65.4)
3.	$CH_3—\overline{CH—CH_2—CH_2}$			
	→ n-C_4H_8 (cis and trans)	740	15.40	65.0
	→ i-C_4H_8		14.62	66.0
4.	$CH_2{=}CH—\overline{CH—CH_2—CH_2}$			
	→ $\overline{CH_2—CH{=}CH—CH_2—CH_2}$	640	13.6	49.7
	→ pentadiene-1,4		14.4	57.3
	→ pentadiene-1,3		⎰13.0 (trans)⎱ 13.9 (cis)	⎰53.6⎱ 56.2
5.	$CH_3—\overline{CH—CH_2—CH}—CH_3$ (cis) → trans	690	15.25	59.4
6.	$\phi—\overline{CH—CH_2—CH}—\phi$ (cis)			
	→ trans (liquid)	460	11.2	33.5
7.	Cyclobutane → $2C_2H_4$	730	15.6	62.5
8.	cis-Dimethyl cyclobutane → trans	690	14.81	60.1
	→ $2C_3H_6$	680	15.48	60.4
	→ C_2H_4 + butene-2	680	15.57	63.4
9.	Acetyl cyclobutane			
	→ $CH_3COCH{=}CH_2$ + C_2H_4	660	14.53	54.5
10.	Methylene cyclobutane			
	→ $CH_2{=}C{=}CH_2$ + C_2H_4	710	15.7	63.0
11.	Cyclo-C_4F_8 → $2C_2F_4$	830	15.95	74.1
12.	$\overline{FC(Cl)—CF_2—CF_2—CFCl}$			
	→ $2CF_2{=}CFCl$	740	15.4	65.3
	cis → trans	720	15.1	60.2
	trans → cis	720	14.9	60.2
13.	$\overline{CH_2CH_2O}$ → CH_3CHO	670	14.2	57.0
14.	$\overline{CH_2CH_2CH_2O}$ → C_2H_4 + CH_2O	710	14.8	60.0
15.	$\overline{CH_2CH_2CH_2—N{=}N}$ → cyclopropane + N_2 + propylene	500	15.5	42.4
15, 16.	$\overline{CH_3CHCH_2CH(CH_3)N{=}N}$ (cis or trans) → dimethyl cyclopropane + N_2 + pentene-2 (cis and trans)	500	15.2	40.3
17.	$\overline{CH_2CF_2—O}$ → CF_2O + $\ddot{C}F_2$	360	13.7	31.6
18.	Cyclobutene → butadiene	390	13.1	32.6
19.	3-Methyl cyclobutene → 1,3 pentadiene (trans)	390	13.5	31.6
20.	1-Methyl cyclobutene → isoprene	420	13.8	35.1
21.	(Perfluoro) butadiene → cyclobutene	500	12.1	35.4

References for Table 3.8

1. T. S. Chambers and G. B. Kistiakowsky, *J. Am. Chem. Soc.*, **56**, 399 (1934).
2. E. W. Schlag and B. S. Rabinovitch, *J. Am. Chem. Soc.*, **82**, 5996 (1960). Values in parentheses are Arrhenius parameters for propylene formation from $C_3H_4D_2$. Note that because the mechanism proceeds via a biradical that can close with equal probability to yield cis or trans, the rate of ring opening is twice the rate of cis-trans isomerization.
3. D. W. Placzek and B. S. Rabinovitch, *J. Chem. Phys.*, **69**, 2141 (1965). Products include butene-1 and butene-2 (cis and trans) in ratios ~4:2:1.
4. C. A. Wellington, *J. Phys. Chem.*, **66**, 1671 (1962).
5. M. C. Flowers and H. M. Frey, *Proc. Roy. Soc.* (London), **A260**, 424 (1961); **A257**, 122 (1960). Collective production of butenes and pentenes is 100-fold slower.
6. L. B. Rodewald and C. H. dePuy, *Tetrahedron Letters*, **40**, 2951 (1964).
7. R. W. Carr, Jr. and W. D. Walters, *J. Phys. Chem.*, **67**, 1370 (1963).
8. H. R. Gerberich and W. D. Walters, *J. Am. Chem. Soc.*, **83**, 3935, 4884 (1961).
9. L. G. Paignault and W. D. Walters, *J. Am. Chem. Soc.*, **80**, 541 (1958).
10. J. P. Chesick, *J. Phys. Chem.*, **65**, 2170 (1961).
11. B. Atkinson and A. B. Trenwith, *J. Chem. Soc.*, 2082 (1953).
12. B. Atkinson and M. Stedman, *J. Chem. Soc.*, 512 (1962).
13. M. L. Neufeld and A. T. Blades, *Can. J. Chem.*, **41**, 2956 (1963); S. W. Benson, *J. Chem. Phys.*, **40**, 105 (1964).
14. D. A. Bittker and W. D. Walters, *J. Am. Chem. Soc.*, **77**, 1429 (1955).
15. R. J. Crawford, R. T. Dummel, and A. Mishra, *J. Am. Chem. Soc.*, **87**, 3024 (1965).
16. R. J. Crawford and A. Mishra, *J. Am. Chem. Soc.*, **87**, 3768 (1965).
17. M. Lenze and A. Mele, *J. Chem. Phys.*, **43**, 1974 (1965).
18. W. Cooper and W. D. Walters, *J. Am. Chem. Soc.*, **80**, 4220 (1958).
19. H. M. Frey, *Trans. Faraday Soc.*, **60**, 83 (1964).
20. H. M. Frey, *Trans. Faraday Soc.*, **58**, 957 (1962).
21. E. W. Schlag and W. B. Peatman, *J. Am. Chem. Soc.*, **86**, 1676 (1964).

Comparison of any of the alkyl substituted cyclopropanes or cyclobutanes with the corresponding vinyl substituted compounds shows an activation energy for the vinyl compound, lower by about 13 kcal and an *A* factor lower by about a factor of 10. The lowering of the activation energy by 13 kcal is precisely what we would expect if the rate determining step is the formation of the allylic biradical (3.39) because the allyl stabilization energy is 12.6 ± 1 kcal. By the same token, the lower *A* factor is explicable in terms of a net loss of hindered rotation of the vinyl group of about 6 eu.

The substitution of a phenyl group should produce a lowering of *E* of about 13 kcal (the benzyl resonance energy) and a lowering in *A* of about 7 eu due to the loss in phenyl rotation. This is very close to what is observed for *cis*-diphenyl cyclopropane isomerization in Table 3.7. This is not strictly comparable, however, because this was a liquid phase reaction, but the parameters should not be solvent dependent.

The same type of biradical mechanism seems to fit the kinetic data on the pyrolysis of the polycyclic ring systems. Table 3.9 summarizes some of the data for these systems.

(*cis* transition state)   (*trans* transition state)   (3.40)

The cis-trans isomerization of 2-methyl-2,1,0-bicyclopentane affords again a clear example of the biradical mechanism. The path is

(3.41)

The activation energy for the cis-trans isomerization is 7.7 kcal less than for the cyclopentene formation, which has been observed in the unsubstituted case. From the data on H migration in biradicals, we can deduce an activation energy of about 11 kcal for the 2-1 shift of an H atom in a 1,3 biradical. This implies here that both the ring inversion step (r) and the back reaction ($-a$) have 8 kcal less activation energy than the H atom shift.

From the known ΔH_f° of the bicyclopentane, it is possible to compute a ΔH_a for its conversion to the 1,3 biradical.

At 298°K we find $\Delta H_a^\circ = 30$ kcal. The steady state rate of cis → trans isomerization is given by (ignoring back reaction and the other slower steps

$$\frac{-d\,(\text{cis})}{dt} = k'_{-a}(TB) \tag{3.42}$$

$$= \frac{k_r k_a k'_{-a}(\text{cis})}{k_r k'_{-a} + k_{-a}k_{-r} + k_{-a}k'_{-a}}, \tag{3.43}$$

Table 3.9 Arrhenius Parameters for the Pyrolysis of Some Bicyclic Compounds

Reference	Reaction	T_m (°K)	log A (sec^{-1})	E (kcal/mole)
1.	→ cyclopentene	550	14.58 (14.1)[2]	46.6 (46.4)[2]
2.	→ CH_2=$CHCH_2CH$=CH_2	600	14.4	52.3
3.	→ *trans* (cis)	450	14.45	38.9
2.	→ hexadiene-1,5	450	13.4	36.0
4.	→ hexadiene-1,5	630	15.17	55.0
5.	→ cyclohexene	700	13.29	57.4
	→ 1-methyl cyclopentane	730	13.89	61.17
6.	→ CH_2=$CH(CH_3)$—$CH(CH_3)$=CH_2	500	14.5	43.3
7.	→ C_2H_4 + cyclopentadiene	500	13.78	42.8
8.	Bicyclopentadiene → 2 cyclopentadiene	430	13.0	33.7
9.	(β-pinene) → (myrcene)	650	13.5	45.1
		650	15.9	49.9

1. M. L. Halberstadt and J. P. Chesick, *J. Am. Chem. Soc.*, **84**, 2688 (1962).
2. C. Steel, R. Zand, P. Hurwitz, and S. G. Cohen, *J. Am. Chem. Soc.*, **86**, 679 (1964).
3. J. P. Chesick, *J. Am. Chem. Soc.*, **84**, 3250 (1962). $K_{eq.}$ = (cis)/(trans) = 0.58 at 220°C.
4. R. Srinivasan and A. A. Levi, *J. Am. Chem. Soc.*, **85**, 3363 (1963).
5. H. M. Frey and R. C. Smith, *Trans. Faraday Soc.*, **58**, 697 (1962).
6. J. P. Chesick, *J. Phys. Chem.*, **68**, 2033 (1964).
7. W. C. Herndon, W. B. Cooper, and M. J. Chambers, *J. Phys. Chem.*, **68**, 2016 (1964).
8. J. B. Harkness, G. B. Kistiakowsky, and W. H. Mears, *J. Chem. Phys.*, **5**, 682 (1937).
9. J. E. Hawkins and J. W. Vogh, *J. Phys. Chem.*, **57**, 902 (1955).

or for the observed first-order isomerization rate constant,

$$k_{obs.} = \frac{1}{(\text{cis})} \frac{d\,(\text{cis})}{dt} = \frac{k_r K_a}{1 + k_r/k_{-a} + k_r/k'_{-a}} \tag{3.44}$$

where $K_a = k_a/k_{-a}$.

If the ring inversion steps r and r' are slow compared to the ring closing steps $(-a)$ and $(-a')$, this reduces to Case I (slow inversion):

$$k_{obs.} \to k_r K_a. \tag{3.45}$$

If, in contrast, the converse is true, it reduces to Case II (fast inversion):

$$k_{obs.} \to \frac{k_a}{1 + \dfrac{k'_r k_{-a}}{k_r k'_{-a}}} \sim \frac{k_a}{2}. \tag{3.46}$$

In Case I we see that the observed activation energy $E_{obs.}$ is $\Delta H_a + E_r$, so that $E_r = 8.9$ kcal. In Case II $E_{obs.} = E_a$, so that $E_{-a} = 8.9$ kcal. This latter value is comparable to the 10 kcal we find for the activation energy for 1,3 biradicals needed to close the cyclopropane rings; thus it is a quite reasonable result. In order for Case II to apply we would require that the barrier to inversion E_r would be less than 8.9 kcal. Nuclear magnetic resonance data on the inversion barrier in cyclohexanes yields a value of about 10 kcal, so that cyclopentanes must be appreciably less because they have rapid pseudorotation that leads to ring inversion. It thus suggests that Case II applies.

If we make the same steady state calculation of the rate of formation of cyclopentene, we find that the activation energy (E_c) for H migration in the biradical (Step c) is 16.6 kcal rather than the 11 kcal of the trimethylene biradical. We can rationalize this in terms of the fact that the transition state for this step requires that four carbon atoms in the ring be planar and thus includes the barrier to ring inversion, as well as the normal activation energy to H migration. This would suggest a 5 kcal barrier to ring inversion which seems quite reasonable.

The biradical mechanism for small ring pyrolysis has been analyzed quantitatively[19] in terms of a "loose" transition state and shown to give A-factor estimates to within a factor of $10^{\pm 0.3}$ sec^{-1} and activation energies to within ± 2 kcal. What is implied by "loose" is that the transition state for ring opening looks very much like the final state, the free biradical. This is not surprising because the data on radical-radical recombination are all in accord with a "loose" transition state for recombination.

[19] S. W. Benson and H. E. O'Neal, *J. Phys. Chem.*, **72** (1968).

The reaction coordinate changes considerably, however, depending on ring size. Looked at from the reverse direction, ring closing of the biradical, the reaction coordinate for closing of $\dot{C}H_2$—CH_2—$\dot{C}H_2$ to cyclopropane is the low frequency (400 cm^{-1}) C—C—C bending mode. For the tetramethylene biradical, however, the reaction coordinate is the rotation of the two $\dot{C}H_2$—CH_2— groups about the central C—C bond.

As an example, we compute the A factor for cis-trans isomerization of *cis-*dideuterocyclopropane at 800°K. First, let us compute $S°$ and $C_p°$ for the $\dot{C}H_2CH_2\dot{C}H_2$ biradical at 298°K. Starting with C_3H_8, we make the corrections listed in Table 3.10 to $S°_{298}$ and $C°_{pT}$ (we neglect triplet states).

Table 3.10

	$\Delta S°_{298}$ (gibbs/mole)	$\Delta C°_{pT}$ (gibbs/mole)		
		300	500	800
Symmetry	+1.6	—	—	—
Lose two C—H stretches (3100 cm^{-1})	0.0	0.0	−0.1	−0.5
Lose four CH$_2$ bends (1450 cm^{-1})	0.0	−0.4	−2.2	−4.6
Two barriers, reduction from				
3 kcal → 2 kcal	+0.8	−0.2	−0.6	−0.4
Totals	+2.4	−0.6	−2.9	−5.5

From the group tables, $\Delta S°_{298}$ for cyclopropane → propane is 9.9 + $R \ln K_\sigma = 7.7$ gibbs/mole, whereas $\Delta C°_{pT} = 4.4, 4.4,$ and 5.8 gibbs/mole at 300, 500, and 800°K. Hence $\Delta S°_{298}$ (cyclopropane → biradical) = 10.1 and $\Delta C°_{pm} = 1.6$ gibbs/mole.

In the transition state, we change overall symmetry from 8 in the biradical to 2 and, otherwise, lose only the reaction coordinate, the C—C—C bending mode at 420 cm^{-1}. At 800°K, this corresponds to 2.6 gibbs/mole loss in $\Delta S^\ddagger$, compensated by a gain of $R \ln 4$ to give a net $\Delta S^\ddagger_{298}$ of +0.2 eu. Correcting to 800 with $\Delta C°_{pm}$, we find $\Delta S^\ddagger_{800} = 1.8$ eu. Hence the value of $\Delta S^\ddagger_{800}$ starting from cyclopropane is 11.9 eu. The A factor for ring opening is thus

$$A = \left(\frac{ekT}{h}\right)e^{\Delta S^\ddagger/R} = 10^{13.64+2.60} = 10^{16.24} \text{ sec}^{-1}.$$

Assuming that ring opening is rate determining and that cis or trans are formed on closure with equal probability (which can be justified by comparing relative rates of rotation and ring closure), this should be compared with twice the A factor reported for isomerization in Table 3.7, namely, $10^{16.4\pm.3}$ sec^{-1}. The agreement is excellent.

A similar analysis to that made above with equally good results can be made for propylene formation and for the substituted C_3 and C_4 rings.

3.11   STERIC INHIBITION OF RESONANCE IN TRANSITION STATES

Perhaps the most interesting feature of the bicyclopentane (2,1,0) pyrolysis is the slow pace at which the ring is opened by the biradical to form the diene. From our analysis of the cyclobutane system we would conclude that the activation energy for a 1,4 biradical to split into two olefins is about 6 kcal:

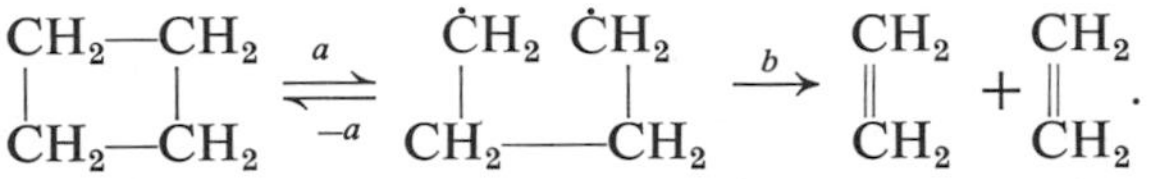

$$\begin{matrix} CH_2-CH_2 \\ | \quad\quad | \\ CH_2-CH_2 \end{matrix} \underset{-a}{\overset{a}{\rightleftharpoons}} \begin{matrix} \dot{C}H_2 \ \dot{C}H_2 \\ | \quad\quad | \\ CH_2-\!\!-CH_2 \end{matrix} \overset{b}{\rightarrow} \begin{matrix} CH_2 \\ \| \\ CH_2 \end{matrix} + \begin{matrix} CH_2 \\ \| \\ CH_2 \end{matrix} . \tag{3.47}$$

This is not the case for the cyclopentane biradical where the activation energy to open the ring is about 22 kcal (Table 3.9). The cause of this large activation energy must be ascribed to steric inhibition of resonance. In order for the cyclopentadiyl-1,3 biradical

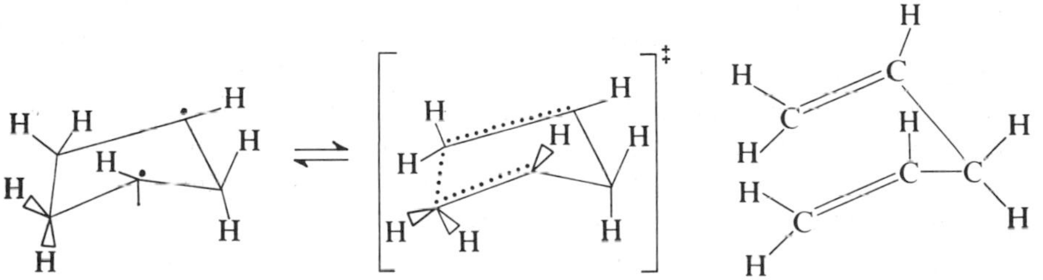

to make the transition to diene, the apex of the ring must be bent almost at right angles, so that the electrons in the breaking C—C bond can interact to form the pi bond in the emergent olefin.

A very similar barrier to that described above has been observed[20] in the decomposition of the cyclopentyl radical to form the pentene-l-yl-5 radical:

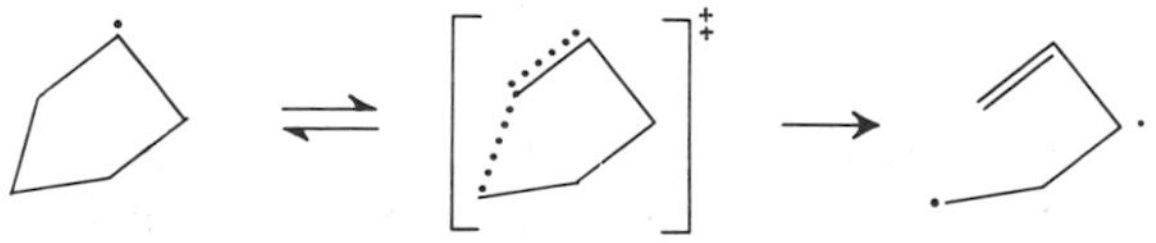

Despite the fact that the reaction above is endothermic by only 17 kcal, the observed activation energy is 37 kcal so that the "excess" activation energy is about 20 kcal, very close to the 22 kcal just estimated for the biradical.

[20] H. E. Gunning and R. L. Stock, *Can. J. Chem.*, **42**, 357 (1964); A. S. Gordon, *Can. J. Chem.*, **43**, 570 (1965).

A striking contrast to the situation just described is provided by the pyrolysis of bicyclohexane $(2, 2, 0)$, which goes to hexadiene-1,5 via a cyclohexadiyl-1,4 biradical:

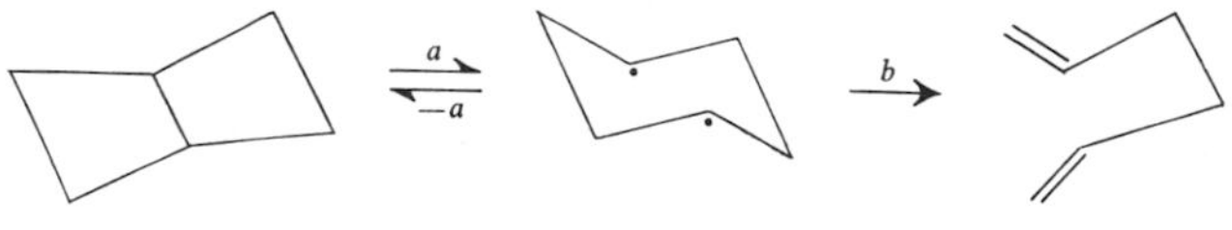

The strain free chair form of the C_6 ring permits the development of the pi bond between the electrons in the breaking bond and the odd electrons without severe distortion of the transition state. We can estimate the ΔH_f° of the bicyclohexane $(2, 2, 0)$ as 29 kcal/mole by assuming double the strain energy of a C_4 ring. With the biradical $\Delta H_f^\circ \sim 55.5$ kcal, we find $\Delta H_a = 27.5$ kcal, compared to an observed activation energy of 36.0 kcal, so that E_b, the activation energy for splitting the ring to yield diene, is now ≤ 8.5 kcal/mole. This can be compared to 22 kcal/mole for the cyclopentyl biradical and 6 kcal/mole for the tetramethylene biradical, showing that there is perhaps 2.5 kcal of strain involved in the C_6 ring transition state. It is, however, more likely that the extra 8.5 kcal of activation should be assigned to E_{-a}, as representing a strain energy developed in closing the biradical to the highly strained bicyclohexane. This would make a the rate determining step.

A final example of such inhibition as that described above is provided by the case of the cyclobutyl radical. The activation energy for its opening to form butene-1-yl-4 radical is reported as 18 kcal,[21] despite the fact that the overall reaction is 3 kcal exothermic:

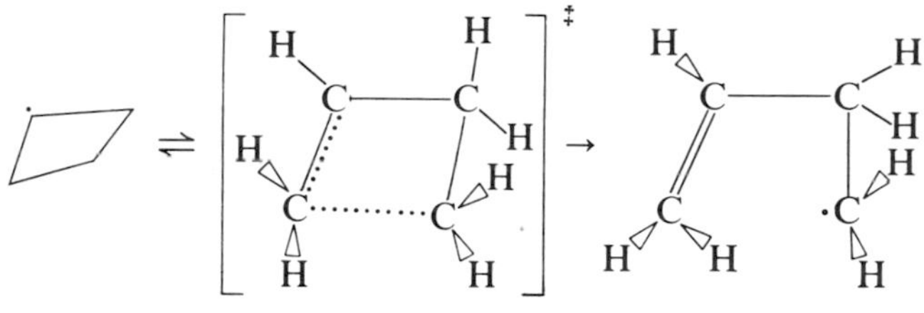

$$(3.48)$$

As we see from the structure, the breaking bond is at right angles to the emerging pi bond and hence there must be very small interaction of pi electrons in the transition state.

3.12   ARRHENIUS A FACTORS FOR RING PYROLYSES

The A factors for bicyclic reactions can only be estimated with less accuracy than those for other reactions because of the absence of data on their

[21] A. S. Gordon, S. Ruthven-Smith, and C. M. Drew, *J. Chem. Phys.*, **36**, 824 (1963).

entropies. However, if we estimate the entropies of the bicyclic species by the empirical methods suggested in the earlier section, we find reasonable agreement between the estimated and observed A factors.

EXAMPLE

Estimate the A factor for the pyrolysis of bicyclopentane (2, 1, 0), BCP, to form cyclopentene at 550°K.

From the preceding discussion, we see that the biradical mechanism predicts that the opening of the ring to form cyclopentadiyl biradical is not rate determining because ring closing is fast compared to H-atom migration. Thus we can assume that the transition state involving H migration is rate determining and calculate $\Delta S^{\ddagger}$ on this basis. The mechanism is

We must first calculate $S°(BCP)$. If we assume that is has a stiff, four-membered ring like cyclobutene rather than cyclobutane (no pseudorotation), we can use the methods of Section 2.16. Starting with dimethyl cyclopropane ($S°_{int.(298)} = 78.2$ eu from groups), we subtract 2×4.0 eu (Table 2.10) to close to the four-membered ring and then subtract 3.2 eu more as the difference between cyclobutene and cyclobutane (Table 2.11). This gives 67.0 eu for $S°_{298}(BCP)$.

For the transition state, we can assume $S°_{298(int.)}$ to be very close to cyclopentene. We correct its entropy by $+1.4$ eu because it has optical isomers, to obtain $S°^{\ddagger}_{298} = 70.6$ eu. The reaction coordinate is the C—H stretch at 3100 cm^{-1} (Table A.13), and its entropy at 550°K (Table A.17) is zero eu. Neglecting any corrections for the moment from ΔC_{pm}, which is expected to be small, we thus calculate $\Delta S^{\ddagger} = 3.6$ eu.

At 550K°, with the Arrhenius A factor given by

$$A = \left(\frac{ekT_m}{h}\right) e^{\Delta S^{\ddagger}/R},$$

we find $A = 10^{14.3}$ sec^{-1}. This is in excellent agreement with the two reported values of $10^{14.1}$ and $10^{14.6}$ sec^{-1} (Table 3.9).

3.13   REVERSE DIELS-ALDER REACTIONS

We have already noted (page 90) that the experimental evidence is fairly compelling that C_3 and C_4 rings pyrolyze by a biradical mechanism. Recent evidence is just as convincing that the same is true for the C_6 rings. The pyrolysis of cyclooctadiene-1,5 has been shown to produce 4-vinyl cyclohexene at low temperatures and butadiene at higher temperature.[22]

---

[22] R. Srinivason and A. A. Levi, *J. Am. Chem. Soc.*, **86**, 3756 (1964).

The inference is very strong from the results mentioned above that both products come from a common precursor because 4-vinyl cyclohexene does not give butadiene at the same higher temperature. The only consistent mechanism is one involving the allylic biradical

$$(3.49)$$

Steady state analysis yields

$$\frac{d(\text{VC})}{dt} = \frac{k_c k_a(\text{CO})}{k_b + k_c + k_{-a}} \; ; \tag{3.50}$$

$$\frac{d(\text{B})}{dt} = \frac{2k_b k_a(\text{CO})}{k_b + k_c + k_{-a}} = 2k_\text{B}(\text{CO}). \tag{3.51}$$

The apparent first-order rate constants are (units of $\sec^{-1}$)

$$k_{\text{VC}} = 10^{14.45-49/\theta} ; \qquad k_\text{B} \sim 10^{15.7-55/\theta}. \tag{3.52}$$

If we assume that the cycloöctadiene-1,5 has the same strain energy as cycloöctene, we can estimate $\Delta H_a^\circ = 49 \pm 1.5$ kcal, with the uncertainty arising chiefly from the uncertainty in strain energy for the diene.

It seems reasonable to assume that there is no activation energy for closing the eight- or six-membered rings. In that case we expect $k_c \gg k_{-a}$, for the A factors should favor six-membered ring formation over eight-membered rings by at least the statistical factor of 4, arising from symmetry differences and optical centers. The apparent activation energy for k_{VC} is given by

$$E_{\text{VC}} \simeq E_a - \left(\frac{k_b}{k_b + k_c}\right) E_b. \tag{3.53}$$

The difference of 6 kcal between k_{VC} and k_B is actually determined from initial ratios of concentration of products and hence equals $(E_b - E_c) \simeq E_b$. Substituting this in the above expression, we find $E_a = 49.6$ because $k_b/(k_b + k_c) \approx 0.10$. This is in excellent agreement with the calculated $\Delta H_a^\circ = 49 \pm 1.5$ and is consistent with our assumption that $E_c \approx 0$.

We can make a further step and calculate $\Delta H_b^\circ = -17.4$ kcal/mole. Because $E_b = 6$ kcal, we would estimate $E_{-b} = 24.6$ kcal/mole. This is so close to the observed activation energy of 26 kcal/mole (concentration unit) for the addition of two butadienes to form vinyl cyclohexene that it give very strong support to the biradical mechanism for this reaction.

From the observed rate constants and thermochemistry, we can now fix the rate constants in the system as follows:[23]

$$k_a = 10^{14.6-49.5/\theta} \ \text{sec}^{-1};$$
$$k_{-a} = 10^{11.3} \ \text{sec}^{-1};$$
$$k_b = 10^{13.3-6/\theta} \ \text{sec}^{-1};$$
$$k_{-b} = 10^{8.0-26.0/\theta} \ \text{liter/mole-sec};$$
$$k_c = 10^{12.1} \ \text{sec}^{-1};$$
$$k_{-c} = 10^{14.2-55.6/\theta} \ \text{sec}^{-1}.$$

$$(3.54)$$

The first-order rate constant for the pyrolysis of 4-vinyl-cyclohexene is given by

$$\frac{k_{-c}k_b}{k_c + k_b} \simeq 10^{15.2-61.0/\theta} \ \text{sec}^{-1}, \tag{3.55}$$

in excellent agreement with the reported value of $10^{15.2-62.00} \ \text{sec}^{-1}$. These data are inferred from the estimated entropy changes, $\Delta S_a = 15.6$ gibbs/mole; $\Delta S_b = 33.4$ gibbs/mole.

In contrast to the dissociation of vinyl cyclohexene-4, in which the rate controlling step is the dissociation of the linear biradical, the dissociation of cyclohexene has the initial step as rate determining:

$$(3.56)$$

We find that $\Delta H_a^\circ = 66.9$ kcal, which is to be compared to an observed activation energy of 66.2 kcal. This implies that $k_b > k_{-a}$, which is consistent with the preceding case if $k_{-a} \sim 10^{12.5} \ \text{sec}^{-1}$ and $k_b \sim 10^{14.6-6/\theta} \ \text{sec}^{-1}$. This would give the latter an activation energy lower than that for the doubly conjugated dibutadienyl radical, a quite reasonable result. The A factor for Step $(-a)$ is expected to be lower than for that of dibutadienyl by a factor of 2 due to symmetry, whereas the A factor for ring opening may be considerably higher, due to the fact that there is more entropy loss in forming the C_8 transition state than in forming the C_6 transition state biradical.

The observed A factor of $10^{15.2} \ \text{sec}^{-1}$ (Table 3.6) yields $\Delta S^{\ddagger} = 7$ gibbs/mole, which is consistent with a transition state about halfway in entropy between the ring and the free biradical.

[23] For more detail, consult S. W. Benson, *J. Chem. Phys.*, **46**, 4920 (1967).

3.14   BIMOLECULAR REACTIONS—CATEGORIES

Transition-state theory yields for the A factor of a bimolecular reaction the value (ekT/h) exp $(\Delta S_p^{\ddagger}/R)$ where $\Delta S_p^{\ddagger}$ is the entropy change (always negative) for forming a mole of transition state complex from the two reactants:[24]

$$A + B \rightleftarrows (AB)^{\ddagger} \rightarrow \text{products.} \qquad (3.57)$$

Three categories of reactions may be distinguished for bimolecular reactions. The first is a metathesis in which an atom is transferred from A to B. An example is the well-known chain step:

$$H + Br_2 \rightleftarrows (H \cdots Br \cdots Br)^{\ddagger} \rightleftarrows HBr + Br. \qquad (3.58)$$

The second is a displacement or exchange reaction, quite frequent in the chemistry of unsaturated molecules:

$$(3.59)$$

The last category is the association reaction. A typical example is the recombination of radicals:

$$2 \cdot CH_3 \rightleftarrows (CH_3 \cdots CH_3)^{\ddagger} \rightarrow C_2H_6. \qquad (3.60)$$

It should be noted that the displacement reaction is a complex process involving the formation of a true intermediate by an association reaction. Because these reactions are generally exothermic, the adduct is usually a vibrationally excited species, which in the gas phase may have a very short lifetime. Such reactions thus involve two discrete transition states.

Unless the vibrationally excited species formed in an association reaction loses its energy by a collision, it will inevitably dissociate back into original or into more stable species. Where the rate of this dissociation is rapid compared to collision frequencies, we find that the reaction rate is controlled by the rate of these deenergizing collisions and the kinetics tend toward third order. Such processes are called energy transfer processes because the rate limiting step is the transfer of energy between species.

Note that in every case of the formation of a transition state from two reactants the reverse process is a unimolecular dissociation, the rate constant

---

[24] This depends again on standard states. The discussion above is correct for pressure units. With $\Delta S_c^{\ddagger}$, based on concentration units, the activation energy is higher by RT, and we get a factor of e^2. However, the same is true for the Arrhenius equation for second-order reactions.

of which is derivable from the considerations presented in the preceding sections.

3.15   LOWER LIMITS TO BIMOLECULAR A FACTORS

The calculation of $\Delta S^{\ddagger}$ for a bimolecular process requires the knowledge of the structure of the $AB^{\ddagger}$ complex. Some useful information in this regard can be obtained very quickly by fixing a lower limit to $\Delta S^{\ddagger}$, which is always negative, by assuming that $AB^{\ddagger}$ is a very tight complex. In such cases, lower limits of $AB^{\ddagger}$ can be quickly fixed by comparison with known molecules. Thus, in the metathesis reaction

$$H + C_2H_6 \rightarrow \left(\begin{array}{c} H \\ | \\ H \cdots H \cdots C-CH_3 \\ | \\ H \end{array} \right)^{\ddagger} \rightarrow H_2 + C_2H_5. \qquad (3.61)$$

We can assign $S^{\ddagger}(C_2H_7^{\cdot})$ a value by comparison with C_2H_6. We note that its translation and rotational entropy should not be seriously increased over C_2H_6 by the additional light H atom, so that the chief changes will be in symmetry and spin. Hence

$$S^{\circ \ddagger}(C_2H_7^{\cdot}) \geq S^{\circ \ddagger}(C_2H_6) + R \ln 6 + R \ln 2, \qquad (3.62)$$

and

$$\Delta S^{\ddagger} = S^{\circ \ddagger}(C_2H_7^{\cdot}) - S^{\circ}(C_{26}H) - S^{\circ}(H)$$
$$\geq -S^{\circ}(H) + R \ln 12. \qquad (3.63)$$

At $400°K$, $\Delta S^{\ddagger}(400) \geq -24.1$ with a standard state of 1 atmosphere. Transforming to molarity by adding $R \ln (eRT) = 9.0$ gibbs/mole, we find $\Delta S_c^{\ddagger}(400) \geq -15.1$ gibbs/mole, so that $A = (ekT/h) \exp (\Delta S^{\ddagger}/R) \geq 10^{10.1}$ l/mole-sec. This is reasonably close to most of the A factors reported for this reaction, which are in the neighborhood of 10^{11} (Table 3.10). To account for the difference, we should have to make the quite reasonable assumption of two H·H—C bends with frequencies at about 400 cm^{-1} in the transition state.

For a reaction of a heavy atom, we can take as an example

$$I + CH_4 \rightleftarrows (I \cdots H \cdots CH_3)^{\ddagger} \rightarrow HI + CH_3. \qquad (3.64)$$

Here $S^{\ddagger} \geq S^{\circ}(CH_3I) + R \ln 2$. To improve the comparison, we should add a correction for the increased rotational entropy of CH_3I due to a long $C \cdots I$ distance. This latter can be estimated by adding 1.4 Å to the sum of the normal C—H and H—I covalent lengths. This yields $r(C \cdots I) = 4.3$ Å, compared to a normal $r(C-I) = 2.10$ Å. Because the entropy goes as

$\frac{1}{2}R \ln (I_A I_B I_C)$, where I_A, I_B, and I_C are the principal moments of inertia and vary as $\Sigma m_i r_i^2$, this changes two of these moments each by a factor of nearly 4. Hence we should add $R \ln 4$ to our estimate:

$$S^{\ddagger} \geq S^{\circ}(CH_3I) + R \ln 8;$$

$$\underset{60.6}{\Delta S^{\ddagger}} \geq \underset{}{S^{\circ}(CH_3I)} - \underset{45.4}{S^{\circ}(CH_4)} - \underset{43.2}{S^{\circ}(I)} + 4.2$$

(3.65)

at 300°K. $\Delta S_c^{\ddagger} > -15.3$ gibbs/mole, so that $A > 10^{10.1}$ liter/mole-sec.

The observed value of $10^{11.7}$ is considerably above this (Table 3.10), indicating the presence of very low frequency bending modes in the transition state. At 700°K, these would have to be two degenerate rocking vibrations at ~ 200 cm^{-1} each to account for the difference, again a quite unreasonable result. An equivalent explanation is an internal rotation of CH_3 in a non-linear complex.

Table 3.11   Arrhenius Parameters for Some Metathesis Reactions Involving Atoms[a]

Reference	Reaction	T_m° (°K)	$\log A$ (sec^{-1})	E (kcal/mole)
1.	$Br + H_2 \rightarrow HBr + H$	620	10.8 (11.4)	18.2 (19.7)
2.	$I + H_2 \rightarrow HI + H$	680	11.4	34.1
1.	$Cl + H_2 \rightarrow HCl + H$	500	10.9 (10.7)[8]	5.5 (5.3)[8]
3.	$O + O_3 \rightarrow 2O_2$	380	10.5	5.7
1.	$Br + C_2H_6 \rightarrow HBr + C_2H_5$	500	10.8	13.5
1.	$Cl + C_2H_6 \rightarrow HCl + C_2H_5$	500	11.0	1.0
4.	$I + CH_4 \rightarrow HI + CH_3$	630	11.7	33.5
5.	$H + C_2H_6 \rightarrow H_2 + C_2H_5$	300 to 1100	11.1	9.7
6.	$H + D_2 \rightarrow HD + D$	900	10.6	8.0
4.	$I + CH_3I \rightarrow I_2 + CH_3$	600	11.4	20.5
7.	$O + NO_2 \rightarrow O_2 + NO$	330	10.3	1.0

[a] A comprehensive review of the data on metathesis reactions of atoms is given by A. F. Trotman-Dickenson, *Advances in Free Radicals*, Academic, New York, 1967, Vol. I, p. 1.
1. G. C. Fettis and J. H. Knox, *Progress in Reaction Kinetics,* Macmillan, New York, 1964, Vol. 2, p. 26. Also see p. 17 for $Cl + H_2$. Values in parentheses are "best" estimates by F and K.
2. J. H. Sullivan, *J. Chem. Phys.*, **30**, 1292 (1959).
3. S. W. Benson and A. E. Axworthy, Jr., *J. Chem. Phys.*, **42**, 2614 (1965).
4. M. C. Flowers and S. W. Benson, *J. Chem. Phys.*, **38**, 882 (1963). See corrections noted by D. M. Golden, R. Walsh, and S. W. Benson, *J. Am. Chem. Soc.*, **87**, 4053 (1965).
5. R. R. Baldwin and A. J. Melvin, *J. Chem. Soc.*, 1785 (1964).
6. G. Boato *et al.*, *J. Chem. Phys.*, **24**, 783 (1956).
7. F. S. Klein and J. T. Herron, *J. Chem. Phys.*, **41**, 1285 (1964).
8. S. W. Benson, F. R. Cruikshank and R. Shaw, *Int. J. Chem. Kin.* **1** (1968).

For a case, such as $CH_3 + I_2$ where there is no close analogue for $(CH_3 \cdots I \cdots I)^{\ddagger}$, we will use $S(I_2)$, corrected for the extra CH_3 group. At $400°K$ this adds an external rotation worth about 4.0 gibbs/mole. Let us also add 1.4 for spin, 1.4 for symmetry, 2.0 for increased principal moments of inertia, and 6.4 for two degenerate bending modes $(C \cdot I \cdot I)$ at $150 \, cm^{-1}$. Then at $400°K$,

$$\Delta S_c^{\ddagger} \geq -48.8 + 15.2 + 9.1 = -24.5;$$

$$A_c \geq 10^{8.0} \, liter/mole\text{-}sec. \tag{3.66}$$

Once again, the observed value of $10^{9.5}$ is much higher, indicating that we need about 6.9 gibbs/mole more looseness in the transition state. It seems reasonable to assign 1.5 of this to further reduced bending modes, $(C \cdot I \cdot I)$ at $100 \, cm^{-1}$, and another 5.4 to the two CH_3 rocking modes at $200 \, cm^{-1}$. Note that the I—I stretch becomes the reaction coordinate and is cancelled by the weakened $C \cdots I$ stretch of about the same frequency. The low CH_3 rocking modes are almost equivalent to free rotation in the transition state.

A final example comes from the attack of CH_3 on C_2H_6 to abstract H. Correcting only for symmetry and spin,

$$S^{\ddagger°}(CH_3 \cdots H \cdots CH_2—CH_3) \geq S°(C_3H_8) + R \ln 4;$$

$$\Delta S_c^{\ddagger} \geq S°(C_3H_8) + 11.2 - S°(C_2H_6) - S°(CH_3)$$

$$\geq -25.4 \, gibbs/mole$$

At $400°K$,

$$A_c \geq 10^{8.0} \, liter/mole\text{-}sec, \tag{3.67}$$

which is reasonably close to the reported value of $10^{8.3}$, indicating that the transition state is fairly stiff. In fact, the reasonable corrections for one free CH_3 internal rotation and increased moment of inertia give $A_c = 10^{8.5}$ in slight excess of the measured value!

3.16 METATHESIS REACTIONS

A number of metathesis reactions between atoms and molecules are shown in Table 3.11, from which we see that the bulk of these reactions have A factors that may be represented as $10^{11.0 \pm 0.5} \, liter/mole\text{-}sec$. This type of representation is probably as accurate a one as is given by any of the more complex treatments that have been done. The uncertainty in A is in most cases also of this order. Minimum A factors, as calculated in the last section, tend to be in excess of $10^{10} \, liter/mole\text{-}sec$, in good agreement with this generalization.

Table 3.12   Arrhenius Parameters for Some Metathesis Reactions Not Involving Atoms

Reference	Reaction	T_m (°K)	$\log_{10} A$ (liter/mole-sec)	E (kcal/mole)
1.	$CH_3 + \overset{*}{C}H_4 \rightarrow CH_4 + \overset{*}{C}H_3$	500	8.8	14.6
2.	$CH_3 + C_2H_6 \rightarrow CH_4 + \cdot C_2H_5$	420	8.5	10.8
2.	$CH_3 + C(CH_3)_4 \rightarrow CH_4 + \cdot CH_2C(CH_3)_3$	420	8.5	10.4
2.[a]	$CH_3 + benzene \rightarrow CH_4 + phenyl$	450	7.5	9.6
3.	$C_2H_5 + C_2H_5COEt \rightarrow C_2H_6 + \dot{C}_2H_4COEt$	450	8.0	7.8
4.	$2C_2H_5 \rightarrow C_2H_4 + C_2H_6$	450	9.6	0
5.	$C_2H_6 + C_2H_4 \rightarrow 2C_2H_5$	450	11.3	60.0
6.	$2C_2H_4 \rightarrow C_2H_5 + C_2H_3$	1300	11.1	62
7.	$2NO_2 \rightarrow (sym) NO_3 + NO$	800	9.7	23.6
8.	$CH_3 + CCl_4 \rightarrow CH_3Cl + CCl_3$	400	10.2	13.4
11.	$CF_3 + CCl_4 \rightarrow CF_3Cl + CCl_3$	450	8.5	10.4
9.	$CF_3 + CHD_3 \rightarrow CF_3H + CD_3$	420	8.1	10.5
	$\rightarrow CF_3D + CHD_2$		8.5	12.7
10.	$C_6H_5 + CH_4 \rightarrow C_6H_6 + CH_3$	450	8.6	11.1
12.	$CF_3 + CH_3Br \rightarrow CF_3Br + CH_3$	420	7.5	8.1
	$+ CH_3Cl \rightarrow CF_3Cl + CH_3$	420	—	>17.0
	$+ CH_3I \rightarrow CF_3I + CH_3$	420	6.8	3.3

1. F. S. Dainton, K. J. Irvin, and F. Wilkinson, *Trans. Faraday Soc.*, **55**, 929 (1959); F. S. Dainton and D. E. McElcheran, *Trans. Faraday Soc.*, **51**, 657 (1955).
2. A. F. Trotman-Dickinson and E. W. R. Steacie, *J. Chem. Phys.*, **19**, 329 (1951).
2[a]. It is doubtful if these are the correct parameters of this reaction.
3. M. H. J. Wijnen and E. W. R. Steacie, *J. Chem. Phys.*, **20**, 205 (1952).
4. A. Shepp and K. O. Kutschke, *J. Chem. Phys.*, **26**, 1020 (1957).
5. Calculated from reference 4 and thermochemical data.
6. Estimates by S. W. Benson and G. R. Haugen, *J. Phys. Chem.* **71**, 1735 (1967), from data on hydrogenation of C_2H_4.
7. P. G. Ashmore and M. G. Burnett, *Trans. Faraday Soc.*, **58**, 253 (1962).
8. D. M. Tomkinson, J. P. Galvin, and H. O. Pritchard, *J. Phys. Chem.*, **68**, 541 (1964).
9. T. E. Sharp and H. S. Johnston, *J. Chem. Phys.*, **37**, 1541 (1962).
10. F. J. Duncan and A. F. Trotman-Dickinson, *J. Chem. Soc.*, 4672 (1962).
11. W. G. Alcock and E. Whittle, *Trans. Faraday Soc.*, **62**, 139, 664 (1966).
12. W. G. Alcock and E. Whittle, *Trans. Faraday Soc.*, **61**, 244 (1965).

Table 3.12 shows the Arrhenius parameters for some atom transfer reactions between two molecules or radicals and molecules. Again, about the best generalization that we can make for these types of reactions is that, for the radical-molecule reactions, most A factors are $10^{8.5 \pm 0.5}$ liter/mole-sec. Two exceptions are noted to this rule in Table 3.10, and both are probably in error. In the case of the CH_3 + benzene abstraction, the data are not compatible with the reverse reaction $C_6H_5 + CH_4$ (Reference 10). The entropy change in the reaction

$$\cdot CH_3 + C_6H_6 \underset{-b}{\overset{b}{\rightleftarrows}} \cdot C_6H_5 + CH_4 \qquad (3.68)$$

is 3.6 gibbs/mole, so that if the back reaction has an A factor of $10^{8 \cdot 6}$, the forward must be $10^{9 \cdot 4}$ liter/mole-sec, not the $10^{7 \cdot 5}$ indicated. It is more likely that both are in error, more reasonable values for both being $A_b = 10^{8 \cdot 9}$ and $A^-_b = 10^{8 \cdot 1}$. Also $\Delta H_b = 8$ kcal so that $E_b = 19.1$ kcal.

The value of A for $CH_3 + CCl_4$ is probably too high by about $10^{1 \cdot 5}$. This system is made complex by secondary reactions, which introduce systematic errors into the study. Similarly the value for the disproportionation of $2NO_2$ is undoubtedly too high. The transition state here represents a quasistable O_2N—O—N—O intermediate, which is isomeric with the known stable O_2N—NO. An estimated value of $\Delta S^{\ddagger}$ leads, at $300°K$, to an A factor of $10^{8 \cdot 5}$ liter/mole-sec, which would imply the more reasonable value of $10^{9 \cdot 2}$ for the back reaction.

A few generalizations are worth noting. The activation energies for H-atom abstractions by organic radicals from organic molecules in exothermic reactions are all about 8 ± 2 kcal and are not too sensitive to the overall exothermicity of the reaction. The same appears to be true for Cl atoms. Atoms of F appear never to be abstracted or to shift in cyclopropane pyrolyses, and we can estimate a lower limit for such abstractions of about 16 kcal/mole. Activation energies for Br atom abstraction appear to be about 6 kcal, although very little quantitative data are available. From a few unpublished experiments in the author's laboratories, I atom abstractions may have activation energies anywhere from zero to about 6 kcal mole (see Table 3.12).

The activation energies presented above follow the order of the H—X bond strength in that they are lowest for the weakest bonds (for example, C—I) and highest for the strongest C—F bonds. HF has the highest bond strength (134 kcal); H—Cl and H—H are about equal (104, 103), and $DH°$ (H—Br) = 87, whereas $DH°$ (H—I) = 71. These numbers also follow the ionization potentials of the atoms involved. This latter is understandable if the atom abstraction goes through a polar state involving electron donation by the atom

The fact that there is a measured activation energy for halogen-atom abstractions can be considered strong evidence against the existence of weakly stable complexes of the type R—X—R. Such complexes have been postulated to exist as stable bridged species in α-halogen radicals:

The truly exceptional values in Table 3.11 are those for the disproportionation of radicals and the inverse processes of disproportionation of stable molecules. If, for example, we estimate the lower limit to the A factor for disproportionation of $C_2H_6 + C_2H_4 \rightarrow 2C_2H_5$ by using n-butane as an analogue for the transition state and add $R \ln 6$ for symmetry, we calculate a lower limit of $10^{8.7}$ for this process, compared to an "observed" value $10^{2.6}$-fold larger. The difference amounts to a 12 gibbs/mole larger entropy in the transition state and must arise from one additional internal rotation and from four loose rocking modes of the two heavy groups. The frequencies of these modes must be about 250 cm^{-1}, which would be quite reasonable value for a very loosened C·H·C bending mode in a bond breaking reaction. Structural reasons for such a loose complex have been discussed.[25]

3.17 ASSOCIATION REACTIONS

Association reactions that involve molecules involve the inverse process to the complex dissociation reactions we discuss above. Because we have indicated some very simple rules for estimating the dissociation reaction parameters, the association reaction parameters can be obtained via the equilibrium constant

$$A + B \underset{-a}{\overset{a}{\rightleftharpoons}} AB;$$

$$K_a = \frac{k_a}{k_{-a}} ;$$

$$\frac{A_a}{A_{-a}} = e^{\Delta S_a/R};$$

$$\Delta H_a = E_a - E_{-a}.$$

(3.69)

Note that when k_a is measured in concentration units, we must correct ΔH_a from pressure to concentration units by adding RT (see Section 1.5):

$$\Delta H_a(p) = \Delta H_2(c) + RT(\Delta n) = \Delta H_a(c) - RT. \qquad (3.70)$$

We shall not discuss these further, as far as the molecule-molecule reactions are concerned.

[25] S. W. Benson, *Advances in Photochemistry*, Interscience, New York, 1964, Vol. 2, p. 1.

Two other categories involving radicals are worth discussing. The first of these is the association of radicals. If we used the parent hydrocarbon for estimating the A factors, we would adopt values of about $10^{8.5}$ liter/mole-sec for the recombination reactions. Thus for the reaction

$$2CH_3 \rightarrow C_2H_6$$

$\Delta S° = -37.1$ gibbs/mole and $\Delta S°(c)$ at $400°K \sim -28.7$ gibbs/mole. This would yield a lower limit for the A factor of 10^7 liter/mole-sec, compared to the observed value of $10^{10.5}$ liter/mole-sec. The difference corresponds to about 16 gibbs/mole and at $400°K$ could only be accounted for mainly by four very loose rocking modes of the CH_3 groups with $\tilde{v}$ about 100 cm^{-1} for each. The result is very close to that already found for the disproportionation complex and implies a force constant of about 100-fold weaker than that accompanying the normal CH_3 rocking modes. An alternative way of looking at these results is to say that the transition state has almost freely rocking groups, and its formation corresponds to a loss only in translational entropy.

As we can see from Table 3.13, the results described above are typical for radical-radical reactions.

For rapid association reactions, which proceed with little or no activation energy, an upper limit to the A factor is provided by collision theory. The collision rate constant is given by (units liter/mole-sec)

$$k_Z = \frac{\pi d_{AB}^2}{\sigma_{AB}} \left(\frac{8RT}{\pi\mu_{AB}}\right)^{1/2} \frac{N_{Av.}}{1000} \tag{3.71}$$

where d_{AB} is the "collision" diameter of the colliding pair. $\mu_{AB} = M_A M_B/(M_A + M_B)$, and σ_{AB} is the symmetry number for the pair (1 for $A \neq B$ and 2 for $A = B$). Using $d_{AB} = 3.5 \times 10^{-8}$ cm, we find $k_Z(CH_3)_{400} = 10^{11.0}$ liter/mole-sec. If we further assume that only that fraction of all collisions ($\frac{1}{4}$) leading to singlet C_2H_6 are to be counted (that is, triplet C_2H_6 is repulsive), we find $10^{10.4}$ liter/mole-sec as the upper limit to the CH_3 recombination. This is actually 25% smaller than the reported recombination rate and raises some questions concerning this latter value. The number can be raised by boosting the collision diameter to 4.0 or 4.5 Å, or else allowing some triplet recombination. The latter assumption is somewhat dubious, and the former reasonable, but the implication is, in any case, clear: that *every* gas-kinetic collision of two CH_3 radicals in the singlet state leads to C_2H_6 formation. Even if the measured recombination rate constant is too high by a factor of 2, the result is very unexpected.

The result gained above implies that at distances of 3.5 to 4.0 Å, the interaction of two CH_3 radicals is sufficiently large, compared to RT (0.8 kcal), that the methyl groups have time to rotate into a proper relative orientation, which will lead to C_2H_6 formation before they separate. If we

Table 3.13 Arrhenius Parameters for Some Association Reactions Involving Radicals[a]

Reference	Reaction	T_m (°K)	$\log_{10} A$ (sec^{-1})	E (kcal/mole)
1.	$2CH_3 \rightarrow C_2H_6$	400	10.5 (10.35)[a]	0
2.	$2C_2H_5 \rightarrow C_4H_{10}$	400	10.4	0
3.	$CH_3 + C_2H_5 \rightarrow C_3H_8$	400	10.7	0
4.	$CH_3 + n\text{-Pr} \rightarrow n\text{-}C_4H_{10}$	400	(10.7)	(0)
5.	$2\,i\text{-Pr} \rightarrow (i\text{-Pr})_2$	400	10.8 (9.9)	0
6.	$2\,t\text{-Bu} \rightarrow (t\text{-Bu})_2$	373	9.5	0
7.	$2\,t\text{-BuO·} \rightarrow (t\text{-BuO})_2$	420	8.8	0
8.	$2CF_3 \rightarrow C_2F_6$	420	10.4	0
9.	$CH_3 + O_2 \rightarrow CH_3O_2^{\cdot}$	300	9.5*	0* (3rd order)
10.	$C_2H_5 + O_2 \rightarrow C_2H_5O_2^{\cdot}$	400	9.6	0
9.	$CH_3 + NO \rightarrow CH_3NO$	300	8.8	0
11.	$CH_3 + C_2H_4 \rightarrow n\text{-}C_3H_7^{\cdot}$	400	8.1 (7.3)[15]	8.6 (7.0)[15]
12.	$CH_3 + n\text{-}C_3H_6 \rightarrow sec\text{-Butyl}$	400	8.9 (8.0)[15]	8.8 (6.0)[15]
13.	$H + C_2H_4 \rightarrow C_2H_5$	300	10.5	4.1
14.	$CH_3 + \text{butadieen} \rightarrow$ $CH_3\text{—}CH_2\text{—}\dot{C}H\text{—}CH\text{=}CH_2$	400	6.9	2.5
15.	$2CF_2 \rightarrow C_2F_4$	300	8.4	1.6

[a] A. Shepp, has calculated the value in parentheses, using an improved theory. He reports $10^{10.6}$ for $CD_3 + CD_3$. See *J. Chem. Phys.*, **24,** 939 (1956).

1. G. B. Kistiakowsky and E. K. Roberts, *J. Chem. Phys.*, **21,** 1637 (1953).
2. A. Shepp and K. O. Kutschke, *J. Chem. Phys.*, **26,** 1020 (1957).
3. J. C. J. Thynne, *Trans. Faraday Soc.*, **58,** 676 (1962).
4. These values were estimated from the observed ratio to Me + Me and n-Pr + n-Pr [J. Grotewald and J. A. Kerr, *J. Chem. Soc.*, 4337 (1963)] and the assumption that n-Pr + n-Pr is the same as Et + Et.
5. E. L. Metcalfe and A. F. Trotman-Dickenson, *J. Chem. Soc.*, 4620 (1962). These values are undoubtedly too high, and the values in parenthesis estimated by bond additivity are to be preferred.
6. E. L. Metcalfe, *J. Chem. Soc.*, 3560 (1963).
7. These values were estimated from the A factor of the back reaction and ΔS overall [L. Batt and S. W. Benson, *J. Chem. Phys.*, **36,** 895 (1962)]; correction by R. Shaw.
8. P. B. Ascough, *J. Chem. Phys.*, **24,** 944 (1956).
9. W. C. Sleppy and J. G. Calvert, *J. Am. Chem. Soc.*, **81,** 769 (1959). The reaction is third order at 75°C.
10. D. P. Dingledy and J. G. Calvert, *J. Am. Chem. Soc.*, **85,** 856 (1963).
11. R. K. Brinton, *J. Chem. Phys.*, **29,** 781 (1958).
12. M. Miyoshi and R. K. Brinton, *J. Chem. Phys.*, **36,** 3019 (1962). About 10% of the addition goes to form i-butyl radical.
13. B. de B. Darwent and R. Roberts, *Disc. Faraday Soc.*, **14,** 55 (1953).
14. L. Mandlecorn and E. W. R. Steacie, *Can. J. Chem.*, **32,** 79, 474 (1954).
15. F. W. Dalby, *J. Chem. Phys.*, **41,** 2297 (1964).

assume that the CH_3—CH_3 bond energy can be represented by a Lennard-Jones potential, at large distances only the attractive term $-2V_0(r_0/r)^6$ is important. The repulsion is provided by the centrifugal energy, which can be written as $p_\theta^2/2\mu r^2$, where p_θ is the constant angular momentum of a colliding pair; $\mu = M_{CH_3}/2$; r is the internuclear distance; $r_0 = 1.54$ Å, the C—C bond distance in C_2H_6; and $V_0 =$ the C—C bond dissociation energy in C_2H_6 corrected for zero point energy. This latter can be estimated at about 6 kcal, and yields a value of $V_0 = 94$ kcal.

The total energy of the pair considered as a quasidiatomic molecule is then (at large distances)

$$E = -2V_0\left(\frac{r_0}{r}\right)^6 - \frac{p_\theta^2}{2\mu r^2}. \tag{3.72}$$

On differentiation and setting $(\partial E/\partial r) = 0$, we find an extremum for $r = r_m$, corresponding to a centrifugal barrier

$$\left(\frac{r_m}{r_0}\right) = \left(\frac{6V_0}{P_\theta^2/2\mu r_m^2}\right)^{1/6} = \left(\frac{6V_0}{E_{rot.}}\right)^{1/6} \tag{3.73}$$

because the rotational energy at the top of the barrier $E_{rot.} = p_\theta^2/2\mu r_m^2$.

The significance of r_m is that, for a given value of $E_{rot.}$, all molecules with impact parameters (that is, the distance between projected trajectories) greater than r_m cannot come into range of the attractive forces, and only collisions with impact parameter $<r_m$ leads to effective contact. Thus, r_m is a collision diameter. If we assume that $E_{rot.} = RT = 0.8$ kcal at 400°K, $(r_m/r_0) \simeq 3.0$ and is not very sensitive to temperature. Other potential curves, such as the Morse curve, lead to equivalent results with slightly smaller values. This calculation forms the basis for assigning r_m as a collision diameter to the radical collision.

If we apply the same analysis we made above to the other alkyl radicals, ethyl, propyl, butyl, etc., we see that because V_0 changes negligibly even for the isomeric radicals, r_m/r_0 is nearly a constant, and the only difference between them arises from a decreasing k_Z due to increasing mass. Thus for Et we estimate $k_Z(Et) \sim 0.71k_Z(Me)$ and $k(n\text{-}Bu) \sim 0.5k_Z(Me)$. This is roughly in keeping with the observed values. However, for t-Bu, the k recombination is ~ 0.1 that for methyl. In explanation, it must be noted that the disproportionation of two t-Bu radicals is about 3.2 times the rate of recombination. The implication here is that an improperly oriented collision of two t-Bu radicals may react to form i-butene + i-butane, before the complex has a chance to rotate to the recombination position. In the case of two C_2H_5 radicals, the disproportionation rate is only one-seventh the recombination rate, so this is not a seriously competing process.

A further point of interest to our discussion is the orientation time and the effective collision times. When two CH_3 radicals "collide," we can estimate a crude collision time as about one-half the period of a rotation:

$$\tau_{\text{coll.}} \approx \frac{1}{2\nu_{\text{rot.}}} = \pi \left(\frac{\mu r_m^2}{2E_{\text{rot.}}}\right)^{1/2} \tag{3.74}$$

at $400°K$ $\tau_{\text{coll.}} \sim 1.3 \times 10^{-12}$ sec. This is to be compared with the relative rate of internal reorientation of the two CH_3 radicals to a proper angle which is about six times faster, due to the smaller moment of inertia of each. This ratio is the same for the heavier radicals.

The calculation made above provides a partial explanation for the significantly lower values of recombination observed for the alkoxy radicals. In the case of t-BuO, compared to CH_3, the rate will be down by a factor of 2 due to mass, and another factor of about $(2.5)^{1/3} = 1.35$ due to 2.5-fold weaker bond. However, the principal factor must be due to the unfavorable forces, probably of repulsion for improperly oriented collisions (that is, back-to-back). This type of analysis predicts only a small change in radical recombination rate with temperature.

Whereas the association of two radicals appears to have no activation energy, the addition of a radical to a stable unsaturated species generally requires a small activation energy of the order of 6 ± 2 kcal when the reaction is exothermic. The implication of such a result is that the electronic state of the reactants is different from that of the product (adduct), and the activation energy results from a crossing of two potential curves. (The same type of analysis may be applied to abstraction reactions.) The electronic reorganization that takes place is usually a rehybridization of the electronic orbitals.

To attach a CH_3 radical to C_2H_4 we must rehybridize the olefin electrons at one end from sp^2 to sp^3 bonding, making a similar change in the radical. We may expect such changes to take place at relatively close contacts between partners, implying a "tight" transition state, similar to those found in abstraction reactions. This is best witnessed from the point of view of the reverse unimolecular reaction.

To take the decomposition of n-propyl radical as an example,

$$n\text{-}CH_3\text{—}CH_2\text{—}\dot{C}H_2 \underset{-1}{\overset{1}{\rightleftarrows}} \dot{C}H_3 + CH_2\text{=}CH_2.$$

We calculate $\Delta H° = 25.5$ kcal/mole and $\Delta S° = 31.6$ gibbs/mole. If we estimate the transition state as about half-bonded, for example, the only important contributions to $\Delta S^{\ddagger}$ comes from two lower CH_3 rocking modes (500 cm^{-1} compared to 950 cm^{-1}), an internal symmetry change (for $\dot{C}H_2$) of $R \ln 2$, one lower C—C—C bend (175 cm^{-1} compared to 350 cm^{-1}), a reduced HCC bend (950 → 475 cm^{-1}), and a CH_2 stiffer semitorsion (500 cm^{-1}), as opposed to a nearly free rotation in the radical. The reaction coordinate is the C—C stretch (900 cm^{-1} ground state) with -0.4 eu. At 400°K these contributions yield $\Delta S^{\ddagger} = +0.5$, so that $A_1 \sim 10^{13.6}$ sec^{-1} and for the addition reaction $A_{-1} \sim 10^{8.5}$ l/mole sec, in reasonable agreement with the reported values.

3.18   DISPLACEMENT   REACTIONS

A related type of association reaction is one in which the intermediate state is not a stable species. These occur in the displacement reactions, of which atom transfer (metathesis) can be considered a special case. Some examples are

$$D + HOH \;\rightleftarrows\; \left[H\overset{\overset{\displaystyle D}{|}}{\underset{O}{\diagup}} {}^{\diagdown} H \right]^{\ddagger} \;\rightarrow\; H\!-\!\overset{\overset{\displaystyle D}{|}}{O} + H; \qquad (3.75)$$

$$CH_3 + H\!-\!O\!-\!O\!-\!H \;\rightleftarrows\; \left[H\overset{\overset{\displaystyle CH_3}{|}}{\underset{O-O}{\diagup}} {}^{\diagdown} H \right]^{\ddagger} \;\rightarrow\; CH_3\!-\!O\!-\!H + \dot{O}H;$$

$$(3.76)$$

$$I + \overset{\overset{\displaystyle CH_2}{\diagup\;\;\diagdown}}{CH_2\!-\!\!-\!CH_2} \;\rightleftarrows\; \left[I\!-\!\overset{\overset{\displaystyle CH_2}{\diagup\;\;\diagdown}}{CH_2\!-\!\!-\!CH_2} \right]^{\ddagger} \;\rightarrow\; I\!-\!CH_2\!-\!CH_2\!-\!\dot{C}H_2.$$

$$(3.77)$$

Very little quantitative data exists for the reactions described above. For attachment to elements of the first row (C to F) we expect such reactions to have appreciable activation energies because they would require expansion of the valence shells (for example, pentavalent C, trivalent O, etc.), which for these elements is energetically unfavorable. With this reasoning, we should expect boron compounds to have low activation energies for such reactions, and that is indeed the case.

For the reaction in (3.77) above, which is thermoneutral, E is about 18 kcal, which is about the best guide we have to activation energies in these systems. We may expect atoms of the later rows (P, S, Si, Pb, etc.) to extend their valence shells more readily and have lower activation energies, but no good data exist for comparison.

Another known example is the epoxidation, which occurs in the HCl catalyzed pyrolysis of $(t\text{-BuO})_2$:

$$Cl + (CH_3)_3C\text{---}O\text{---}O\text{---}t\text{-Bu} \rightarrow HCl + \overset{\displaystyle Me}{\underset{\displaystyle Me}{\overset{|}{\underset{|}{\dot{C}H_2\text{---}C}}}}\text{---}O\text{---}O\text{---}t\text{-Bu};$$

$$\tag{3.78}$$

It is estimated that the activation energy for this very rapid exothermic step $\leq 17\ \text{kcal/mole}$. This is not surprising, for in the cyclopropane system it takes 11 kcal of activation energy just to close the ring from trimethylene biradical.

Displacement reactions by radicals on saturated C, O, or N have not been observed, aside from the examples above. Such reactions have been reported for S and P and Si, but no quantitative details are available.

3.19   ENERGY TRANSFER PROCESSES—DIAGNOSIS

As we have noted, association reactions produce an energized product, which, if left to itself, must ultimately redissociate. The alternative is to make a collision with some chemically inert species in which the product loses sufficient energy to become stable. When the total energy of the adduct is large and there are many internal degrees of freedom into which to share this energy, the lifetime of the adduct is long and collisions may be sufficiently frequent to deactivate the species. On the contrary, if these conditions are not satisfied, the rate of reaction can be determined by the rate of collisional deactivation, and the process is said to be controlled by the rate of energy transfer.

Schematically, we can write

$$A + B \underset{-1}{\overset{1}{\rightleftarrows}} A\text{---}B^*;$$

$$A\text{---}B^* + M \overset{2}{\longrightarrow} A\text{---}B + M$$

$$\tag{3.79}$$

where we neglect all the intermediate energy states of AB between AB^* and ground state AB. Using the steady state method for the intermediate AB^*, we find for the overall rate

$$k_2 K_1(A)(B)(M) \qquad (3.80)$$

$$k_{-1} \gg k_2 \,(M)$$

$$\frac{d\,(AB)}{dt} = \frac{k_2 k_1(A)(B)(M)}{k_{-1} + k_2(M)}$$

$$k_{-1} \ll k_2 \,(M)$$

$$k_1(A)(B) \qquad (3.81)$$

Equations (3.80) and (3.81) are the reverse of the Lindemann scheme, which has been used to describe the collisional mechanism for the unimolecular decomposition of $A-B$. At high pressures, $[k_2(M) \gg k_{-1}]$, the reaction is second order, whereas at low enough pressures, $k_2(M) \ll k_{-1}$, it becomes third order. Conversely, from the point of view of the inverse reaction, the fission of $A-B$, we can see that the rate is first order at high pressures and second order at low pressures.

In principle, any association or inverse decomposition can go from one extreme to another with sufficiently large change in pressure. However, as of the present time, no single reaction has been followed from one extreme order to the other.

The Rice-Ramsperger-Kassel (RRK) model for these reactions gives a reasonably precise picture from which we can draw some diagnostic conclusions. Let us first see when we need to concern ourselves about pressure effects.

The mean rate constant at which an activated species $A-B^*$ will decompose is given by the RRK theory (classical form) as

$$k_{-1}(E) = A_{-1}\left(\frac{E - E^*}{E}\right)^{s-1} \qquad (3.82)$$

where A_{-1} is the usual Arrhenius A factor for the unimolecular decomposition of $A-B$; E is the total energy of the complex; E^* is the activation energy for decomposition of $A-B$; and S is the number of "effective" internal degrees of freedom that can store energy in the $A-B^*$. In principle, $S \leq 3N - 6$, where $N = $ number of atoms in $A + B$. In reactions where A and B are both large groups, and the complex is loose, there is no reason that two or three rotational degrees of freedom should not participate.[26]

[26] That is, rotational energy may contribute to bond breaking. However energy cannot transfer from rotational degrees of freedom to vibration because of the need to conserve angular momentum. The net effect is that the total energy required for bond breaking may be divided into two parts, $E_{rot} + E_{vib} = E$ and only E_{vib} is to be used in (3.82), whereas E^* should then be reduced by E_{rot} if most of the energy in rotation is available for bond breaking. Studies of the photolysis of NO_2 by Pitts, Sharp, and Chan have shown that about 90% of the energy in the three rotational modes can be used in bond breaking. See J. N. Pitts, Jr., J. H. Sharp, and S. I. Chan, *J. Chem. Phys.*, **40**, 3655 (1964).

As an example, we can estimate the lifetime of NO_2^* formed from the attachment of O atoms to NO in the gas phase at $1000°$ as follows.

EXAMPLE

Assuming a loose complex, $A = (ekT/h) \exp \{\Delta S^{\ddagger}/R\}$. $\Delta S^{\ddagger}$ is calculated for $NO_2 \rightarrow NO_2^{\ddagger}$. If we assume a simple extension of the N—O bond by a factor of 2.5, it can be shown that the product of the three moments of inertia changes by a factor of about 4. If we also lower the bending mode by a factor of about 5, these two and the symmetry ($R \ln 2$) contribute 6.0 eu to $\Delta S^{\ddagger}$. We have a stretch (reaction coordinate) of about 1100 cm^{-1}, equivalent to 1.3 eu for a net of 4.7 eu. Hence $A = 10^{14.9}$ sec^{-1}. Because $\Delta S_{1000} \sim 34.3$ eu $\rightarrow 23.8$ (concentration units), this implies, for the addition of 0 to NO, an A factor of $10^{9.7}$ liter/mole-sec, in reasonable agreement with the observed data.[27]

When $O + NO \rightarrow NO_2^*$, the energy of three translations ($\frac{3}{2}RT$) plus the two rotations of NO (RT), go into the internal modes of NO_2^*. Actually, only a fraction $I_{NO_2}/(I_{NO} + I_{AB(NO_2)}) \sim \frac{3}{4}$ of the rotational energy of NO goes into NO_2 due to conservation of angular momentum. Here I_{NO} is the moment of inertia of NO and $I_{AB(NO_2)}$ is the product of the two large principal moments of inertia of NO_2. Furthermore, of the $\frac{3}{2}RT$ of translation, only RT goes into vibration. The other $\frac{1}{2}RT$, again because of conservation of angular momentum, will go into rotation. Thus, only $\frac{3}{4}RT + RT = 1.75RT$ goes into internal modes. At $1000°K$ this is 3.5 kcal. Moreover, not all of the 72 kcal of the newly formed bond will be found in internal modes. Because of the large change (factor of 4) in two principal moments of inertia in going from transition state to ground state, the $\frac{1}{2}RT$ of rotational energy at the transition state becomes $4 \times \frac{1}{2}RT = 4$ kcal of rotational energy in ground state geometry. Thus, the difference of 4 kcal $- \frac{1}{2}RT = 3$ kcal of bond energy, winds up in rotation.

This implies that the nascent molecules formed from "loose" transition complexes have large amounts of excess rotational energy, in this case, $\frac{1}{4}RT + 4 \times \frac{1}{2}RT = 2.25RT = 4.5$ kcal. This also introduces a statistical weight of $(E_R^*/RT)^{1/2} \approx 1.5$, favoring these rotationally hot species.

Substituting all these numbers, we find

$$k_{1000}(NO_2) = 10^{14.9} \left(\frac{3.5}{72.5}\right)^2 = 10^{12.3} \text{ sec}^{-1};$$

$$\tau_{NO_2} \sim \frac{1}{k(NO_2)} = 10^{-12.3} \text{ sec.}$$

This number can be compared with the collision rate constant of about $10^{9.3}$ sec^{-1} at 1 atmosphere and $1000°K$. We see that on the average NO_2^*

---

[27] J. T. Herron and F. S. Klein, *J. Chem. Phys.*, **40**, 2731 (1964) report a value of $10^{9.4}$ l/mole-sec at $300°K$, which would imply a slightly tighter transition state.

makes only one collision per 10^3 decompositions and therefore is in the low-pressure limit for the association.

If $O + NO$ go into an upper electronic state the bond energy of which is estimated at only 40 kcal, its lifetime would have been about fourfold smaller.

At 300°K we can estimate $A \sim 10^{14.2}$ sec^{-1} and $\tau \sim 10^{-10.5}$ sec. The recombination at 1 atmosphere is still in the third-order region because collisional deactivation must be at least $10^{1.2}$ slower than decomposition. At low temperatures (for example, 300°K) one must use caution in estimating lifetimes by reason of the low energy content of the associating species. The classical formula (3.92) can be replaced by one due to Marcus and Rice:

$$k(E) = \frac{kT}{h} \frac{\rho^\ddagger(E - E^*)}{\rho(E)} \left(\frac{I^\ddagger_{ABC}}{I_{ABC}}\right)^{1/2} \tag{3.83}$$

where $\rho(E)$ is the number of ways of distributing energy E among the ground state molecules, and $\rho^\ddagger(E - E^*)$ is the corresponding quantity for the transition state. We have less energy to distribute, because E^* the activation energy, must be localized in the potential energy of the molecule to reach the transition state. This result assumes that energy is redistributed rapidly over the internal degrees of freedom of the molecule, compared to the rate of passage to the transition state. The ratio $I^\ddagger_{ABC}/I_{ABC}$ is the ratio of the principal products of inertia in transition and ground states and differs from unity significantly only for "loose"complexes, such as NO_2.

For "s" harmonic oscillators with a geometric mean frequency ν_m, ρ is given by $(\nu_m{}^s = \nu_1 \cdot \nu_2 \cdots \nu_s)$:

$$\rho(E) \approx \frac{1}{(S - 1)!} \left(\frac{E}{h\nu_m}\right)^{s-1}. \tag{3.84}$$

Inserting this, (3.83) leads to the form of (3.82).

When the total excess energy in the molecule $(E - E^*)$ is of the order of that needed to excite one quantum, (3.84) can be badly in error, and it is preferable to make a discrete counting of the number of different distributions. For NO_2^* at 300°K, with only 1.0 kcal of excess energy, this is not enough to excite even one quantum of stretch, and it must all be either in the weakened bending mode or the rotations.

The frequencies of NO_2 are 1800, 1100, and 600 cm^{-1} with a geometric mean of about 1100 cm^{-1}. $(E/h\nu_m)$ at $E = 73.5$ kcal is about 24, so that $\rho(E) \sim 280$. In the excited state with assumed frequencies of 1800, 400, and 120 cm^{-1}, there is again not enough excess energy to make more than one vibrational state, and hence (3.83)

$$k_{300} = 2 \times 2 \times 10^{12.8}(\tfrac{1}{280}) = 10^{11} \text{ sec}^{-1};$$

$$\tau_{300} = \frac{1}{k_{300}} = 10^{-11} \text{ sec.}$$

In this case the two methods give about the same results.

EXAMPLE

Calculate the lifetime at 800°K of $C_2H_6^* \rightarrow 2CH_3$, if the $C_2H_6^*$ has been formed by $H + C_2H_5 \rightarrow C_2H_6^*$.

Using an average A factor (Table 3.1) of 10^{17} sec^{-1}, we assume two-thirds of the modes are active. Thus $S = \tfrac{2}{3}(3N - 6) = 12$. Note that if we count all the modes and exclude the internal rotation, and all C—H stretches, we find $S = 11$. The internal energy of C_2H_5 can be estimated by summing $C_V(\text{int.}) \, \Delta T$ from 0°K to 800°K. From our table of radical groups, we find $C_p{}^0(300) = 11.1$; $C_p(500) = 16.5$; and $C_p(800) = 23$. Subtracting $\tfrac{5}{2}R$ for translation plus external work, $\tfrac{1}{2}R$ for the internal rotation, and $\tfrac{5}{2}R$ for the external rotations, we find $C_V(300) = 2.1$; $C_V(500) = 7.5$; and $C_V(800) = 14$ gibbs/mole. This leads to $E_V(\text{int.}) = 4.6$ kcal/mole. Adding $\tfrac{3}{2}RT = 2.4$ kcal/mole for the translational energy of H gives $E_V(C_2H_6)^* = 7.0$ kcal/mole. The C—H bond energy is 98 kcal, whereas the C—C is 88 kcal. Hence $E - E^* = 10.0 + 7.0 = 17.0$, and $E = 98 + 7.0 = 105.0$. Thus, $\tau(C_2H_6^*) \sim 10^{-17.0}(105.0/17.0)^{11} \sim 10^{-8.2}$ seconds, which is to be compared to $10^{-9.3}$ seconds between collisions at 1 atmosphere pressure. We expect less than 10% of such complexes to decompose before their next collision.

The other kind of lifetime we need to calculate is that for an ordinary thermally equilibrated molecule. In this case, we estimate the average energy content from the assumption that the transition state is at thermal equilibrium. The number of effective oscillators s can be estimated by our $\tfrac{2}{3}$ rule, or by estimating $C_V = C_p - 8$ at the temperature in question, and dividing by R (that is, $s \sim C_V/R$).

EXAMPLE

Calculate the lifetime of an average energized molecule of C_2H_6 at 1000°K.

ANSWER

$$s = \frac{C_V}{R} (C_2H_6) \quad \text{at } 1000°K = \frac{29.5 - 9}{2} = 10.3;$$

$$E_V = \int_0^{1000} C_V \, dT \sim 9.4 \text{ kcal};$$

$$\tau \sim 10^{-17} \left(\frac{97.4}{9.4}\right)^{9.3} \sim 10^{-7.4} \text{ sec.}$$

Here we have treated the internal rotations as not contributing to the energy transfer. This result is slightly high because of the low excess energy involved.

If we estimate a collisional deactivation efficiency of about $\frac{1}{3}$ per collision, then because $k_z \sim 10^{9.0}$ sec^{-1} for C_2H_6 (1000°K, 1 atmosphere), we see that the pyrolysis of C_2H_6 will be showing very slight fall-off from unimolecular behavior at 1000°K and 1 atmosphere pressure.

If we want to find a more accurate measure of the pressure effects, the more complex method of Marcus[28] (RRKM) must be employed. This requires assignment of all frequencies in the ground state and transition state and, for complex molecules, a computer program.

For very rapid estimates, the RRK method with E_v between $1/sRT$ and sRT at very high temperatures is usually accurate to better than a power of 10 when E_v exceeds two quanta. When it is less, it is best to count the distributions of energy among the oscillators and use RRK for the ground state.

3.20 ATOM RECOMBINATION

The recombination of two atoms X in the presence of simple third bodies M (for example, Ar, Ne, H_2, etc.) can be considered to occur by a sequence of bimolecular steps:

$$X + X \rightleftarrows X_2^*;$$
$$X_2^* + M \rightleftarrows X_2^v + M;$$
$$X_2^v + M \rightleftarrows X_2^{v-1} + M$$
$$\cdot$$

(3.85)

$$\cdot$$
$$\cdot$$

$$X_2^1 + M \rightleftarrows X_2^0 + M$$

where X_2^* is an unstable atoms pair and X_2^v is among the top vibrational states of X_2. It has been shown[29] that such a scheme leads to very good agreement with experimental results over a large temperature range.

Steady state treatment of the excited vibrational states leads to an apparent third-order rate constant:

$$\frac{d(X_2)}{dt} = \text{Rate} = k_r(X)^2(M);$$
$$k_r = K^* k_z^* \lambda G(T)$$

(3.86)

with K^* the equilibrium constant between X and X_2^*; k_2^* the rate constant for collision of X_2^* with M; and λ the probability that such a collision leads to deactivation of X_2^* to one of the bound levels. $G(T) = 1 -$ (the probability that $X_2^{(v)}$ will be reactivated to X_2^*) and is approximately equal to $(N + 1)^{-1}$ where N is the number of vibrational levels of X_2 within energy range RT of

[28] See discussions in B. S. Rabinovitch and D. W. Setzer, *Advances in Photochemistry*, Interscience, New York, 1964, Vol. 3, p.1.
[29] S. W. Benson and T. Fueno, *J. Chem. Phys.*, **36**, 1597 (1962).

the dissociation threshold. It can be shown that $K^* \sim \frac{4}{3}\pi r_m^3 Q^*/Q_x^2$ where Q^*/Q_x^2 is the ratio of electronic partition functions for the particular ground state chosen for X_2 and for X. Thus, for $H + H \rightleftarrows H_2^*$, $Q^*/Q_2^x = \frac{1}{4}$, whereas for $2I \rightleftarrows I_2^*$; $Q^*/Q_{e1}^2 = \frac{1}{16}$, it being assumed that only $^1\Sigma$ ground state species are formed as X_2^*.

The efficiency of deactivation λ^* is usually close to unity but can decrease if X and M differ greatly in their masses.[30] The quantity r_m is calculated by the same methods as those employed in discussing radical recombinations (3.73) and has a negative temperature coefficient if we use the Boltzmann distribution to assign the rotational energy of the colliding pair at RT.

The value of k_z^* is different for symmetrical and unsymmetrical molecules. Excited unsymmetrical molecules with atoms of appreciably different masses, such as HCl^* or SO^*, have most of the kinetic energy of the vibration present in the lighter atom. Hence collision of M with the molecule can only be effective in deactivation if the lighter atom is struck by M. In cases such as HCl or HF, it means that less than half of the collisions are effective.

Although the measurements on atom recombination are not very precise, it is well established that the rate constant has a negative temperature coefficient. This arises in the present theory from the negative temperature contribution of K^* and $G(T)$. The contribution from K^* just about cancels the $T^{1/2}$ of k_z^*, whereas $G(T) \propto 1/T$ for most molecules except H_2 and $H—X$ at low temperatures. Experimentally, T^{-1} seems to be about what is observed for the recombination rate constant.

A negative activation energy of the order of RT implies that in the reverse reaction (dissociation of X_2) the activation energy is less than the energy of dissociation at the mean reaction temperature by RT. At $3500°K$, this amounts to 7 kcal, and most workers using shock tubes to follow dissociation reactions find activation energies appreciably below the ΔE_T° for the reaction. Many workers choose to refer their observed dissociation energies to ΔE_0°, the dissociation energy at absolute zero. However, $\Delta E_T^\circ = \Delta E_0^\circ + \langle \Delta C_v \rangle T$, and $\langle \Delta C_v \rangle = +1.0$ gibbs/mole at low T and changes over to -1.0 at high T. It changes sign at about $T = h\nu/3k$, where $\nu = $ vibration frequency. For I_2, this is $70°K$; for Cl_2, $140°K$, and for H_2, $2000°K$. For practically all molecules except H_2 and HX, $\langle \Delta C_v \rangle \sim -1$ above $500°K$, and $\Delta E < \Delta E_0^\circ$. For H_2 above $3000°K$, this is also true, and if the recombination rate constant at high temperatures varies at T^{-1}, the activation energy for dissociation should be $\Delta E_0^\circ - \frac{3}{2}RT$.

Table 3.14 lists some typical atom recombination rate constants. Note that they all seem to lie close to $10^{9.5 \pm 0.5}$ liter^2/mole^2 sec at $300°K$, and about a power of 10 smaller at $3000°K$.

[30] S. W. Benson and G. Berend, *J. Chem. Phys.*, **40**, 1289 (1964); **44**, 470 (1966).

Table 3.14 Termolecular Rate Constants for Some Atom Recombination

Reference	Reaction	Temperature °K	log k^a (M)
1.	$H + H + M \rightarrow H_2 + M$	1072	9.5 (H_2)
			9.3 (N_2, H_2O)
2.		3500	9.3 (H_2), 8.3 (Ar)
3.		4500	8.6 (Ar)
4.		300	10.0 (H_2)
5.		300	10.1 (H_2)
6.	$D + D + M \rightarrow D_2 + M$	3500	8.5 (D_2), 9.3 (D)
5.	$O + O + M \rightarrow O_2 + M$	300	8.9 (O_2)
7.			9.0 (N_2), 8.5 (Ar, He),
			9.2 (N_2O)
8.		2200	8.85 (O_2)
9.		2000	7.4 (Ar)
10.		4000	7.3 (Ar), 7.6 (Kr), 8.1 (Xe)
4.	$N + N + M \rightarrow N_2 + M$	300	8.9 (N_2)
5.		300	9.5 (N_2)
11.		300	9.3 (N_2)
12.	$I + I + M \rightarrow I_2$	300	9.3 (Ne)
13.			9.50 (He), 9.64 (Ar)
14.			10.82 (n-C_5H_{12}), 9.36 (n-C_4H_{10})
3.	$H + F + M \rightarrow HF + M$	4500	8.7 (Ar)
15.	$H + Cl + M \rightarrow HCl + M$	3500	(Ar)
4.	$N + O + M \rightarrow NO + M$	300	9.5 (N_2)

^{a} Units are l^2/mole^2-sec.

1. G. Dixon-Lewis, M. M. Sutton, and A. Williams, *Disc. Faraday Soc.*, **33**, 205 (1962).
2. R. W. Patch, *J. Chem. Phys.*, **36**, 1919 (1962).
3. T. A. Jacobs, R. R. Giedt, and N. Cohen, *J. Chem. Phys.*, **43**, 3688 (1965).
4. C. B. Kretschmer and H. L. Peterson, *J. Chem. Phys.*, **39**, 1772 (1963).
5. T. C. Marshall, *Phys. Fluids*, **5**, 743 (1962).
6. J. P. Rink, *J. Chem. Phys.*, **36**, 1398 (1962).
7. J. E. Morgan and H. I. Schiff, *J. Chem. Phys.*, **38**, 1495 (1963).
8. J. H. Kieffer and R. W. Lutz, *J. Chem. Phys.*, **42**, 1709 (1965).
9. K. L. Wray, *J. Chem. Phys.*, **38**, 1518 (1963).
10. J. P. Rink, *J. Chem. Phys.*, **36**, 572 (1962).
11. L. I. Avramenko and V. M. Krasnen'kov, *Izv. Akad. Nauk USSR, Otd. Khim. Nauk*, 1196 (1963).
12. G. Porter, Z. G. Szabo, and M. G. Townsend, *Proc. Roy. Soc.* (London), **A270**, 493 (1962).
13. M. I. Christie et al., *Proc. Roy. Soc.* (London), **A216**, 152 (1953).
14. R. Marshall and N. Davidson, *J. Chem. Phys.*, **21**, 659 (1953).
15. T. A. Jacobs, N. Cohen, and R. R. Giedt, *J. Chem. Phys.*, **46**, 1958 (1967).

An alternative mechanism exists for recombination if the third body M is a polyatomic molecule capable of forming a long-lived complex with one of the recombining atoms X. Thus, it is observed that n-pentane (Table 3.13) is ten times more effective than Ar in recombining I atoms. In these cases, we write the mechanism as:

$$M + X + M \underset{-1}{\overset{1}{\rightleftharpoons}} MX + M;$$

$$MX + X \overset{2}{\longrightarrow} X_2 + M. \tag{3.87}$$

Note that the formation of the MX complex is itself termolecular. The overall steady state rate is now ($K_1 = k_1/k_{-1}$);

$$\frac{d(X_2)}{dt} = \frac{k_1 k_2 (X)^2 (M)^2}{k_{-1}(M) + k_2(X)} \approx K_1 k_2 (X)^2 (M) \tag{3.88}$$

with an apparent termolecular rate constant k_r:

$$k_r = K_1 k_2. \tag{3.89}$$

If MX is a reasonably tight complex, we can expect $\Delta S_1^\circ \approx -29$ gibbs/mole, which is about -20.5 in molar units. If k_2 has a typical atom abstraction, A factor of $10^{10.5}$,

$$\log(k_r) \approx 16 - \frac{E_2 + \Delta H_1}{\theta} \ (1^2/\text{mole}^2\text{-sec}) \tag{3.90}$$

with an abnormally small pre-exponential factor.

If E_2 is small or nearly zero, there will be a relatively large negative activation energy because ΔH_1 is negative for an exothermic reaction. Such a case occurs in the O_2 or NO catalyzed recombinations of O atoms at low pressures where the steps $O + NO_2 \rightarrow O_2 + NO$ and $O + O_3 \rightarrow \sim O_2$ are both very fast (Table 3.11). NO acts as a catalyst for I atom recombination in the same way.

For the more weakly bound van der Waals or charge-transfer complexes, such as I atom forms with large molecules or unsaturates, the complex is extraordinarily loose; $\Delta S_1^\circ \sim -6$ gibbs/mole (molar units),[31] and the A factor appears normal, that is $\sim 10^{9.8}$ $1^2/\text{mole}^2$-sec. It is only the magnitude of the negative temperature coefficient of k_r, -1 to -3 kcal, rather than $-RT$, which is a clue to the behavior.

3.21   ENERGY TRANSFER PROCESSES—LOW-PRESSURE LIMIT

When the process of energy transfer becomes rate limiting, decomposition reactions become second order and association processes become third order.

[31] O. K. Rice and D. Atack, *J. Phys. Chem.*, **58**, 1017 (1954).

From the analysis given in Section 3.19, we should expect this to be true (at 1 atmosphere) of most three- or four-atom molecules above 300°K and for five- to seven-atom molecules above 1000°K. The rate constants for such processes can be examined from the point of view of the association. The dissociation reaction can then be deduced by use of the dissociation equilibrium constant.

Let us consider the association of NO + O:

$$O + NO \underset{-1}{\overset{1}{\rightleftharpoons}} NO_2^*;$$

$$NO_2^* + M \xrightarrow{2} NO_2 + M; \tag{3.91}$$

$$[O + NO_2 \xrightarrow{3} O_2 + NO] \qquad (fast).$$

The steady state rate of disappearance of O atoms at low pressure is given by

$$\frac{-d(O)}{dt} = \frac{2k_1 k_2(M)(O)(NO)}{k_{-1} + k_2(M)} \tag{3.92}$$

$$\xrightarrow[k_{-1} \gg k_2(M)]{\text{low pressure}} 2K_1^* k_2(O)(NO)(M) = 2k_r(O)(NO)(M) \tag{3.93}$$

where $K_1^* = k_1/k_{-1}$, and k_r is the termolecular recombination rate constant.

We can estimate K_1^* from the individual rate constants k_1 and k_{-1}, assuming one average energy state only for the NO_2. However, it is much simpler to estimate K_1^* if we assume an average energy state at 1000°K for the energized NO_2^*. Because NO_2^* is in equilibrium with NO and O, we need not concern ourselves with the transition state.

The equilibrium constant for NO_2^* is given by

$$K_1^* = e^{\Delta S_1^\circ/R} \cdot \rho(E) \cdot \left(\frac{I_{NO_2}^{\ddagger}}{I_{NO_2}}\right)^{1/2} \tag{3.94}$$

where the last term in parentheses corrects for the excess rotational energy of NO_2^* and is ~ 1.5, ΔS_1° is the normal entropy change for the association to ground state, NO_2, and $\rho(E)$ is the number of ways in which the internal energy of NO_2^* can be distributed among the three internal vibrational modes the mean frequency of which is taken at 1100 cm^{-1}. The total energy E can be taken as the bond dissociation energy E° (72 kcal) plus the thermal energy of the recombination RT. From the formula for $\rho(E)$ [(3.84)] and $\Delta S_{300}^\circ = -31.3$ gibbs/mole $\rightarrow -23.0$ (molar units), $\langle \Delta C_v \rangle = 0$:

$$K_1^* = 10^{-5.0} \times \frac{1.5}{2}\left(\frac{72.5}{3.2}\right)^2 = 10^{-2.4} \text{ liter/mole.} \tag{3.95}$$

Table 3.15 Arrhenius Parameters for Some Third-Order Addition Reactions Involving Molecules

Reference	Reaction	$T_m(°K)$	$\log k_1 (l^2/mole^2\text{-}sec)$
1.	$O + O_2 + M \rightarrow O_3 + M$	380	8.1 (O_2), 8.2 (N_2), 8.5 (O_3)
2.		300	8.1 (O_2)
3.	$O + NO + M \rightarrow NO_2 + M$	300–500	$9.16 + 1.9/\theta$ (O_2)
4.		200–300	$8.9 + 1.8/\theta$ (O_2)
5.		300	10.46 (O_2)
6.	$H + NO + M \rightarrow HNO + M$	300	10.17 (H_2)
7.	$H + O_2 + M \rightarrow HO_2 + Ar$	300 and up	$8.67 + 1.6/\theta$
8.	$Cl + NO + M \rightarrow NOCl + M$	245 ± 50	9.7 + 1.1/θ (Ar), 10.5 (He), 10.5 (N_2), 10.6 (O_2), 10.5 (Cl_2), 10.5 (SF_6)

1. S. W. Benson and A. E. Axworthy, Jr., *J. Chem. Phys.*, **42**, 2614 (1965).
2. N. Basco, *Proc. Roy. Soc.* (London), **A283**, 302 (1965).
3. F. S. Klein and J. T. Herron, *J. Chem. Phys.*, **41**, 1285 (1964).
4. M. A. A. Clyne and B. A. Thrush, *Proc. Roy. Soc.* (London), **A269**, 404 (1962).
5. A. A. Westenberg and N. DeHass, *J. Chem. Phys.*, **40**, 3087 (1964).
6. M. A. A. Clyne and B. A. Thrush, *Disc. Faraday Soc.*, **33**, 139 (1962).
7. M. A. A. Clyne and B. A. Thrush, *Proc. Roy. Soc.* (London), **A275**, 559 (1963).
8. T. R. Clark, M. A. A. Clyne, and D. H. Stedman, *Trans. Faraday Soc.*, **62**, 3354 (1966).

Then using a collision diameter of 4.0 Å and assuming deactivation at every collision, with N_2 as the third body, $k_2 = 10^{11.6}$ liter/mole-sec, and $k_r(1000) \sim 10^{9.2}$ liter^2/mole^2-sec. This can be compared with the extrapolated value $k_r(1000) = 10^{9.3 \pm 0.3}$ (Table 3.15).

3.22 REACTIONS OF IONS

A number of ion reactions are of interest and have been studied in the gas phase. These include dissociative recombination of ion pairs ($A^+ + B^- \rightarrow A + B$), displacement reactions ($H_2^+ + H_2 \rightarrow H_3^+ + H$), and charge transfer ($N_2^+ + NO \rightarrow N_2 + NO^+$).

Without going into details[32] here, a few generalizations are in order. For the exothermic metathesis reactions, such as $CH_4^+ + CH_4 \rightarrow CH_5^+ + CH_3$, the rate constants are all very close to collision frequencies. However, the dissociative recombination processes have rate constants about $10^{2.5 \mp 0.5}$ higher than collision frequencies; this has been rationalized[33] in terms of the

---

[32] An excellent summary of recent work has been provided by B. Mahan. See *Ann. Rev Phys. Chem.*, **17**, 173 (1966).
[33] B. H. Mahan and J. C. Person, *J. Chem. Phys.*, **40**, 285 (1964).

large coulomb interaction of opposite charges. This causes A^+ and B^- to be able to form effective collision pairs at very large distances r, where $r \sim kT/e^2$ (after the theory of J. J. Thomson). At 300°K, $r \sim 500$ Å! It has been shown, however, that one must follow the subsequent reactivation of such pairs to smaller distances because redissociation is important.

We do not expect activation energy for exothermic ion-molecule reactions because the polarization energy of the collision pair $E_p \sim (e^2\alpha/2r)$ is usually far in excess of any expected activation process for the neutral. Because it has an empty low-lying orbital, we do not expect to see any activation required for the ion. This would not be the case for closed-shell ions, such as HeH^+, H_3^+, CH_5^+, etc. in contrast to radical ions, such as H^+, H_2^+, CH_4^+, etc.

4

Analysis of Complex
Reaction Systems

4.1 CHAIN REACTIONS

In Chapter 3 we have been primarily concerned with the kinetics of what
may be described as elementary chemical reactions. These are reactions that
proceed from reactants to products by passage over a single energy barrier.
Very few chemically reacting systems are so simple. Most can be shown to
be complex in that usually two or more elementary reaction steps can be
demonstrated to coexist. The most common type of complexity found is that
in which highly reactive intermediates, atoms, or free radicals are formed
and act as catalysts for the reaction. The mechanism of this catalysis con-
sists of a cycle of elementary steps (propagations), each involving the reaction
of a free radical and, finally, reforming the original chain carrier. The net
effect of the chain cycle is to produce a molecular reaction without changing
the concentrations of chain carriers. The reaction of $H_2 + Br_2$ provides a
classical example:

$$\text{Chain} \quad \begin{cases} H + Br_2 \rightleftarrows HBr + Br \\ Br + H_2 \rightleftarrows HBr + H. \end{cases} \tag{4.1}$$

Net reaction: $H_2 + Br_2 \rightleftarrows 2HBr$

At each propagation step in the chain, one chain carrier is converted into
another ($H \rightleftarrows Br$), but the sum of the total carrier concentrations [(H) +
(Br)] is left unchanged.

120

Reactions in which the total carrier concentration is increased by the chain are called branching chains, the $H_2 + O_2$ reaction providing an important example.

$$H + O_2 \rightleftarrows HO + O;$$
$$O + H_2 \rightleftarrows OH + H; \qquad (4.2)$$
$$HO + H_2 \rightleftarrows HOH + H.$$

There is no way of adding these equations to yield a net molecular reaction. The first two reactions in the scheme give two chain carriers for one ($H \rightarrow HO + O$, or $O \rightarrow OH + H$), and the result is an exponential growth of radicals in the system once the chain has been initiated. We shall restrict our discussion here to the nonbranching chains.

4.2 SOME CRITERIA FOR SIGNIFICANCE OF CHAINS

In principle, there is no unique path from some particular set of reactants to products. The possible number of alternative paths is limited only by the imagination of the kineticist analyzing the reaction. However, in the laboratory system, "the race is to the swiftest," and, of the infinity of possible paths, only those leading most rapidly to products under the experimental conditions will be observed. In trying to make an *a priori* assessment of the preferred path for a chemical reaction, we should compare all possible paths. One of these may be the "concerted" process involving a single transition state. Thus, in the reaction $H_2 + Br_2 \rightarrow 2HBr$, the simplest path would be the four-center path involving $H_2 + Br_2$, for example

$$H\text{—}H + Br\text{—}Br \rightleftarrows \begin{bmatrix} H \cdot H \\ \cdot \\ \dot{B}r \cdot Br \end{bmatrix}^{\ddagger} \rightleftarrows 2HBr \qquad (4.3)$$

Such concerted paths involving stable molecules generally have high activation energies, and if they are bimolecular, low A factors. Radical chains can compete favorably with them only if the propagation steps are sufficiently rapid, meaning usually that they have low activation energies. In our analyses of complex reaction systems, we always have to consider the competition of concerted processes with radical processes. Pyrolysis of large molecules, particularly unsaturates, may show the coexistence of both paths.

Not all molecules are capable of decomposing by fast, simple chains. For example, the pyrolysis of C_2H_6 to $H_2 + C_2H_4$ admits of a simple chain:

$$\text{Chain} \quad \begin{cases} H + C_2H_6 \rightarrow H_2 + C_2H_5 \\ \quad C_2H_5 \rightarrow C_2H_4 + H. \end{cases} \qquad (4.4)$$

Net reaction: $\qquad C_2H_6 \rightarrow H_2 + C_2H_4$

However, there is no simple chain decomposition of CH_4 to form either $C_2H_6 + H_2$ or $C_2H_2 + 2H_2$. Let us see why.

A simple method of testing to see if a molecule X can undergo chain decomposition is to start with an unspecified radical R that can attack the molecule X in any of the standard bimolecular reactions to propagate a new radical, which will ultimately give back R. We shall consider the reactions of addition, atom abstraction, and unimolecular fission among our possible propagation steps. In order to be fast bimolecular steps must have low activation energies ($E/\theta \le 5.5$), whereas, for unimolecular steps, $E/\theta \le 14$.[1] These restrictions come about from the requirement that the rate of the chain cycle be reasonably rapid (ten to 100-fold), compared to the rate of formation of chain centers. If this is not the case, the initiation reactions will begin to dominate the system, and the chain is not important.[2]

The activation energy restrictions usually rule out steps in which saturated C, N, O, F atoms, etc., increase their valence shells (that is, pentavalent carbon or trivalent O). Thus we rule out

$$CH_3 + CH_4 \rightarrow \left[\begin{array}{c} H \quad\quad H \\ \diagdown \;\; \diagup \\ H_3C \cdots C \cdots H \\ | \\ H \end{array} \right]^{\ddagger} \rightarrow C_2H_6 + H$$

as an important propagation step in the CH_4 pyrolysis.

Let us consider a pyrolytic chain (one reactant) decomposition of C_2H_5Cl, as an example. A radical R can only abstract an atom, hence

$$R + C_2H_5Cl \begin{array}{l} \xrightarrow{\;1\;} \cdot CH_2CH_2Cl + RH \\ \xrightarrow{\;1'\;} CH_3\dot{C}HCl + RH \\ \xrightarrow{\;1''\;} CH_3\dot{C}H_2 + RCl \end{array} \qquad (4.5)$$

are the three possible propagation reactions. The subsequent steps would have to be

$$\dot{C}H_2CH_2Cl \xrightarrow{\;2\;} C_2H_4 + Cl$$
$$CH_3\dot{C}HCl \xrightarrow{\;2'\;} C_2H_3Cl + H \qquad (4.6)$$
$$CH_3\dot{C}H_2 \xrightarrow{\;2''\;} C_2H_4 + H$$

and to constitute a chain, the radical R would have to be H or Cl.

---

[1] $\theta = 2.303\ RT$ in kcal/mole.
[2] It must not be too rapid, that is, too long a chain length, or else the system may not reach a stationary state.

From our bond energy tables, we see that a Cl atom could not abstract Cl because it would be endothermic by 22 kcal and thus have too high an activation energy. Therefore only HCl and H_2 are possible products of the various combinations of the chain cycles. These are $1 + 2$ yielding $C_2H_4 +$ HCl with $R = Cl$; $1' + 2'$ yielding $C_2H_3Cl + H_2$ with $R = H$; and, $1'' + 2''$ with $R = H$ yielding $C_2H_4 + HCl$. Again, from bond dissociation energies we can show that $2'$ and $2''$ are endothermic by $\sim$39 kcal, whereas 2 is only 20 kcal endothermic. Hence only the sequence $1 + 2$ can give a fast chain with $C_2H_4 + HCl$ as products and Cl· and ·C_2H_4Cl as chain carriers.

The molecule Cl_2O cannot undergo simple chain pyrolysis. Abstraction of a Cl atom leads to the tightly bound radical ClO·, which has no effective path for reacting with Cl_2O, according to our rules above. The same is true of F_2O, N_2O, and ClO_2.[3]

The molecule H_2O_2, by our rules, does not lend itself to a fast chain, for only abstraction of H can occur from it, leading to HO_2:

$$R\cdot + H_2O_2 \rightarrow RH + HO_2^{\boldsymbol{\cdot}} \qquad (4.7)$$

However, $HO_2^{\boldsymbol{\cdot}}$ cannot undergo ready decomposition because the bond strengths are $DH°(H-O_2) = 47$ kcal and $DH°(HO-O) = 67$ kcal. This is in accord with the facts that show H_2O_2 decomposing by a simple nonchain, radical process, even up to 550°C.

$$H_2O_2 + M \rightarrow 2OH + M;$$

$$HO + H_2O_2 \rightarrow HOH + HO_2; \qquad (4.8)$$

$$2HO_2 \rightarrow H_2O_2 + O_2.$$

4.3 RATES OF CHAIN CYCLES

The rate of a cycle consisting of elementary steps is measured by the reciprocal of the total time required to pass through each step in the cycle. Thus, in the H_2—Br_2 chain [(4.1)] the mean time required for a H atom to react, τ_H is given by

$$\tau_H \equiv \frac{(H)}{d(H)/dt} = \left[\frac{d[\ln(H)]}{dt}\right]^{-1} = \frac{1}{k_a(Br_2)} \qquad (4.9)$$

---

[3] However, a chain propagation involving two radicals is possible:

$$2ClO\cdot \rightarrow Cl-O-O\cdot + Cl\cdot;$$

$$Cl-O-O\cdot + M \rightleftarrows Cl\cdot + O_2 + M;$$

$$Cl\cdot + Cl_2O \rightleftarrows Cl_2 + ClO\cdot;$$

where we have neglected the reverse of this reaction ($H + Br_2 \rightarrow HBr + Br$). Similarly, for Br atoms ($Br + H_2 \rightarrow HBr + H$),

$$\tau_{Br} = \frac{1}{k_b(H_2)}. \tag{4.10}$$

If we wish to correct for the back reaction, we would multiply this by $1/(1 - \alpha)$ where α is the fraction of Br atoms returned by the back reaction.

The total chain cycle requires a time $\tau = \tau_{Br} + \tau_H$. For a chain of m steps, the chain cycle time is given by a similar sum, and we can see that, if one of the steps k is significantly slower than the rest, the chain time τ can be approximated by τ_k, and this becomes the rate determining step in the chain. Not all chains admit of such simplification, but many do.

Although the total concentration of all radicals is unaffected by the propagation steps, the ratio of radical concentrations is given uniquely by the propagation steps under the conditions of the usual quasisteady state analysis. Thus in the H_2–Br_2 reaction,

$$H + Br_2 \underset{-a}{\overset{a}{\rightleftarrows}} HBr + Br,$$
$$Br + H_2 \underset{-b}{\overset{b}{\rightleftarrows}} HBr + H, \tag{4.11}$$

the condition of long chain lengths ($\lambda \geq 10$) implies that the slowest chain step is at least ten times faster than any step involving initiation or destruction of radicals. Hence the quasisteady state hypothesis applied either to (H) or (Br) leads to the same equation:

$$\frac{d(H)}{dt} = \frac{d(Br)}{dt} \approx 0, \tag{4.12}$$

$$k_a(H)(Br_2) + k_{-b}(HBr)(H) = k_{-a}(Br)(HBr) + k_b(Br)(H_2),$$

or, neglecting the slow, very endothermic, reaction step $-a$,

$$\frac{(H)}{(Br)} = \frac{k_b(H_2)}{k_a(Br_2) + k_{-b}(HBr)}. \tag{4.13}$$

The rate of reaction $R(HBr)$ is given by

$$R(HBr) = R_a - R_{-a} + R_b - R_{-b}, \tag{4.14}$$

which, on substituting from (4.12), becomes

$$R(HBr) = 2(R_a - R_{-a}) \approx 2R_a$$
$$= 2k_a(H)(Br_2), \tag{4.15}$$

or, in terms of (Br) atoms from (4.13),

$$R(HBr) = \frac{2k_a k_b(H_2)(Br_2)(Br)}{k_a(Br_2) + k_{-b}(HBr)}. \tag{4.16}$$

In similar fashion, it will always be possible to write a steady state rate expression for long-chain reactions in terms of the concentration of any one of the chain carriers. As we shall see later, the absolute concentrations of the chain carriers will be determined by the initiation and termination reactions.

As an additional example, consider the chain pyrolysis of neopentane (NpH) to form isobutene + CH_4. Applying our usual test, we write:

$$R + C(CH_4)_4 \xrightarrow{a} RH + \dot{C}H_2{-}C(CH_3)_3;$$
$$\dot{C}H_2{-}C(CH_3)_3 \xrightarrow{b} \dot{C}H_3 + CH_2{=}C(CH_3)_2. \tag{4.17}$$

If R is CH_3, we have a chain with two carriers, the neopentyl radical ($\dot{N}p$) and ($\dot{C}H_3$).

The steady state concentration ratio for long chains is given by

$$\frac{(\dot{N}p)}{(\dot{C}H_3)} = \frac{k_a(NpH)}{k_b}, \tag{4.18}$$

whereas the steady state rate is

$$\frac{-d(NpH)}{dt} = R_a = R_b = k_a(CH_3)(NpH) = k_b(\dot{N}p). \tag{4.19}$$

4.4 PRODUCTS OF COMPETING CHAINS

For more complex molecules, more than one chain cycle is possible, as we noted for C_2H_5Cl. If the chain lengths of any one of these is long, the relative product distribution is determined uniquely by the propagation steps. Thus in the pyrolysis of n-butene we find by our usual method the following chain cycles:

$$R\cdot + CH_3CH_2CH_2CH_3 \left[\begin{array}{l} \xrightarrow{a} \dot{C}H_2CH_2CH_2CH_3 + RH; \\ \xrightarrow{b} CH_3\dot{C}HCH_2CH_3 + RH \end{array} \right.$$
$$\dot{C}H_2CH_2CH_2CH_3 \xrightarrow{c} C_2H_4 + \dot{C}_2H_5; \tag{4.20}$$
$$CH_3\dot{C}HCH_2CH_3 \xrightarrow{d} C_3H_6 + \dot{C}H_3.$$

Hence the two cycles produce $CH_4 + C_3H_6$ if abstraction occurs at the secondary H atom and $C_2H_6 + C_2H_4$ if it occurs at the primary H atom. However, either carrier $\dot{C}H_3$ or $\dot{C}_2H_5$ can abstract at either position, so steps a' and b' must be added to steps a and b to represent this.

The ratio of C_2H_4 to C_3H_6 is given by

$$\frac{R(C_2H_4)}{R(C_3H_6)} = \frac{k_c(n\text{-Bu}\cdot)}{k_d(sec\text{-Bu}\cdot)} = \frac{R_a + R_a'}{R_b + R_b'} \tag{4.21}$$

where primes refer to $\dot{C}_2H_5$ abstraction, and unprimed R to $\dot{C}H_3$.

The steady state equations are

$$R_c = R_a + R'_a = R'_a + R'_b;$$
$$R_d = R_b + R'_b = R_a + R_b; \tag{4.22}$$

so that

$$\frac{(CH_3)}{(C_2H_5)} = \frac{k'_b}{k_a}$$

and

$$\frac{R(C_2H_4)}{R(C_3H_6)} = \frac{k'_b + k'_a}{k_b + k_a}. \tag{4.23}$$

We have, of course, neglected any secondary reactions, so that the simple expressions above apply only to the initial stages of the reaction.

The overall logarithmic rate of decomposition of the n-butane is

$$\frac{R(C_4H_{10})}{(C_4H_{10})} \equiv \frac{-d(C_4H_{10})}{(C_4H_{10}) \, dt} = \frac{(R_a + R'_a + R_b + R'_b)}{(C_4H_{10})}$$

$$= [(k_a + k_b)(\dot{C}H_3) + (k'_a + k'_b)(\dot{C}_2H_5)]$$

$$= \left[(k_a + k_b)\frac{k'_b}{k_a} + (k'_a + k'_b) \right](\dot{C}_2H_5). \tag{4.24}$$

As a final example, let us consider the chain pyrolysis of n-PrCl. The chain test leads to

$$R + CH_3CH_2CH_2Cl \rightarrow \begin{array}{l} \xrightarrow{1} \dot{C}H_2CH_2CH_2Cl + RH \\ \xrightarrow{2} CH_3\dot{C}HCH_2Cl + RH \\ \xrightarrow{3} CH_3CH_2\dot{C}HCl + RH \\ \xrightarrow{4} CH_3CH_2\dot{C}H_2 + RCl \end{array} \tag{4.25}$$

followed by

$$\dot{C}H_2CH_2CH_2Cl \xrightarrow{5} C_2H_4 + \dot{C}H_2Cl$$

$$CH_3\dot{C}HCH_2Cl \xrightarrow{6} C_3H_6 + Cl$$

$$CH_3CH_2\dot{C}HCl \xrightarrow{7} CH_2{=}CHCl + \dot{C}H_3 \tag{4.26}$$

$$CH_3CH_2\dot{C}H_2 \xrightarrow{8} C_2H_4 + \dot{C}H_3$$

We have neglected back reactions, abstraction reactions by large radicals, secondary reactions with products, and the more endothermic competing reactions, which eliminate H atoms ($\dot{C}H_2CH_2CH_2Cl \rightarrow CH_2{=}CHCH_2Cl + H$). We note three competing paths, leading to $C_3H_6 + HCl$ ($R = Cl$); $C_2H_4 + CH_3Cl$ ($R = \dot{C}H_2Cl$ or $\dot{C}H_3$); and $CH_2 = CHCl + CH_4$ ($R = CH_3$).

The steady state relations yield

$$R_1' + R_2' + R_3' + R_4' = R_1 + R_1' + R_1'' = R_5;$$

$$R_1 + R_2 + R_3 \qquad = R_2 + R_2' + R_2'' = R_6;$$

$$R_3 + R_3' + R_3'' = R_7; \qquad (4.27)$$

$$R_4' + R_4'' = R_8;$$

$$R_1'' + R_2'' + R_3'' + R_4'' \qquad\qquad = R_7 + R_8$$

where unprimed rates are for Cl, primed for $\dot{C}H_2Cl$, and R'' for $\dot{C}H_3$.

Solution of the relations given above can be accomplished, and they lead to unique solutions for all radical ratios and rates. Inspection of these equations will show that the products are given by

$$\frac{R(C_2H_4)}{R(C_3H_6)} = \frac{R_1 + R_1' + R_1'' + R_4' + R_4''}{R_1 + R_2 + R_3};$$

$$\frac{R(CH_2CHCl)}{R(C_3H_6)} = \frac{R_3 + R_3' + R_3''}{R_1 + R_2 + R_3}. \qquad (4.28)$$

More detailed analysis will show that not all of the paths described above are followed appreciably because the rate of splitting of C—C bonds is sufficiently slow, compared to the reverse reaction of the radicals with HCl, that even a few percent of reaction is sufficient to suppress all paths except $C_3H_6 + HCl$.

4.5 SOME SIMPLE CHAIN CATEGORIES

The nonbranching chain reactions fall into three basic categories, corresponding to metathesis, addition, or pyrolysis reactions. The latter gives overall reactions from a single reactant, whereas the former involve the exchange or addition of species between two reactants.

Some examples of pyrolysis reactions that have been studied are

1. $C_2H_6 \rightarrow C_2H_4 + H_2$
2. neopentane $\rightarrow i$-butene $+ CH_4$
3. $(CH_3)_2O \rightarrow CH_2O + CH_4$

$$\qquad\qquad \lfloor\!\!\longrightarrow CO + H_2 \qquad\qquad (4.29)$$

4. $C_2H_5Br \rightarrow C_2H_4 + HBr$
5. $CH_3COCH_3 \rightarrow CH_2CO + CH_4$

$$\qquad\qquad \lfloor\!\!\longrightarrow \tfrac{1}{2}[CH_2{=}C{=}CH_2 + CO_2]$$

The reactions listed above all have in common the fact that they are endothermic and exentropic, so that, in principle, they may run to a measurable equilibrium state and should be characterized by a "ceiling" temperature, below which the equilibrium constant becomes rapidly unfavorable for reaction. The overall driving force is the entropy increase for the reaction.

The reverse reactions should be observable as addition reactions below the ceiling temperature, proceeding by the same chain mechanism. In practice, however, this is rarely the case. Usually the addition rates are too slow to observe below the ceiling temperature, whereas at slightly higher temperatures and concentrations, secondary reactions complicate the system.

During the addition of H_2 to C_2H_4, for example, polymerization of C_2H_4 competes with C_2H_6 formation.[4] The addition of CH_4 to CH_2O to form $(CH_3)_2O$, or of H_2 to CO to form CH_2O, both of which are nearly thermoneutral, are too far above their ceiling temperatures even at 1000 atmospheres pressure to ever yield significant products at any temperature where the reverse homogeneous reactions are measurably rapid.

Some examples of metathesis chains that have been studied are

$$H_2 + Br_2 \rightleftarrows 2HBr$$

$$H_2 + D_2 \rightleftarrows 2HD$$

$$H_2 + CH_2{=}CHCH_3 \rightarrow C_2H_4 + CH_4$$

$$D_2 + C_2H_2 \rightleftarrows C_2HD + HD$$

(4.30)

$$Cl_2 + CH_4 \rightarrow CH_3Cl + HCl$$

$$Cl_2 + C_6H_5Br \rightarrow C_6H_5Cl + BrCl$$

These reactions are generally exothermic, sometimes thermoneutral, and involve very little entropy change. Thus they can frequently be observed to come to equilibrium, and the reverse reaction can be measured independently.

The addition reactions are related to the pyrolysis reactions and are generally exothermic and endentropic. They have ceiling temperatures T_c, above which they may be expected to show decreasing overall rates. In addition, the reactions can show abnormally small activation energies due to a reversible, exothermic step. Telomerization is a special case of an addition reaction,

---

[4] This probably would not be the case for sufficiently high $(H_2)/(C_2H_4)$ ratios (that is, in excess of 20), but the reaction has not been studied under these conditions.

and the simplest case of a polymerization. Thus CCl_4, CF_3CN, or CCl_3Br can add to a double bond, as follows:

$$CCl_4 + \ \ \diagdown_{\diagup}C{=}C_{\diagdown}^{\diagup} \ \rightarrow \ CCl_3{-}\overset{\diagdown}{\underset{\diagup}{C}}{-}\overset{\diagup}{\underset{\diagdown}{C}}{-}Cl$$

$$CF_3CN + \ \ \diagdown_{\diagup}C{=}C_{\diagdown}^{\diagup} \ \rightarrow \ CF_3{-}\overset{\diagdown}{\underset{\diagup}{C}}{-}\overset{\diagup}{\underset{\diagdown}{C}}{-}CN$$

$$CCl_3Br + \ \ \diagdown_{\diagup}C{=}C_{\diagdown}^{\diagup} \ \rightarrow \ CCl_3{-}\overset{\diagdown}{\underset{\diagup}{C}}{-}\overset{\diagup}{\underset{\diagdown}{C}}{-}Br$$

or generally,

$$A{-}X + \ \ \diagdown_{\diagup}C{=}C_{\diagdown}^{\diagup} \ \rightarrow \ A{-}\overset{\diagdown}{\underset{\diagup}{C}}{-}\overset{\diagup}{\underset{\diagdown}{C}}{-}X \qquad (4.31)$$

If the olefin concentration is sufficiently high, polymeric species of various chain lengths can be formed, such as $CCl_3{-}(>C{-}C<)_n{-}Cl$ with $n = 1, 2$, etc. These complexities generally restrict the study of addition reactions to very low olefin concentrations if quantitative data is sought.

Common to each of the chain categories outlined above is a characteristic propagation step. In the pyrolytic chains it is the unimolecular fission of a radical. Thus in the C_2H_6 pyrolysis, the fission step is

$$\dot{C}_2H_5 \rightleftarrows C_2H_4 + H.$$

These steps are generally the principle source of the endothermicity of the overall reaction and have relatively high activation energies.[5] Because of this endothermicity, the back reactions are usually fast and appreciable, even when small amounts of product are formed.

As we note in Chapter 3, very little direct experimental data are available on the rate constants for such propagation steps, and the estimated rate constants, by our usual methods, are probably as reliable as some of the quoted data. The largest uncertainty associated with these fissions is their pressure dependence. They generally tend to be in an intermediate pressure regime, so that the high-pressure Arrhenius parameters are not applicable.

In a similar fashion the reverse addition step is characteristic of addition chains, and there is the same lack of knowledge regarding the pressure

---

[5] For the decomposition $\Delta H° = 39$ kcal, and because the activation energy for the reverse addition reaction is about 3.5 kcal, $E = 42.5$ kcal. At 900°K, which is a typical pyrolysis temperature for C_2H_6, the lifetime of a $\dot{C}_2H_5$ radical would be about 10^{-4} sec, if the reaction were at its high pressure limit. However, $E/RT \sim 23$, a low value, corresponding to relatively few vibrational quanta, and this reaction is almost certain to be in an intermediate pressure region, even at 1 atmosphere total pressure.

dependence of the addition rate. As an example, we can consider the addition of HBr or Br_2 to olefins:

$$Br + \quad \overset{\diagdown}{\diagup}C{=}C\overset{\diagup}{\diagdown} \quad \underset{-1}{\overset{1}{\rightleftharpoons}} \quad Br{-}\overset{\diagdown}{\underset{\diagup}{C}}{-}\overset{\cdot}{\underset{\diagdown}{C}}\diagup \ ,$$

$$Br{-}\overset{\diagdown}{\underset{\diagup}{C}}{-}\overset{\cdot}{\underset{\diagdown}{C}}\diagup + Br_2 \quad \overset{2}{\longrightarrow} \quad Br{-}\overset{\diagdown}{\underset{\diagup}{C}}{-}\overset{\diagup}{\underset{\diagdown}{C}}{-}Br + B\dot{r} \qquad (4.32)$$

$$+ \, HBr \quad \overset{2'}{\longrightarrow} \quad Br{-}\overset{\diagdown}{\underset{\diagup}{C}}{-}\overset{\diagup}{\underset{\diagdown}{C}}{-}H + B\dot{r}.$$

Here the second step (2) is irreversible, being about 35 kcal exothermic (2' is about 11 kcal/mole exothermic). The steady state rate of the disappearance of Br_2 is given by

$$\frac{-d(Br_2)}{dt} = \frac{k_1 k_2 (Br_2)(\text{olefin})(Br)}{k_{-1} + k_2 (Br_2)}. \qquad (4.33)$$

This has two limiting cases:

$$\frac{-d(Br_2)}{dt} \xrightarrow{k_{-1} \ll k_2 (Br_2)} k_1 (Br)(\text{olefin}) \qquad (4.34)$$

$$\xrightarrow{k_{-1} \gg k_2 (Br_2)} K_1 k_2 (Br_2)(\text{olefin})(Br) \qquad (4.35)$$

where $K_1 = k_1/k_{-1}$. (Note that both 1 and -1 may be in pressure dependent regions.)

In the second, or equilibrium case, the activation energy for the propagation scheme is $\Delta E_1 + E_2$. Because $\Delta E_1 \sim -12$ kcal (see bond energies), whereas $E_2 \sim 1.5$ kcal, we see that the propagation scheme can have an overall negative activation energy of about -10.5 kcal/mole. In point of fact the photochemical bromination of C_2H_4, in which the $(Br)_{ss}$ concentration has no temperature dependence, does decrease markedly with increasing temperature.[6]

For the metathesis chains that can reach equilibrium, and that are nearly thermoneutral, all of the chain steps are, in principle, metathetical, and reversible. The H_2–D_2 exchange is a simple example:

$$H + D_2 \underset{-1}{\overset{1}{\rightleftharpoons}} HD + D; \qquad (4.36)$$

$$D + H_2 \underset{-2}{\overset{2}{\rightleftharpoons}} HD + H.$$

[6] G. B. Kistiakowsky and J. C. Sternberg, *J. Chem. Phys.*, **21**, 2218 (1953).

The rate of exchange at steady state is

$$\frac{d(HD)}{dt} = (R_1 - R_{-1}) + (R_2 - R_{-2})$$

$$= 2(R_1 - R_{-1})$$

$$= 2k_1(H)(D_2)\left\{1 - K_{-1}\frac{(HD)}{(D_2)}\frac{(D)}{(H)}\right\} \tag{4.37}$$

where

$$(D)/(H) = \frac{k_1(D_2) + k_{-2}(HD)}{k_2(H_2) + k_{-1}(HD)}, \tag{4.38}$$

so that

$$\frac{d(HD)}{dt} = \frac{2k_1(H)(D_2)}{1 + \left(\dfrac{k_{-1}}{k_2}\right)\left(\dfrac{HD}{H_2}\right)}\left\{1 - \frac{(HD)^2}{K_{eq.}(H_2)(D_2)}\right\} \tag{4.39}$$

where $K_{eq.}$ is the equilibrium constant for the net reaction, $H_2 + D_2 \rightleftarrows 2HD$. Because k_{-1} and k_2 are comparable to each other in absolute magnitude, we note that the effect of (HD) inhibition appears long before the overall reverse reaction is significant.[7]

4.6 INITIATION STEPS

For long chain reactions, we have seen that the rates can be derived from the propagation steps and expressed in terms of the concentration of any one of the radical carriers. The absolute concentrations of these carriers is fixed by the rates at which initiation and termination of radicals occur. If we restrict ourselves for the moment to homogeneous systems, stable molecules can only give rise to mono radicals in pairs, and conversely, mono radicals can only disappear two at a time.

All possible reactions must be considered as radical sources, the rule being that the most rapid will be the one observed. The same is true for the termination reactions. Our criteria for selecting initiation steps is based on the lowness of the activation energy and the order of the reaction. Because unimolecular fission reactions have generally high A factors, $10^{16\pm1}$ sec^{-1}, they will be favored over bimolecular processes, which have A factors of about $10^{9\pm1}$ l./mole sec for radical disproportionations.

[7] Thus, when $(HD)/(D_2) = 0.20$ ($\sim 9\%$ reaction), the denominator in (4.39) is 1.2, whereas the bracketed term is negligibly different from unity [0.99 for $(H_2) = (D_2)$].

Consider the hypothetical example of radical production by competing unimolecular and bimolecular paths from a reactant A:

$$A \xrightarrow{\ 1\ } 2 \text{ radicals}$$

$$2A \xrightarrow{\ 2\ } 2 \text{ radicals}$$

(4.40)

At a pressure of 100 torr ($\sim 10^{-2.4}\ M$), the ratio of rates is

$$\frac{R_1}{R_2} = \frac{k_1(A)}{k_2(A)^2} \approx \frac{10^{16 \pm 1 - E_1/\theta}}{10^{9 \pm 1 - E_2/\theta}(A)}$$

$$\approx 10^{9.4 \pm 2 - (E_1 - E_2)/\theta}.$$

(4.41)

The rates R_1 and R_2 are competitive when $E_1 - E_2 = (9.4 \pm 2)\theta$. At 2000°K, a typical temperature for shock tube studies, $\theta = 9.2$ kcal/mole, which corresponds to about 88 ± 18 kcal. This is so high that we can reasonably conclude that bimolecular initiations will almost never compete with unimolecular at 2000°K. At 1000°K, a typical pyrolysis temperature for hydrocarbons, $\theta = 4.6$ kcal/mole and $E_1 - E_2 = 44 \pm 9$ kcal/mole. This is still sufficiently large that unimolecular steps are still by far the favored ones at 1000°K. That is, it will be exceptional for a bimolecular initiation step to have an activation energy lower than that for a unimolecular step by 44 kcal.

Such exceptions may occur in the pyrolysis of the olefins. Thus for C_3H_6 the two competing paths will be

$$C_3H_6 \xrightarrow{\ 1\ } \dot{C}_3H_5 + H, \qquad \Delta H_1^\circ = 87 \text{ kcal/mole};$$

$$2C_3H_6 \xrightarrow{\ 2\ } \dot{C}_3H_5 + \dot{C}_3H_7, \qquad \Delta H_2^\circ = 48 \text{ kcal/mole}.$$

(4.42)

At 900°K, $\Delta E_1^\circ = \Delta H_1^\circ - RT \simeq 85$ kcal/mole, and the difference in activation energies is expected to be ~ 37 kcal/mole, which would account for a factor of $10^{9.0}$ in the ratio of rates. This is close enough to the expected differences in A factors to make it likely that both paths will play a role at various pressures and temperatures in this range. Unfortunately, the pyrolysis itself is sufficiently complex to obscure the details of the precise initiation.

In a number of instances, positive, quantitative evidence has been adduced for bimolecular initiation processes. Stable radicals, such as NO and NO_2, are capable of abstracting atoms to form molecules and initiate chains. Thus it is found that NO_2 is a very powerful chain initiator for hydrocarbon reactions. The reaction is

$$NO_2 + RH \rightarrow HONO + \dot{R}.$$

Because the H—ONO bond strength is about 78 kcal/mole, and $DH^\circ(R\text{—}H)$ is in the range 85–100 kcal/mole, such initiation reactions will have extremely low activation energies, about 2 to 5 kcal in excess of the endothermicity of the reactions, that is from 10 to 25 kcal/mole. In similar fashion, $DH°(H—NO) \sim 49$ kcal/mole, so that NO is expected to act as an initiator of chain reactions at sufficiently high concentrations. This, in fact, is well documented.[8]

In recent years, it has been proposed that termolecular processes of initiation are possible. An example would be olefins reacting with diatomic molecules:

$$2\ \diagdown\!\!\diagup{C}\!\!=\!\!{C}\diagup\!\!\diagdown + Cl_2 \rightleftarrows \left[\diagdown\!\!\diagup{C}\overset{\cdot}{-}{C}\diagup\!\!\diagdown \cdot Cl \cdot Cl \cdot \diagdown\!\!\diagup{C}\overset{\cdot}{-}{C}\diagup\!\!\diagdown \right]^{\ddagger}$$

$$\downarrow$$

$$2\ \diagdown\!\!\diagup\overset{\cdot}{C}\!\!-\!\!{C}\!\!-\!\!Cl\diagup\!\!\diagdown$$

(4.43)

Such a reaction would be endothermic by only about 20 kcal/mole. However, because the intermediate is not a stable species, there would be an appreciable activation energy in addition to this endothermicity, which would make the overall step prohibitive.[9] Even more important, however, is the unfavorable A factor. The entropy change for three molecules forming a single transition state can be estimated at $\sim -60 \pm 10$ gibbs/mole. At 1 mole/liter standard state, this would become -46 gibbs/mole, yielding an A factor of about $10^{4\pm2}$ liter^2/mole^2-sec with an accompanying increase in activation energy of $2RT$.

Another example of a bimolecular initiation is afforded by the HBr catalyzed isomerization of olefins. Butene-1 undergoes a chain catalyzed isomerization[10] initiated by

$$CH_3CH_2—CH\!\!=\!\!CH_2 + HBr \rightleftarrows CH_3CH_2—\overset{\cdot}{C}H—CH_3 + Br \quad (4.44)$$

which $\Delta H° = +48$ kcal/mole. The most rapid competing unimolecular reaction would be the scission of the C—C bond to form CH_3 + allyl at a cost of

---

[8] P. Goldfinger et al., *Trans Faraday Soc.*, **57**, 2197, 2210, 2220 (1961); L. V. Karmilova, N. S. Enikolopyan, and A. B. Nalbandjan, *Zhur. Fiz. Khim.*, **30**, 748 (1956); B. W. Wojciechowski and K. J. Laidler, *Can. J. Chem.*, **38**, 1027 (1960).

[9] What is implied here is that the exothermic back reaction of two chloroalkyl radicals to give two olefins + Cl$_2$ is expected to have an appreciable activation energy. This is not the case for the analogous observed reaction, $2ROO \cdot \rightleftarrows [ROOOOR] \rightarrow 2RO \cdot + O_2$, which proceeds by way of a stable tetraoxide.

[10] A. Maccoll and R. A. Ross, *J. Am. Chem. Soc.*, **87**, 4997 (1965). The authors have offered a molecular mechanism for the reaction, but the radical chain gives an excellent quantitative fit.

74 kcal/mole. At 550°K, $\theta = 2.5$ kcal/mole, so that the difference of 26 kcal/mole amounts to a difference of $10^{10.2}$ in relative rates, making the bimolecular act the favored one. The rest of the chain is

$$Br + CH_3-CH_2-CH=CH_2 \rightleftarrows CH_3-\overset{\cdot}{C}H-CH=CH_2 + HBr;$$
$$HBr + CH_3\overset{\cdot}{C}H-CH=CH_2 \rightleftarrows CH_3-CH=CH-CH_3 + Br. \tag{4.45}$$

Each step in the chain is very fast with an activation energy in the range of 3 to 8 kcal/mole.

The competing reaction of HBr addition is considerably slower because of the unfavorable precursor equilibrium step:[11]

$$Br + CH_3-CH_2-CH=CH_2 \rightleftarrows CH_3-CH_2-\overset{\cdot}{C}H-CH_2Br. \tag{4.46}$$

A very unexpected initiation step turns out to be important in many reactions. This is the case in which initiation involves products, so that the reaction becomes autocatalytic. An excellent example occurs in the metathesis reactions of organic iodides with HI:

$$RI + HI \rightleftarrows RH + I_2. \tag{4.47}$$

This reaction can be recognized as the reverse of the usual halogenation reaction, $RH + X_2 \rightarrow RX + HX$. For iodine the equilibrium lies well over in favor of I_2, in contrast to the reverse case for F_2, Cl_2, and Br_2. In the HI reactions, very rapid initiation is provided by I_2:[12]

$$I_2 \underset{\longleftarrow}{\overset{\longrightarrow}{}} 2I \text{ (rapid, equilibrium } K_{I_2});$$

$$\left.\begin{array}{l} I + RI \overset{1}{\underset{\longleftarrow}{\rightleftarrows}} R\cdot + I_2 \\[2mm] R\cdot + HI \overset{2}{\underset{\longleftarrow}{\rightleftarrows}} RH + I \end{array}\right\} \text{ chain.} \tag{4.48}$$

The overall rate of reaction is given by

$$\frac{d(I_2)}{dt} = -\frac{d(RI)}{dt} = \frac{k_2 k_1(I)(RI)(HI)}{k_{-1}(I_2) + k_2(HI)}$$

$$= \frac{k_1 K_{I_2}^{1/2}(I_2)^{1/2}(RI)}{1 + k_{-1}(I_2)/k_2(HI)} \tag{4.49}$$

$$\xrightarrow{k_{-1}(I_2) < k_2(HI)} k_1 K_{I_2}^{1/2}(I_2)^{1/2}(RI). \tag{4.50}$$

[11] $K \approx 10^{-6.3+10/\theta}$ atm^{-1} from our tables.
[12] It should be pointed out that in these systems the chain length $\lambda \ll 1$. Under the usual experimental conditions, it is in the range of from 10^{-2} to 10^{-3}. This does not quite fit the usual concept of chain reaction, but there is no reason to exclude it.

The last equation predicts a rate approaching zero in the early stages of the reaction when $I_2 \to 0$. This in principle would imply an induction period early in the reaction, during which some less favorable initiation, such as $RI \to R + I$ would occur. These latter reactions are so much slower than I_2 initiation that even at 0.01% reaction, with $(I_2)/(RI) = 10^{-4}$, the I_2 initiation is competing favorably. In practice, such early regimes are never seen because spurious, though slow, wall reactions make it almost impossible to avoid small initial traces of I_2 in these systems.

An equally interesting example is provided by the hydrogenation of C_2H_4 at high temperatures (800 to 1200°K). In the early stages of the reaction, initiation is provided by the bimolecular process:

$$C_2H_4 + H_2 \underset{}{\overset{1}{\rightleftarrows}} H + \dot{C}_2H_5.$$

However, depending on the precise conditions, the competing unimolecular initiation by the product can become of comparable importance:

$$C_2H_6 \overset{1'}{\rightleftarrows} 2\dot{C}H_3.$$

The relative rates of the two steps above are given by

$$\frac{R_1'}{R_1} = \frac{k_1'(C_2H_6)}{k_1(C_2H_4)(H_2)} \approx \frac{10^{16.5-87/\theta}[(C_2H_6)/(C_2H_4)]}{10^{10.1-64/\theta}(H_2)} \tag{4.51}$$

and at $(H_2) = 10^{-2}$ M and 750°K $(\theta = 3.4$ kcal/mole)

$$\frac{R_1'}{R_1} \approx 10^{8.5-23/\theta} \frac{(C_2H_6)}{(C_2H_4)} \tag{4.52}$$

$$= 10^{1.7} \frac{(C_2H_6)}{(C_2H_4)} \tag{4.53}$$

We see that $R_1 = R_1'$ at $(C_2H_6)/(C_2H_4) = 0.02$, whereas at higher temperatures, such as 1000°K (or lower H_2 concentrations), this is true at $(C_2H_6)/(C_2H_4) = 3 \times 10^{-4}$.

In the calculation above we estimate the rate of $H_2 + C_2H_4$ by estimating the rate constant for the back reaction (-1), (the disproportionation of $H + \dot{C}_2H_5$) as 10^{10} liters/mole-sec with no activation energy.

4.7 TERMINATION REACTIONS

We have already seen in Chapter 3 that recombination reactions of large radicals do not show much variation with structure and mostly fall in the range $10^{9.8\pm0.5}$ liters/mole-sec for either recombination or disproportionation. Under these conditions, the termination reaction in a complex chain is predominantly between the radicals present in largest concentrations. Because this is determined by the propagation steps, it is possible to make a fairly direct choice of termination reaction, or reactions, from estimates of the chain steps. Difficulties intrude into this picture as soon as we are involved with small radicals or atoms. For these species, recombination may frequently be pressure dependent. Thus, in the case just considered, present experimental evidence indicates that at $1000°K$, $2CH_3 \rightarrow C_2H_6$ is pressure dependent below 400 torr.[13] This means that we must make some estimate of the correction to be applied for this falloff in rate. A relatively rapid, though crude, method for doing this is to decompose the recombination into the steps

$$R + R \underset{-1}{\overset{1}{\rightleftarrows}} R_2^*;$$

$$R_2^* + M \xrightarrow{k_z} R_2 + M. \tag{4.54}$$

The steady state rate of recombination is then given by

$$\frac{-d(R)}{dt} = \frac{2d(R_2)}{dt} = \frac{2k_1 k_z (R)^2 (M)}{k_z (M) + k_{-1}} \tag{4.55}$$

As a first approximation, we take k_z equal to 0.3 times collision frequencies, and k_{-1} would be estimated by the methods discussed in Section 3.19. The rate constant k_1 could be taken as the normal pressure-independent rate constant. Thus in the case of CH_3 recombination at $1000°K$, and 100 torr, we can choose $k_1 = 10^{10.5}$ liter/mole-sec, $k_z = 10^{10.5}$ liter/mole sec, and $(M) = 10^{-2.8}$ M; k_{-1} is given by:

$$k_{-1} = 10^{16.5} \left(\frac{E - E^*}{E} \right)^{s-1} \sec^{-1}$$

with $s = [C_{p1000}(C_2H_6) - 9]/R = 10.2$; $E^* = 87$ kcal and

$$E - E^* = \int_0^{1000} (C_p - 9)\, dT \approx 9.4 \text{ kcal/mole},$$

so that $k_{-1} = 10^{16.5}(9.4/96.4)^{9.2} \approx 10^{7.2} \sec^{-1}$.

The ratio of the pressure dependent rate to pressure independent rate is given by

$$\frac{k_z(M)}{k_z(M) + k_{-1}} = \frac{10^{7.7}}{10^{7.7} + 10^{7.2}} \approx 0.83. \tag{4.56}$$

[13] M. C. Lin and M. H. Back, *Can. J. Chem.*, **44**, 2357 (1967).

This is a negligible correction in view of the uncertainty of the various estimates. However, at 10 torr, it is down to $\frac{1}{4}$ and significant. Of particular importance is the apparent negative activation energy in the recombination rate constant.

The case of atoms is of special interest because the atom-atom, or atom-diatomic molecule, recombination is always in the third-order region with a recombination rate constant of about $10^{9.5 \pm 0.5}$ liter^2/mole^2-sec. At $(M) = 10^{-2.8}$ this is sufficiently slow that these combinations are only important when the atom concentrations exceed the concentrations of complex radicals by at least 10^3. This can happen in reaction systems containing I_2 and I, but in very few others.

In the $C_2H_6 \rightleftarrows C_2H_4 + H_2$ chain, the radical species are C_2H_5, CH_3, and H. We can neglect $H + H + M$, as an important recombination under all conditions. In the system $CHCl_3 + Br_2 \rightleftarrows CBrCl_3 + HBr$, in contrast, we can neglect $\dot{C}Cl_3$ radicals in termination because their concentration is indeed less than $10^3(Br)$.

Once we have passed the small radicals, such as CH_3, termination need not be restricted by third body effects because disproportionation is always in competition with combination and is not pressure dependent. Thus two C_2H_5 radicals will disproportionate at about one-seventh their rate of recombination, whereas branched or polar radicals will prefer disproportionation. Two $CH_3\dot{O}$ radicals will disproportionate with a rate constant estimated at $10^{10.5}$, whereas the recombination rate constant is about $10^{9.0}$ liter/mole sec. Similarly, two t-butyl radicals disproportionate about 3.5 times faster than they recombine.

4.8 TRANSFER REACTIONS AND SENSITIZATION

Because the dominant initiation reaction is always the most rapid of the possible initiation reactions in the system, it does not necessarily give rise to the active chain carriers. The metathetical reactions relating active chain carriers to other nonpropagating radicals are referred to as transfer reactions, and they constitute an important aspect of chain systems.

The C_2H_6 pyrolysis provides a good example of a transfer reaction. The initiation produces $2CH_3$ radicals, whereas the chain carriers are H and C_2H_5. The scheme is as follows.

$$
\begin{aligned}
\text{Initiation:} \quad & C_2H_6 \rightarrow 2\dot{C}H_3; \\
\text{Transfer:} \quad & \dot{C}H_3 + C_2H_6 \rightleftarrows CH_4 + \dot{C}_2H_5; \\
\text{Chain:} \quad & \begin{cases} \dot{C}_2H_5 \rightleftarrows C_2H_4 + H \\ H + C_2H_6 \rightleftarrows \dot{C}_2H_5 + H_2. \end{cases}
\end{aligned}
\tag{4.57}
$$

In many cases the transfer is so rapid and irreversible that the initial radicals never appear in the scheme. The thermal decomposition of F_2O_2 provides another example. The products at -80 to $0°C$ are almost solely $F_2 + O_2$, whereas the initiation could be the cleavage of the O—O bond.

$$\text{Initiation:} \quad F_2O_2 + M \rightarrow 2F\dot{O} + M;$$

$$\text{Transfer:} \quad F\dot{O} + F_2O_2 \rightarrow F_2O + FO\dot{O};$$

$$\text{Chain:} \quad \begin{cases} M + FO\dot{O} \rightarrow \dot{F} + O_2 + M \\ F + F_2O_2 \rightarrow F_2O_2 + FO\dot{O} \end{cases} \tag{4.58}$$

Here the chain lengths are extremely long, so that F_2O is a very minor product of the reaction. It is not clear in this system, however, what the termination is.

Many systems are induced to undergo chain reactions by initiating them with radicals introduced by either photochemical means or from thermally unstable species.

In the range 40 to 80°C diacyl peroxides (for example, CH_3COO—$OCOCH_3$) are excellent thermal sensitizers. They produce acyl radicals that cleave to form alkyl or aryl radicals:

$$(RCOO)_2 \rightarrow 2RC\dot{O}_2 \rightarrow 2\dot{R} + 2CO_2. \tag{4.59}$$

These radicals can then, by transfer, initiate a chain.

In the range 100 to 150°C dialkyl peroxides can provide the same initiation. They form alkoxy radicals, which can further cleave into alkyl radicals plus ketones or aldehydes. Ditertiary butyl peroxide is a well known example.

$$(t\text{-BuO})_2 \rightarrow 2t\text{-Bu}\dot{O} \rightarrow 2CH_3 + 2 \text{ acetone}. \tag{4.60}$$

In the range from 250 to 350°C azo compounds form radicals:

$$R—N{=}N—R \rightarrow 2\dot{R} + N_2. \tag{4.61}$$

Above 300°C a variety of substances ranging from metal alkyls, such as HgR_2, to ethylene oxide can act as radical sensitizers. The reactions are

$$HgR_2 \rightarrow Hg + 2\dot{R}$$

$$\overset{\overline{\quad\quad\quad\quad}}{CH_2—CH_2—O} \rightarrow (CH_3CHO)^* \rightarrow \dot{C}H_3 + \dot{C}HO \tag{4.62}$$

In the latter instance the intermediate acetaldehyde is vibrationally excited and a competing side reaction is its quenching to ground state, stable CH_3CHO.

4.9   PYROLYSIS OF CH₃CHO

One of the most thoroughly studied pyrolysis systems that undergoes a simple chain decomposition, is that of CH_3CHO. The reaction is easily studied from 450 to 550°C. It forms $CH_4 + CO$ as major products and minor amounts of H_2, CH_3COCH_3, and C_2H_4.[14] The main features of the chain are very much what we would expect from our preceding discussion.

Initiation:
$$CH_3\text{---}CHO \xrightarrow{i} \dot{C}H_3 + \dot{C}HO;$$

Chain:
$$\begin{cases} \dot{C}H_3 + CH_3CHO \xrightarrow{1} CH_4 + CH_3\dot{C}O \\ CH_3\dot{C}O + M \xrightarrow{2} \dot{C}H_3 + CO + M; \end{cases}$$

(4.63)

Termination:
$$2CH_3 \xrightarrow{t} C_2H_6;$$

Transfer:
$$\begin{cases} \dot{C}HO + M \xrightarrow{3} H + CO + M \\ H + CH_3CHO \xrightarrow{4} CH_3\dot{C}O + H_2. \end{cases}$$

The steady state radical concentrations are given by (long chains):

$$(CH_3\dot{C}O)/(\dot{C}H_3) \simeq \frac{k_1(CH_3CHO)}{k_2(M)}, \tag{4.64}$$

or with

$$(CH_3CHO) = (M) \sim 10^{-2.5}\ M$$

$$(CH_3\dot{C}O)/(\dot{C}H_3) \approx \frac{10^{8.0-8.0/\theta}}{10^{11.0-10/\theta}} \sim 10^{-3.0+2.0/\theta}$$

$$\simeq 10^{-2.3} \quad \text{at} \quad 700°\,K.$$

$$(\dot{C}HO) = \frac{k_i}{k_3} = \frac{10^{16-80/\theta}}{10^{11.5-20/\theta}} = 10^{4.5-60/\theta}$$

$$\approx 10^{-14.5}\ M\ (700°K).$$

$$(\dot{H}) = \frac{k_i}{k_4} \approx \frac{10^{16-80/\theta}}{10^{10.3-5/\theta}} = 10^{5.7-75/\theta}$$

$$\approx 10^{-17.7}\ M\ (700°K)$$

$$(CH_3) = \left[\frac{k_i(CH_3CHO)}{k_t}\right]^{1/2} \simeq \left[\frac{10^{16-80/\theta}(10^{-2.5})}{10^{10.5}}\right]^{1/2}$$

$$\approx 10^{-11.3}\ M\ (700°K). \tag{4.65}$$

[14] The most recent study is to be found in K. J. Laidler and M. T. H. Lin, *Proc. Roy. Soc.* (London), **A297**, 365 (1967); *Can. J. Chem.*, **46** (1968).

We can see that only CH_3 radicals are of importance, and this justifies using a single termination reaction of $2CH_3$. The overall rate of the chain is

$$\frac{-d(CH_3CHO)}{dt} = k_1(CH_3)(CH_3CHO) = k_1\left(\frac{k_i}{k_t}\right)^{1/2}(CH_3CHO)^{3/2}. \quad (4.66)$$

This equation is in excellent agreement with the observed data which verify the $\frac{3}{2}$ order and also the assignments of the individual rate constants and activation energy:

$$k_{obs.} = 10^{10.8-48/\theta}(liter/mole)^{1/2}\ sec^{-1}.$$

The rate of H_2 production should be equal to the rate of initiation, so that the kinetic chain length λ is given by[15]

$$\lambda = \frac{d(CH_4)/dt}{d(H_2)/dt} = \frac{k_1(CH_3CHO)^{1/2}}{(k_ik_t)^{1/2}}$$

$$= \frac{10^{8.0-8.0/\theta}(10^{-2.5})}{10^{13.3-40/\theta}} = 10^{-7.8+32/\theta} \quad (4.67)$$

$$= 10^{2.2} \quad at \quad 700°K$$

$$= 10^{0.95} \quad at \quad 800°K.$$

The reaction is extremely sensitive to small traces of O_2, and the walls of the vessel must be conditioned to yield reproducible rate data. Ethylene oxide, $Hg(CH_3)_2$, and I_2 all will sensitize the pyrolysis at temperatures about 60°C lower than the usual pyrolysis range.

4.10 "WRONG" RADICALS

As we have already noted, the existence of more than one abstractable atom in a molecule makes for a diversity of possible products and raises, as well, the question of the importance of alternate radical species. The pyrolysis of CH_3CHO presents a simple example. In this case, the abstraction of an alkyl H atom leads to a relatively inert radical, $\cdot CH_2CHO$. The rate at which this may be expected to continue the chain by fission is limited by the endo-thermicity of the reaction

$$\cdot CH_2CHO \xrightarrow{5} CH_2CO + H \quad \Delta H° = 36\ kcal/mole. \quad (4.68)$$

If we assume by analogy with other unsaturates an activation energy of about 3 kcal for the addition of H to ketone, $E_5 \simeq 39\ kcal/mole$. With an A factor of about $10^{13}\ sec^{-1}$, this gives a steady state concentration of

[15] See, however, Section (4.10).

$\cdot$CH$_2$CHO, as follows:

$$\cdot\text{CH}_3 + \text{CH}_3\text{CHO} \xrightarrow{1'} \cdot\text{CH}_2\text{CHO} + \text{CH}_4;$$

$$\dot{\text{C}}\text{H}_2\text{CHO} + \text{CH}_3\text{CHO} \xrightarrow{6} \text{CH}_3\text{CHO} + \text{CH}_3\dot{\text{C}}\text{O}$$

$$\frac{(\cdot\text{CH}_2\text{CHO})}{(\cdot\text{CH}_3)} = \frac{k_1'(\text{CH}_3\text{CHO})}{k_6(\text{CH}_3\text{CHO}) + k_5}$$

$$\approx \frac{k_1'}{k_6} \approx 1. \tag{4.69}$$

This last result[16] is obtained by estimating k_1' and k_6 both as $10^{8.0-10/\theta}$ liter/mole-sec, so that at $(\text{CH}_3\text{CHO}) = 10^{-2.5}$ M $k_6(\text{CH}_3\text{CHO})/k_5 \sim 10^{1.5}$ at 700°K, but only $10^{0.5}$ at 800°K. In such a case, we should change our termination to include this inert radical. We should add the steps

$$\text{CH}_3 + \cdot\text{CH}_2\text{CHO} \xrightarrow{k_t'} \text{CH}_3\text{CH}_2\text{CHO};$$

$$2\cdot\text{CH}_2\text{CHO} \xrightarrow{k_t''} \text{CHOCH}_2\text{CH}_2\text{CHO}. \tag{4.70}$$

The final expression becomes

$$\frac{-d(\text{CH}_3\text{CHO})}{dt} = \frac{k_1 k_i^{1/2}(\text{CH}_3\text{CHO})^{3/2}}{[k_t + (k_1'/k_6)k_t' + (k_1''/k_6)^2 k_t'']^{1/2}}. \tag{4.71}$$

Using the generally valid geometric mean rule, $k_t' = 2(k_t k_t'')^{1/2}$, we obtain

$$\frac{-d(\text{CH}_3\text{CHO})}{dt} = k_1\left(\frac{k_i}{k_t}\right)^{1/2} \frac{(\text{CH}_3\text{CHO})^{3/2}}{[1 + (k_1'/k_6)(k_t''/k_t)^{1/2}]}$$

$$\approx \frac{k_1}{2}\left(\frac{k_i}{k_t}\right)^{1/2}(\text{CH}_3\text{CHO})^{3/2}. \tag{4.72}$$

In the last step we have assumed that $k_1' \sim k_6$ and $k_t'' \sim k_t$.

The path taken above also gives an additional contribution to H$_2$ production, which is almost exactly equal to the initiation rate at $10^{-2.5}$ M of CH$_3$CHO. The total H$_2$ production is now

$$\frac{d(\text{H}_2)}{dt} = k_i(\text{CH}_3\text{CHO}) + \left(\frac{k_i}{k_t}\right)^{1/2}\left(\frac{k_1'}{k_6}\right)k_5(\text{CH}_3\text{CHO})^{1/2}. \tag{4.73}$$

---

[16] K. J. Laidler and M. T. H. Lin arrive at about the same ratio, but for different reasons. They omitted reaction 6 and underestimated the rate of step 1'. See *Proc. Roy. Soc.* (London), **A297**, 365 (1967); *Can. J. Chem.*, **46** (1968).

This will modify our previous discussion of H_2 production and chain length. We note that C_2H_5CHO should be as abundant as H_2 production, and CH_2CO should be about half of H_2. Acetone production has been reported as another minor component, comparable to H_2.[17] Acetone can arise from two sources. The major one appears to be the endothermic displacement of H from CH_3CHO:

$$CH_3 + CH_3CHO \rightleftharpoons (CH_3)_2CHO \rightarrow (CH_3)_2CO + H.$$

A second is the addition of CH_3 to ketone to produce the inert radical $\cdot CH_2COCH_3$, which can abstract from CH_3CHO to form acetone:

$$\cdot CH_3 + CH_2CO \rightarrow \cdot CH_2COCH_3;$$

$$CH_3CO\dot{C}H_2 + CH_3CHO \rightarrow CH_3COCH_3 + CH_3\dot{C}O. \tag{4.74}$$

The alternative source of acetone from $CH_3\dot{C}O + CH_3$ is not significant because the $(CH_3\dot{C}O)$ concentration is so low.

We see that in the present instance the production of "inert" or "wrong" radicals does not produce a significant change in the kinetics or rate law. Although this may often be the case, it also may happen that such species will be important in modifying the rate law or quantitative Arrhenius parameters.

Another example is to be found in the chain pyrolysis of C_2H_5Br, where the "wrong" radical is $CH_3\dot{C}HBr$. The chain steps are

$$Br + C_2H_5Br \underset{1}{\overset{1}{\rightleftharpoons}} HBr + \dot{C}H_2CH_2Br$$

$$\underset{-1'}{\overset{1'}{\rightleftharpoons}} HBr + CH_3\dot{C}HBr.$$

$$M + \dot{C}H_2CH_2Br \underset{-2}{\overset{2}{\rightleftharpoons}} C_2H_4 + Br + M \tag{4.75}$$

$$CH_3\dot{C}HBr \overset{3}{\longrightarrow} CH_2{=}CHBr + H\cdot.$$

Step 3 in (4.75) has an endothermicity of about 35 kcal and an expected activation energy of about 39 kcal. It is very slow compared to the exo-thermic, bimolecular reaction with HBr $(-1')$, which has an estimated rate constant $10^{9.5-6/\theta}$ liter/mole-sec. Even at $(HBr) = 10$ torr $= 10^{-3.5}$ M, Step $-1'$ will be 10^3 to 10^4 times faster than Step 3.

[17] K. J. Laidler and M. T. H. Lin, *Proc. Roy. Soc.* (London), **A297**, 365 (1967); *Can. J. Chem.*, **46** (1968).

The steady state concentration of the $CH_3\dot{C}HBr$ is then given by

$$\frac{(CH_3\dot{C}HBr)}{(B\dot{r})} = K_1'\left(\frac{C_2H_5Br}{HBr}\right) \tag{4.76}$$

$$\approx 10^{1.3-7/\theta}\left(\frac{C_2H_5Br}{HBr}\right)$$

$$\approx 10 \ (700°K \text{ and } 1\% \text{ decomposition}) \tag{4.77}$$

$$\approx 1 \ (700°K \text{ and } 10\% \text{ decomposition}).$$

Here the wrong radical is a major species early in the reaction and can account for much of the termination because the other radical $\dot{C}H_2CH_2Br$ is present in equal ($>10\%$ reaction) or smaller amounts. We can estimate its steady state concentration from the near equilibrium which is established in Step 2:[18]

$$\frac{(\dot{C}H_2CH_2Br)}{(Br)} = \frac{k_{-2}(C_2H_4)(M) + k_i(EtBr)}{k_2(M) + k_{-1}(HBr)} \tag{4.78}$$

$$\approx \frac{k_{-2}(C_2H_4)}{k_2} = K_{-2}(C_2H_4). \tag{4.79}$$

At $700°K$ and 10 torr C_2H_4, $(\dot{C}H_2CH_2Br)/(Br) \approx 10^{-3.4}$. At $650°K$, which is the middle of the temperature range and with 100 torr of added C_2H_4, it becomes $10^{-2.6}$, or of the same order as the $CH_3\dot{C}HBr$. Because $Br + Br + M$ is prohibitively slow, due to its third-order rate constant, all termination is with these two minor radicals:

$$\text{Termination:} \begin{cases} Br + \dot{C}H_2CH_2Br \xrightarrow{\ t\ } C_2H_4Br_2 \\ +CH_3\dot{C}HBr \xrightarrow{\ t'\ } CH_3CHBr_2. \end{cases} \tag{4.80}$$

The absolute concentration of Br atoms is then determined by the initiation, which is most probably the unimolecular fission of the weakest bond, the C—Br bond. However, bimolecular metathesis from products can become competitive:

$$C_2H_5Br \xrightarrow{\ i\ } C_2\dot{H}_5 + Br; \tag{4.81}$$

$$C_2H_4 + HBr \xrightarrow{\ i'\ } C_2\dot{H}_5 + Br.$$

---

[18] In making these estimates we assign values as follows:

$k_{-2} \sim 10^{10-2/\theta} \text{ liter}^2/\text{mole}^2\text{-sec}; \quad k_1 = 10^{10.5-13/\theta} \text{ liter/mole-sec};$

$k_{-1} = 10^{9.5-2/\theta} \text{ liter/mole-sec}; \quad k_2 = K_2k_{-2} \text{ with } K_2 \sim 10^{3-9/\theta} \text{ mole/liter}.$

The ratio of rates by our usual methods is

$$\frac{R_i}{R_i'} = \frac{10^{14.8-68/\theta}(Et\text{Br})}{10^{10-46/\theta}(C_2H_4)(HBr)}$$

$$= 10^{4.8-22/\theta}\,\frac{(Et\text{Br})}{(C_2H_4)(HBr)}.\tag{4.82}$$

At $650°K$ and 10% decomposition with $(Et\text{Br})_0 = 10^{-2.5}\,M$, this ratio has the value 10^2. However, large added quantities of either HBr or C_2H_4 at $600°K$, or at 50% decomposition, could reduce it to below unity and shift the initiation mechanism. With C_2H_5Br as the source, however, we have

$$(\text{Br})^2 = \frac{k_i(C_2H_5Br)}{k_tK_1'\left(\dfrac{C_2H_5Br}{HBr}\right) + k_t'K_{-2}(C_2H_4)}$$

$$= \frac{k_i(HBr)}{k_tK_1'}\bigg/\left[1 + \frac{k_t'K_{-2}}{k_tK_1'}\frac{(C_2H_4)(HBr)}{(C_2H_5Br)}\right]\tag{4.83}$$

Inserting the first-order concerted, four-center path, k_A, the overall rate of the reaction becomes

$$\frac{-d(Et\text{Br})}{dt} = k_A(Et\text{Br}) + k_1(\text{Br})(Et\text{Br})$$

$$\frac{-d(Et\text{Br})}{(Et\text{Br})\,dt} = k_A + k_1\left(\frac{k_i}{k_tK_1'}\right)^{1/2}\frac{(HBr)^{1/2}}{(1 + k_t'K_{-2}[(C_2H_4)(HBr)/(C_2H_5Br)])^{1/2}}\tag{4.84}$$

$$\approx k_A + k_1\left(\frac{k_i}{k^tK_1'}\right)^{1/2}(HBr)^{1/2}.\tag{4.85}$$

The apparent first-order chain contribution term can be estimated from our previous assignments (with $HBr = 10$ torr $\sim 10^{-3.6}$ M) as $10^{10.5-43.5/\theta}$ $\sec^{-1}$. This is in excellent agreement with the observations of Goldberg and Daniels[19] who reported, between 310 to 476°C, an overall first-order rate law $10^{11.8-46.4/\theta}$ $\sec^{-1}$.

In agreement with (4.84), Goldberg and Daniels observed catalysis by HBr, inhibition by large amounts of C_2H_4, and an induction period that was extremely pronounced at the lowest temperatures and that was decreased markedly by HBr addition. They also verified the autocatalytic behavior. However, they ascribed the catalysis to Br_2 production arising from the reaction of HBr with EtBr. This seems very unlikely.

The preceding analysis, on the contrary, shows that at low HBr the "wrong" radical cuts the chain lengths down to negligible proportions, and

[19] A. E. Goldberg and F. Daniels, *J. Am. Chem. Soc.*, **79**, 1314 (1957).

the major effect of HBr is on suppressing this species. There is, as well, a small suppression of the "right" radical, $\cdot CH_2CH_2Br$.

With minor modifications, we may expect the same behavior to occur in most pyrolyses of alkyl chlorides and bromides.

4.11 SELECTIVITY OF RADICALS

Because exothermic radical metathesis reactions have very small activation energies, we do not expect them to be very selective in the exothermic direction. For example, the radical chlorination of a hydrocarbon will proceed via

$$Cl + RH \rightarrow HCl + \dot{R}. \tag{4.86}$$

This is a reasonably exothermic reaction, having $\Delta H_r^0 = -5$ kcal for primary C—H bonds; $\Delta H_r^0 = -9$ kcal for secondary, -12 kcal for tertiary C—H, and $\Delta H_r^0 \sim -22$ kcal for allylic or benzylic C—H bonds. However, the activation energy is already so small (~ 1 kcal) for the primary C—H bond metatheses that there can be no appreciable variation in activation energy with bond strength. We thus expect Cl atoms to abstract H atoms, almost indiscriminately from organic compounds with little concern for their bond strengths. An example of this is provided by the gas phase, free radical chlorination of butane that gives (sec-butyl chloride)/(primary butyl chloride) ratios of 2.4, almost independent of temperature. Correcting by the statistical number of abstractable atoms, the per-atom, metathesis rate ratio becomes 3.6.

A similar example to that given above is provided by the liquid phase chlorination of n-butyl benzene in dilute CCl_4 solution.[20] The statistically corrected, relative rate ratios[21] are indicated in the following:

$$\underset{5.9\ :\ 2.7\ :\ 4.0\ :\ 1.0}{C_6H_5-\overset{\alpha}{C}H_2-\overset{\beta}{C}H_2-\overset{\gamma}{C}H_2-\overset{\delta}{C}H_3.} \tag{4.87}$$

By way of contrast, we should then expect to see a very strong effect of bond strength on selectivity in atom abstraction reactions which occur in the endothermic direction. Abstraction of H atoms by Br atoms will be generally endothermic with endothermicities of 17 kcal for CH_4, 11 kcal for primary C—H, 7.5 kcal for secondary C—H, and 4.5 kcal for tertiary C—H. The exothermic reactions of all of these radicals with HBr have similar activation energies of about 1.5 ± 0.5 kcal.

We expect to see the full differences in bond strengths reflected in the activation energies of Br atom attack, and this is indeed the case. As an

[20] G. A. Russell, A. Ito, and D. G. Hendry, *J. Am. Chem. Soc.*, **85**, 2976 (1963).
[21] To make explicit the counting, the actual ratios of $\alpha : \beta : \gamma : \delta$ chlorides, which are observed, are 5.9 : 2.7 : 4.0 : 1.5.

example, the ratio of secondary/primary bromides produced by vapor phase bromination of n-butane at 160°C is about 55, to be compared to the quoted 2.4 for Cl atom attack.

One has, however, to exercise some caution in interpreting such results as those gained above because the final products may be affected by unimolecular abstraction reactions. Thus, in the case of n-pentane, a primary radical may isomerize as follows:

$$\dot{C}H_2CH_2CH_2CH_2CH_3 \xrightarrow{1} CH_3CH_2CH_2\dot{C}HCH_3$$

$$+Cl_2 \xrightarrow{2} ClCH_2CH_2CH_2CH_2CH_3 + Cl. \qquad (4.88)$$

The ratio of these two paths is given by

$$\frac{R_1}{R_2} = \frac{k_1}{k_2(Cl_2)} \approx \frac{10^{11-15/\theta}}{10^{9.5-1/\theta}(10^{-2.5})} \qquad (4.89)$$

$$= 10^{4-14/\theta}$$

The ratio is very small below 180°C (10^{-3} at 450°K) but becomes significant above 700°K, or at lower Cl_2 concentrations.

The A factor for the internal abstraction is estimated from our A factors for five-membered ring reactions, and the activation energy is obtained by adding to the expected 8 kcal for H atom abstraction, 7 kcal of ring strain in the five-membered ring.

4.12   OXIDATION

One of the most intriguing of the complex chain reactions is the oxidation of organic molecules. At low temperatures ($<190°C$) the main products are hydroperoxides and oxygenated species obtained from their secondary reactions. These include alcohols, ketones, aldehydes, and acids, as well as CO and CO_2.

A simple chain mechanism can account for the species listed above.

$$\text{Chain:} \begin{cases} R\dot{O}_2 + RH \xrightarrow{1} RO_2H + \dot{R}; \\ \dot{R} + O_2 \xrightarrow{2} R\dot{O}_2 \end{cases}$$

$$\text{Transfer:} \begin{cases} 2R\dot{O}_2 \xrightarrow{3} 2R\dot{O} + O_2 \\ R\dot{O} + RH \xrightarrow{4} ROH + \dot{R} \\ R\dot{O} \xrightarrow{5} R''R'C{=}O + \dot{R}'''; \\ \dot{R}''' + O_2 \xrightarrow{6} R'''O_2 \end{cases} \qquad (4.90)$$

and so on.

The complexity in these oxidations is introduced by the unusual Step 3, which is only slightly exothermic ($\Delta H_3 \sim -6$ kcal) and which proceeds through the formation of a weekly bonded tetraoxide. It is estimated that the concerted split of the tetraoxide to give $2R\dot{O} + O_2$ is about thermoneutral.

The $RO\cdot$ radicals can undergo fission to produce stable ketones or aldehydes and a smaller radical. Thus with $t\text{-BuO}\cdot$, $t\text{-amyl O}\cdot$, or cumyl $O\cdot$:

$$(CH_3)_3C\text{---}\dot{O} \rightarrow (CH_3)_2CO + \dot{C}H_3,$$
$$(CH_3)_2(C_2H_5)C\text{---}\dot{O} \rightarrow (CH_3)_2CO + \dot{C}_2H_5, \qquad (4.91)$$
$$\phi(CH_3)_2C\text{---}\dot{O} \rightarrow \phi COCH_3 + \dot{C}H_3.$$

In general the weakest bond, as may be expected, is one that undergoes fission.

Near 100°C, with an excess of O_2, it is possible to get very long chains and almost quantitative production of the RO_2H from RH. However, for saturated secondary or primary hydroperoxides, the yield is limited by the very slow abstraction step

$$R\dot{O}_2 + RH \underset{-1}{\overset{1}{\rightleftarrows}} RO_2H + \dot{R}, \qquad (4.92)$$

and the competing side paths via Step 3 can become dominant. The RO_2H is, itself, protected from attack on its weak O—H bond by the excess O_2 that converts all $R\cdot$ radicals to RO_2^- with extremely high rate constants ($10^{9.5}$ liter/mole-sec) with no activation energy. $RO\cdot$ radicals are generally scavenged by the large excess of RH.

The initiation in the systems discussed above is generally provided by sensitizers. Spontaneous thermal initiation of saturated alkanes with O_2 is too slow to be of importance below 150°C. The same is true of olefins $+O_2$. For the latter, both addition or abstraction reactions will have activation energies in excess of 35 kcal.

As examples, consider $C_2H_4 + O_2$ addition reactions:

$$(4.93)$$

Step 1 is endothermic by about 32 kcal and reverses quickly unless followed by the exothermic Step 3, which is expected to have an activation energy of another 5 kcal and then lead rapidly to formaldehyde. Step 2 is estimated to have an activation energy of about 16 kcal. It is the only one which leads to a propagating radical.

Abstraction of allylic, or benzylic, H is more favorable. With 3-methyl butene-1, we would expect

$$(CH_3)_2CH\!-\!CH\!=\!CH_2 + O_2 \rightarrow (CH_3)_2\dot{C}\!-\!CH\!=\!CH_2 + H\dot{O}_2$$

with an activation energy just equal to the endothermicity of 31 kcal. Above $100°K$ in neat liquid phase, this would be a quite significant radical source, even at low O_2 concentrations $(10^{-4}\ M)$.

The overall net reaction, which is the production of RO_2H from $RH + O_2$, is exothermic by about 20 kcal and can become a source of self-ignition only at very high O_2 concentrations, or at temperatures near $300°C$ where gas mixtures exhibit the well-studied phenomenon of "cool" flames.

Above $160°C$ the hydroperoxides themselves begin to undergo homogeneous decompositions into $RO + OH$ radicals and so can act as secondary initiation centers for further oxidation. Above $300°C$ with estimated rate constants for this fission of about $10^{15-43/\theta}\ sec^{-1}$, the lifetimes of RO_2H are of the order of 10 seconds and their slow formation and rapid decomposition may be shown to account for the long induction periods and periodic flames characterizing the cool-flame region. The overall phenomenon is described as "degenerate" chain branching because a product in the reaction is giving rise to chain center multiplication.

Because of the RO_2H pyrolysis, the rate of reaction of hydrocarbons with O_2 shows an auto-acceleration from about 200 to $350°C$. At the latter temperature the homogeneous gas phase rate reaches a maximum, and then declines to the point where it is almost immeasurably slow at $400°C$ in a flow system.[22] In a static system this region of negative temperature coefficient is observed to be accomplished by a change over in products from oxygen containing compounds, such as RO_2H, and its secondary products to olefins and $H_2O + H_2O_2$.

All of the results described above are accounted for by a very simple scheme:

$$\dot{R} + O_2 \underset{-1}{\overset{1}{\rightleftarrows}} R\dot{O}_2$$

$$\underset{-1'}{\overset{1'}{\rightleftarrows}} H\dot{O}_2 + \text{olefin};$$

$$R\dot{O}_2 + RH \overset{2}{\longrightarrow} RO_2H + \dot{R}; \qquad\qquad (4.94)$$

$$H\dot{O}_2 + RH \overset{2'}{\longrightarrow} HO_2H + \dot{R}.$$

The abstraction of H from $R\cdot$ to give $HO_2^{\cdot} + $ olefin (Step $1'$) is at least 200 times slower than the addition of O_2 to $R\cdot$ to give $RO_2^{\cdot}$. The latter is a radical recombination with a rate constant measured at $10^{9.5}$ liter/mole-sec

[22] K. C. Salooja, *Combustion and Flame*, **6**, 275 (1962); **8**, 311 (1964); **9**, 219 (1965). Y. H. Chung and S. Sandler, *Combustion and Flame*, **6**, 295 (1962).

in its high-pressure region. The competing abstraction step though exothermic by about 7 kcal/mole or more, has a rate constant estimated at
$10^{9.2-4/\theta}$ liter/mole-sec. It can never be significant compared to addition.

However, Step 1, which below 200°C is the rate determining step in oxidation, becomes significantly reversible above 250°C, so that Step 2 becomes
the slow, rate-determining oxidation step. This is indicated in the overall
oxidation rate

$$\frac{d(RO_2H)}{dt} = \frac{k_1 k_2 (RH)(\dot{R})(O_2)}{k_{-1} + k_2(RH)} \tag{4.95}$$

$$\xrightarrow{T<200°C} k_1(\dot{R})(O_2)$$

$$\xrightarrow[T>250°C]{} K_1 k_2 (RH)(O_2)(\dot{R}). \tag{4.96}$$

The turnover point in the rate law will occur when $k_{-1} = k_2(RH)$. With
$k_{-1} \sim 10^{14.5-29/\theta}$, $k_2 \sim 10^{8-12/\theta}$, and E_2 depending somewhat on the nature
of the hydrocarbon, turnover will occur at about 450 to 500°K for $(RH) =$
1 atmosphere. Let us compare this with the rate law for olefin production
via exothermic Step 1', which can be taken as effectively irreversible in the
system,

$$\frac{d(\text{olefin})}{dt} = k_1'(\dot{R})(O_2). \tag{4.97}$$

The ratio of rates is given by

$$\frac{R(\text{olefin})}{R(RO_2H)} = \frac{k_1'[k_{-1} + k_2(RH)]}{k_1 k_2(RH)} \qquad \begin{array}{l} \xrightarrow{T<200°C} \dfrac{k_1'}{k_1} \ll 1 \\[2ex] \xrightarrow{T>250°C} \dfrac{k_1'}{K_1 k_2(RH)} \end{array} \tag{4.98}$$

Using the values of the assigned rate constants, we find that above 250°C,
the ratio becomes

$$\frac{R(\text{olefin})}{R(RO_2H)} \approx 10^{7.9-13/\theta}. \tag{4.99}$$

This relation quantitatively fits the observed data for a number of hydrocarbon oxidations under very varied conditions.[23] In particular, the inverse
dependence on (RH) has been observed as well.

Above 400°C the rates of oxidation in flow systems begin to rise again as
the product H_2O_2 begins to decompose homogeneously to provide a new
source of radicals $(M + H_2O_2 \rightarrow 2OH + M)$ and play the role of the missing
RO_2H. Above 500°C this is sufficiently rapid that secondary oxidation of the

[23] See S. W. Benson, *J. Am. Chem. Soc.*, **87**, 972 (1965) for a summary; also see S. W.
Benson, *Adv. in Chem.* (1968).

product olefin provides sufficient heat to cause self-ignition and explosion. Note that the overall reaction to produce H_2O_2 is nearly thermoneutral and involves a very small entropy change:

$$O_2 + RH \rightarrow \text{olefin} + H_2O_2 + 2 \text{ kcal.} \tag{4.100}$$

Olefins turn out to be more easily oxidized than alkanes. The mechanism involves addition to the double bond and/or abstraction of allylic H atoms:

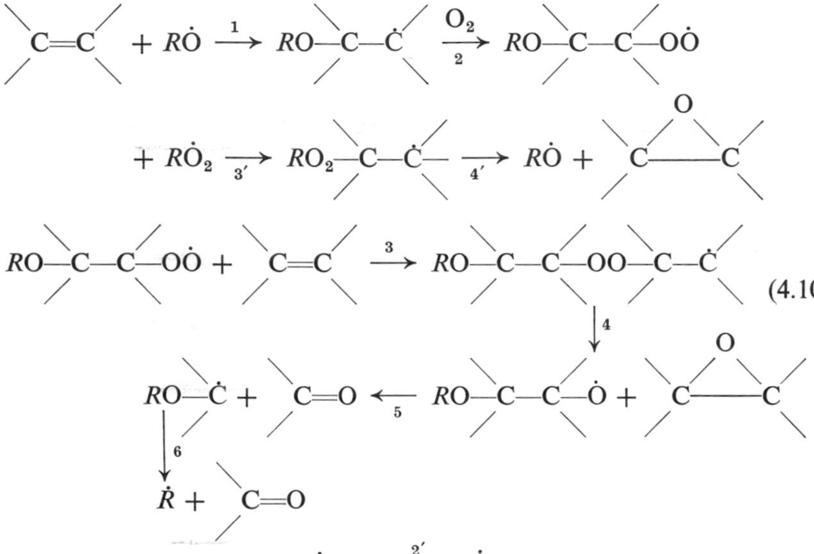

$$\text{(4.101)}$$

The sequence above provides a chain mechanism for conversion of original olefins into epoxides and aldehydes, via $R\cdot$, $RO\cdot$, and $RO_2^{\cdot}$.

Allylic H atom abstraction leads to

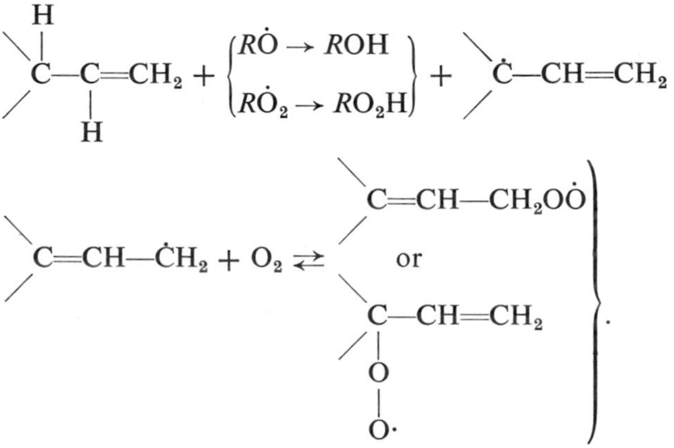

$$\text{(4.102)}$$

The allyl peroxy radicals are even more weakly bound than the alkyl peroxy, and at $O_2 = 0.1$ atm will be in labile equilibrium with an equal concentration of allyl radicals above $500°K$. This tends to make diene formation more likely by the $HO_2^{\cdot}$ mechanism at the higher temperatures for C_4 or higher olefins. It also lowers the turnover temperature at which RO_2H production starts to decrease.

4.13 INERT INITIATION RADICALS

We have seen how in complex compounds, abstraction from a wrong position can lead to an inert radical that cannot react rapidly to propagate the chain. These inert radicals can in many instances arise from initiation reactions. An example arises in the pyrolysis of n-propyl benzene, where the fastest initiation is fission of the weak C—C bond to produce benzyl + ethyl radicals:

$$\phi CH_2 - CH_2 - CH_3 \rightarrow o\dot{C}H_2 + \dot{C}_2H_5. \qquad (4.103)$$

Whereas $\cdot C_2H_5$ can abstract with relatively low activation energy from all $3C$—H bonds, the corresponding reaction for benzyl radical is expected to have about a 4 to 6 kcal higher activation energy for the αC—H, and 19 to 22 kcal total activation energy for β and γ—C—H, and hence be very slow. In this system, competing chains exist by virtue of the different C—H bond abstractions:

$$\dot{R} + \varphi CH_2 - CH_2 - CH_3 \xrightarrow{\;1\;} RH + \varphi \dot{C}H - CH_2 - CH_3,$$

$$\xrightarrow{\;1'\;} RH + \varphi CH_2 - \dot{C}H - CH_3,$$

$$\xrightarrow{\;1''\;} RH + \varphi CH_2 - CH_2 - \dot{C}H_2, \qquad (4.104)$$

$$\varphi \dot{C}H - CH_2 - CH_3 \xrightarrow{\;2\;} \varphi CH = CH_2 + \dot{C}H_3,$$

$$\varphi CH_2 - \dot{C}H - CH_3 \xrightarrow{\;2'\;} \varphi CH = CH - CH_3 + H,$$

$$\varphi CH_2 - CH_2 - \dot{C}H_2 \xrightarrow{\;2''\;} \varphi \dot{C}H_2 + C_2H_4.$$

Of the three possible fission steps, Step $2''$ is the fastest, with an expected activation of about 20 kcal, but a low A factor of about $10^{12.8}$ sec^{-1}. However, it produces an inert $\phi \dot{C}H_2$ radical, which can propagate slowly and only at the α—C—H bond. The next fastest fission step is Step $2'$ with an expected activation energy of 38 kcal and a low A factor of about $10^{12.8}$ sec^{-1} also. It gives rise, however, to a very nonselective H atom, which can attack rapidly at any of the C—H positions, and hence will not produce long chains.

The slowest fission step is Step 2 with an expected activation energy of about 50 kcal and an A factor of about 10^{14} sec^{-1}. It produces a CH_3, which again is not very selective. It can be seen that there are no long chains expected for n-propyl benzene because only inert, or wrong, radicals are produced in one, or both, of the propagation steps.

Another example comes from the pyrolysis of neopentane (NpH). The initiation produces $\cdot CH_3$ + the inert t-butyl radical:

$$(CH_3)_4C \xrightarrow{\ i\ } \dot{C}H_3 + \dot{C}(CH_3)_3.$$

The activation energy for t-butyl attack on the primary C—H bond, which is endothermic by 7 kcal, is expected to be about 17 kcal, making this a very slow step. The alternative route is fission of t-Butyl to give H + isobutene with an expected activation energy of about 43 kcal ($\Delta H^\circ = 41$ kcal/mole). This will be far more rapid than the H atom abstraction, so that the sequence will be

$$(CH_3)_3\dot{C} \xrightarrow{\ I\ } H + CH_2{=}C(CH_3)_2.$$

The stationary concentration of t-Bu$\cdot$ will be

$$(t\text{-Bu}) = \frac{k_i(\text{NpH})}{k_1} \approx \frac{10^{16.5-80/\theta}(18^{-2.5})}{10^{14.0-43/\theta}}$$

$$= 10^{-37/\theta}. \tag{4.105}$$

At $750°K$ ($\theta = 3.5$ kcal/mole) this is $10^{-10.6}\ M$, and relatively minor compared to the concentration of propagating radical CH_3, which is about 100-fold higher ($\sim 10^{-8}\ M$ at $750°K$) at all temperatures. This generally turns out to be the case for inert radicals formed in initiation, but one must analyze the system carefully to be certain.

4.14   SECONDARY REACTIONS

We have already seen that the initial stages of the pyrolysis of molecules with more than three polyvalent atoms is complicated by competing chain reactions. Such complexity is further compounded in the later stages of the decomposition when secondary reactions with product molecules become appreciable. These secondary reactions can also produce inhibition, or acceleration of the initial chain and in extreme cases, completely obscure the nature of the initial products.

We can expect secondary reactions to become important in depleting products when the rates of radical reactions with these products are comparable in magnitude to the parallel rates in the initial chain. Consider, for example, the pyrolysis of dimethyl ether. The initial chain is the very simple pyrolytic, two-center scheme:

Chain: $\begin{cases} \dot{C}H_3 + CH_3OCH_3 \xrightarrow{1} CH_4 + \dot{C}H_2OCH_3 \text{ (slow)} \\ \dot{C}H_2OCH_3 + M \xrightarrow{2} CH_2O + \dot{C}H_3 + M \text{ (fast)}; \end{cases}$ (4.106)

Net reaction: $CH_3OCH_3 \rightarrow CH_2O + CH_4.$

CH_2O is an excellent source of abstractable H atoms, so that it will compete along with the original ether for the CH_3 radicals. The activation energy appears to be about 2 kcal lower for $CH_2O + CH_3$ than that for CH_3 abstraction of H from ether, so that if the A factors can be taken as equal, we expect a $10^{2/\theta}$ faster attack on CH_2O by $\dot{}CH_3$ than on Me_2O. At 800°K ($\theta = 3.6$ kcal) in the middle of the range where the reaction has been studied, this amounts to a factor of about 4, in excellent agreement with the observation that, during the pyrolysis, the CH_2O concentration builds up to a steady state ratio, relative to Me_2O of about $\frac{1}{4}$.

More quantitatively, if CH_2O is destroyed by $\dot{}CH_3$ attack,

Secondary chain: $\begin{cases} \dot{C}H_3 + CH_2O \xrightarrow{1'} CH_4 + \dot{C}HO \\ \dot{C}HO + M \xrightarrow{2'} CO + \dot{H} + M, \end{cases}$ (4.107)

it should approach a stationary state given by

$$\frac{d(CH_2O)}{dt} \simeq k_1(CH_3)(Me_2O) - k_1'(CH_3)(CH_2O).$$

When the steady state is reached and $d(CH_2O)/dt \approx 0$, then

$$\frac{(CH_2O)}{(Me_2O)} \approx \frac{k_1}{k_1'} \approx \frac{1}{4}.$$ (4.108)

The agreement needs to be modified to allow for H atoms, which are also active carriers in the system, produced by the secondary chain. They can attack both Me_2O and CH_2O. The data suggest that the same ratio of about 4 applies to the relative rates of H atom attack on CH_2O and Me_2O:

$$H + (CH_3)_2O \rightarrow H_2 + \dot{C}H_2OCH_3,$$
$$H + CH_2O \rightarrow H_2 + \dot{C}HO.$$ (4.109)

In the ether–CH_2O system just discussed the secondary reactions would not be important at 1% reaction, but they would become appreciable at 20% reaction. The reason for this is that the two chain carriers are the not very selective radicals H and CH_3. We would expect much more significant secondary reactions in chains carried by less active, hence more selective, radicals. An example would be provided by the pyrolysis of t-butyl bromide, where the carriers would be the fairly inert Br atoms. The chain steps are:

Chain:
$$\begin{cases} \text{Br} + (\text{CH}_3)_3\text{C—Br} \underset{2}{\overset{1}{\rightleftarrows}} \text{HBr} + \dot{\text{C}}\text{H}_2(\text{CH}_3)_2\text{C—Br}, \\ \dot{\text{C}}\text{H}_2(\text{CH}_3)_2\text{—Br} \rightleftarrows \text{CH}_2\text{=C}(\text{CH}_3)_2 + \text{Br} \end{cases}$$
(4.110)

Secondary reaction:
$$\text{Br} + \text{CH}_2\text{=C}(\text{CH}_3)_2 \overset{3}{\rightleftarrows} \text{HBr} + \text{CH}_2\text{=C}(\text{CH}_3)\text{—}\dot{\text{C}}\text{H}_2$$

The slow chain carrying step is the endothermic ($\Delta H° = 11$ kcal) abstraction of H by Br atoms (Step 1). The secondary reaction competing with this is the exothermic ($\Delta H° = -2$ kcal) abstraction of H from the isobutylene product to give the stable methyl allyl radical (Step 3). Even with A factors favoring Step 1 by about a factor of 10, the expected difference of 13 kcal in the activation energies of Steps 1 and 3 will make the rate constant for the latter 10^4-fold faster at 300°C. This means that even at 0.01 % decomposition, Br attack on the olefin is as fast as on the parent molecule. As a consequence, Reaction 3 very quickly reaches a state of equilibrium with the (Br)/(methyl allyl) ratio given by

$$\frac{(\text{Br})}{(\text{methyl allyl})} = K_{-3}\frac{(\text{HBr})}{(\text{olefin})} \approx 10^{-1.5/\theta} \approx \frac{1}{4}.$$
(4.111)

The estimate is made by noting that $\Delta S \sim 0$ and that (HBr) = (olefin) by stoichiometry. Because the other radical is negligibly small at 580°K, compared to Br, this immediately establishes Br and methyl allyl as the terminating species. Further analysis will also show that the chain is extremely slow with an overall rate given by

$$\frac{-d(\text{RBr})}{dt} = k_1\left(\frac{k_i K_{-3}}{k_t}\right)^{1/2}\left(\frac{\text{HBr}}{\text{olefin}}\right)^{1/2}(\text{RBr})^{3/2}$$
(4.112)

$$\approx k_1\left(\frac{k_i K_{-3}}{k_t}\right)^{1/2}(\text{RBr})^{3/2}.$$
(4.113)

The initiation and termination steps are

$$t\text{-BuBr} \overset{i}{\longrightarrow} t\text{-B}\cdot + \text{Br},$$
$$\text{methyl allyl} + \text{Br} \overset{t}{\longrightarrow} \text{CH}_2\text{=C}(\text{CH}_3)\text{CH}_2\text{Br}.$$
(4.114)

We have neglected the termination of two methylallyl radicals, which is expected to have a rate constant about ten-fold smaller than k_t. This introduces only a small error. Estimating $k_i = 10^{14.5-68/\theta}$, $k_t = 10^{10}$, and $k_1 = 10^{10.5-13.5/\theta}$, we find for the $\frac{3}{2}$ order rate constant

$$k_{3/2} = k_1(K_i K_{-3}/k_t)^{1/2} \simeq 10^{12.8-48/\theta} \text{ (liter/mole)}^{1/2} \text{ sec}^{-1}.$$
(4.115)

At 550°K and 100 torr of t-BuBr, this predicts a half-life of one year, which is negligible compared to the observed rate and which can thus be properly ascribed to the unimolecular, four-center elimination of HBr (Table 3.5). Similar considerations will show that none of the secondary or tertiary bromides can decompose by chain reactions at the temperatures where they have been studied. This is in agreement with the observations, which show no acceleration of the rate by Br_2 and no effect of radical inhibitors, such as NO or propylene on these reactions.

As already noted, such conclusions do not hold for the chlorides, where the active radical, Cl is nonselective. They do, however, predict substantial chain inhibition in these systems. We would similarly expect that the pyrolysis of amines and alcohols, which give rise to the nonselective $\dot{N}H_2$ and $\dot{O}H$ chain carriers, can also show chain character with inhibition by products and also by "wrong" radicals.

A last, and somewhat unusual example of important secondary reactions, is provided by the chain chlorination of benzene. Because of the high C—H bond energy in benzene ($\sim$112 kcal/mole), very few radicals or atoms can abstract H atoms from benzene. Instead, the preferred mode of reaction is addition. The reaction of Cl_2 + benzene, which leads to C_6H_5Cl + HCl as major products above 220°C, actually proceeds through an addition mechanism to form o- and p-$C_6H_6Cl_2$, as the product. Under the reaction conditions, however, these are very rapidly dehydrohalogenated to yield the observed products.

The scheme is

$$Cl_2 \rightleftarrows 2Cl + K_{Cl_2}$$

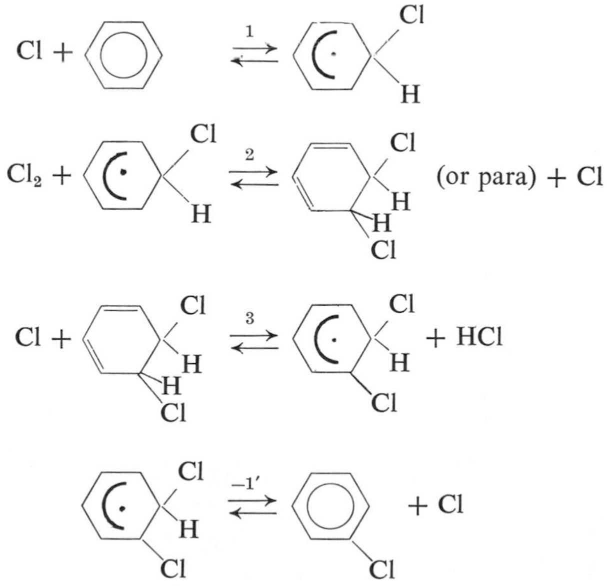

(4.116)

The competing reaction to Step 3 above is Cl atom addition to form tri-chloro-allyl radical. Because of the unfavorable, though exothermic pre-equilibrium (Step 1), the overall rate of attack of Cl on adduct (Step 3) is about 500 times faster than the net rate of formation of dichloride, and hence this latter never appears as a significant product of the reaction, despite the fact that all of the reaction proceeds through it. Its net rate of production is given by

$$\frac{d(RCl_2)}{dt} \simeq k_2 K_1 K_{Cl}^{1/2}(Cl_2)^{3/2}(\phi H) - k_3 K_{Cl}^{1/2}(Cl_2)^{1/2}(RCl_2) \qquad (4.117)$$

where we have neglected back reactions with ϕCl and have assumed that Cl atoms are the only appreciable chain centers in the system.[24] The steady state concentration of RCl_2 is

$$\frac{(RCl_2)_{ss}}{(\phi H)} = \frac{k_2 K_1(Cl_2)}{k_3}. \qquad (4.118)$$

It is likely that $k_2/k_3 \sim 10^{-1-3/\theta}$, so that with $(Cl_2) = 100$ torr and the assigned value of K_1, $(RCl_2)/(\phi H) = 10^{-8.2+7/\theta} = 10^{-4.4}$ at 550°K.

The present mechanism yields for the rate of chlorination

$$\frac{d(\phi Cl)}{dt} \approx \frac{-d(\phi H)}{dt} = k_2 K_1 K_{Cl_2}^{1/2}(Cl_2)^{3/2}(\phi H)$$

$$\simeq 10^{6.6-23.5/\theta}(Cl_2)^{3/2}(\phi H). \qquad (4.119)$$

The apparent 5/2 order rate constant is notable for having an activation energy less than half the dissociation energy of Cl_2 (28.5 kcal). This arises from the exothermic preequilibrium Step 1.

4.15 GAS PHASE POLYMERIZATION

Addition reactions are always subject to a very important species of secondary reactions, polymerization. This is usually not observed in the radical catalyzed additions of small molecules, such as the hydrogen halides, or halogens to unsaturates, but is found in the additions (telomerizations) of more complex species, such as, CCl_3Br, CCl_4, CCl_2O, CF_3CN, or as a special case, H_2 to olefins. Addition to acetylenes or conjugated olefins are almost never without side reactions of polymerization, even for the simple molecules.

The reason for the result described above is that the simple chain telom-erization is always in competition with the addition of a radical to another

---

[24] The ratio $(\cdot RCl)/(Cl) \simeq K_1(\phi H) \approx 10^{-6.2+10/\theta}(\phi H)$ in units of atmospheres. At $(\phi H) = 100$ torr and 550°K, $(\cdot RCl)/(Cl) = 10^{-3.1}$.

molecule of olefin. Let us consider, as an example, the addition of H_2 to C_2H_4 to produce C_2H_6. Above 400°C, where the rate is appreciable, C_4 and higher hydrocarbons are produced, unless $(H_2) \gg (C_2H_4)$. The relevant steps in the chain are

Chain:
$$\left\{ \begin{array}{l} H + C_2H_4 \overset{1}{\rightleftarrows} \cdot C_2H_5 \\ \cdot C_2H_5 + H_2 \overset{2}{\rightleftarrows} C_2H_6 + H \end{array} \right. ,$$
(4.120)

Polymer formation: $\cdot C_2H_5 + C_2H_4 \overset{3}{\rightleftarrows} n\text{-}\dot{C}_4H_9,$

and so on.

The ratio of rates of production of polymer formation $(\geq C_4)$ to C_2H_6 is given by

$$\frac{R_1(\geq C_4)}{\omega(C_2H_4)} = \frac{k_3}{k_2} \frac{(C_2H_4)}{(H_2)}$$

$$\approx 10^{-1+5/\theta} \frac{(C_2H_4)}{(H_2)}$$
(4.121)

where we have used average assignments for A_3 ($10^{9.5}$) and A_2 ($10^{8.5}$). At $(C_2H_4)/(H_2) = 0.10$ and $\theta = 3.5$ ($\sim 750°K$), this would give $R(\geq C_4)/R(C_2H_6)$ $\sim \frac{1}{4}$ in reasonable agreement with observations.[25] We see from this result that it would require $(H_2)/(C_2H_4)$ ratios in excess of 800 to reduce polymerization to 1% of hydrogenation.

Such behavior as that described above is not observed with HCl, HBr, Cl_2, Br_2, etc. because these species have much lower activation energies than H_2 for radical attack. In contrast, acetylenes and conjugated dienes are much more susceptible to polymerization because the activation energy for radical addition to these species is down to about 4 kcal, rather than 8, as it is with the olefins. This is somewhat compensated for in the case of acetylenes by the fact that the product of the addition, vinyl radicals are extremely reactive, having appreciably lower activation energies for atom abstraction than alkyl radicals.

$$\dot{R} + \text{---}C\equiv C\text{---} \rightarrow R\text{---}C\text{=}\dot{C}\text{---},$$

$$R\text{---}C\text{=}\dot{C}\text{---} + \text{---}C\equiv C\text{---} \rightarrow R\text{---}C\text{=}C\text{---}C\text{=}\dot{C}\text{---},$$
(4.122)

$$+ RY \rightarrow R\text{---}C\text{=}C\text{---}C\text{=}C\text{---}Y + \dot{R}.$$

[25] H. A. Taylor and A. Van Hook, *J. Phys. Chem.*, **39**, 811 (1935); R. N. Pease, *J. Am. Chem. Soc.*, **54**, 1877 (1932).

By way of contrast, 1,3-dienes show enhanced polymerization tendencies because of the slowness of the chain carrier allyl radical in abstraction reactions.

$$R\cdot + \quad \overset{\diagdown}{C}=\overset{\diagup}{C}-\overset{\diagup}{C}=\overset{\diagup}{C} \quad \leftrightarrows \quad R-\overset{\diagdown}{C}-\overset{.}{C}-\overset{\diagup}{C}=\overset{\diagup}{C}$$

$$R-\overset{\diagdown}{C}-\overset{.}{C}-\overset{\diagup}{C}=\overset{\diagup}{C} \;+\; \overset{\diagdown}{C}=\overset{\diagup}{C}-\overset{|}{C}=\overset{\diagup}{C} \quad \xrightarrow{\text{(fast)}} \quad \text{allyl adduct} \qquad (4.123)$$

$$+ \; R-Y \; \xrightarrow{\text{(slow)}} \; R-\overset{\diagdown}{C}-\overset{\diagup}{C}=\overset{\diagup}{C}-\overset{\diagup}{C}-Y + \overset{.}{R}.$$

It is difficult to make quantitative studies of gas phase polymerizations or telomerizations because the higher molecular weight products may easily exceed their vapor pressures at the reaction temperatures and condense on the walls. This tends to make for a second phase at the walls and a hetero-geneous system. Even without product condensation, the higher molecular weight radicals tend to be adsorbed at the walls and continue the reaction at fixed surface sites.

4.16   HOMOGENEOUS CATALYSIS

It is in principle possible to catalyze a chain reaction in two ways. One is to increase the stationary supply of radicals by increasing the rate of initiation. This in essence is the method of chain sensitization by species, such as ethylene oxide or peroxides. It does not, however, represent true catalysis because the sensitizers are used up as the reaction proceeds.

The second method is to use a catalyst to speed up the chain itself by providing an alternative, faster path. An excellent example of this is to be found in the catalytic effect produced by H_2 gas on the pyrolyses of dimethyl ether on C_2H_6 and on almost all hydrocarbon pyrolyses. (We should use some caution in interpreting the results because in many cases, the products are affected and H_2 is consumed.) In the case of $(CH_3)_2O$ the effect is truly catalytic, whereas in the case of C_3H_8, large concentrations of H_2 inhibit C_2H_4 and C_3H_6 production, as well as other minor species, and lead to $C_2H_6 + CH_4$ as almost quantitative products.

Because H_2 is a product of many of these pyrolyses, this also leads to some autocatalytic effect on the rate. In the case of $(CH_3)_2O$ the chain mechanism in the presence of large amounts of H_2 is

Catalysis: $\left\{ \begin{array}{l} \cdot CH_3 + H_2 \overset{1}{\rightleftharpoons} CH_4 + H \\ H + CH_3OCH_3 \overset{2}{\rightleftharpoons} H_2 + \cdot CH_2OCH_3 \end{array} \right.$ $\qquad (4.124)$

Chain: $\qquad\qquad \cdot CH_2OCH_3 \overset{3}{\rightleftharpoons} CH_2O + \cdot CH_3.$

The effect of added H_2 is to replace the normal chain step, $\cdot CH_3 + CH_3OCH_3 \xrightarrow{1'} \cdot CH_4 + \cdot CH_2OCH_3$, by two faster propagation steps, Steps 1 and 2. Steps 1 and 1' have about the same activation energy, but Step 1 has an A factor higher by about a factor of 2. The rate constant for Step 2 is extremely fast compared to that for Step 1, owing to a still higher A factor by about a factor of 10 and also a lower activation energy by about 4 kcal. This results in a very low stationary state concentration of H atoms and makes Step 1 essentially irreversible.

The combined pair, Steps 1 and 2, regenerate the H_2 catalyst, and can be looked upon as catalysis by chain transfer. The ratio of rates of $(CH_3)_2O$ pyrolysis with and without H_2 are

$$\frac{R(H_2)}{R \text{ (normal)}} \approx \frac{k_1(\dot{C}H_3)(H_2)}{k_1'(CH_3)(Me_2O)} = \frac{k_1(H_2)}{k_1'(Me_2O)} \qquad (4.125)$$

This is calculated for the initial stages of the reaction before H_2 (from the secondary chain) and CH_2O have accumulated in the system. The maximum catalysis is then a factor of 2 in the initial rate when H_2 and Me_2O are equal— not a very large effect.

A much more pronounced catalysis can be obtained via the use of HCl. Reactions of radicals with HCl tend to have activation energies just slightly (~ 1 kcal) in excess of the endothermicity of the reaction. The second catalytic chain step, involving Cl atom attack on RH to regenerate HCl is extremely rapid, so that small amounts of HCl can produce very pronounced catalysis. In the $(CH_3)_2O$ pyrolysis 20 mole % of HCl is observed to give an eight-fold increase in rate.[26] The catalytic transfer steps are

Catalysis: $\left\{ \begin{array}{l} \dot{C}H_3 + HCl \xrightarrow{1} CH_4 + Cl \\ Cl + (CH_3)_2O \xrightarrow{2} HCl + \dot{C}H_2OCH_3 \ ; \end{array} \right. \qquad (4.126)$

Net reaction: $\quad \dot{C}H_3 + (CH_3)_2O \xrightarrow{1'} CH_4 + \dot{C}H_2OCH_3.$

Here the rate ratios are initially

$$\frac{R(HCl)}{R \text{ (normal)}} \sim \frac{k_1(\dot{C}H_3)(HCl)}{k_1'(\dot{C}H_3)(Me_2O)} = \frac{k_1(HCl)}{k_1'(Me_2O)}. \qquad (4.127)$$

However, A_1 is about three-fold larger than A_1', but E_1 is only 2.5 kcal, as against 9.5 kcal for E_1', so that at 750°K the net acceleration at $(HCl) = (Me_2O)$ is about 300-fold. This effect is rapidly diminished as CH_4 accumulates, for it tends to compete with ether for Cl via Step 1. Including this in the rate expression yields

$$\frac{R(HCl)}{R \text{ (normal)}} = \frac{k_1(HCl)}{k_1'(Me_2O)[1 + k_{-1}(CH_4)/k_2(Me_2O)]}. \qquad (4.128)$$

[26] S. W. Benson and K. H. Anderson, *J. Chem. Phys.*, **39**, 1677 (1963).

Because k_{-1} and k_2 do not differ very much at 750°K, the initial acceleration by HCl is steadily diminished as CH_4 accumulates.

Such catalytic effects as those described above are very useful in providing a very important diagnostic tool for examining chains. In a number of instances *a priori* estimates are not sufficiently reliable to establish which of two chain steps is the faster in a simple scheme. Let us consider the Me_2O pyrolysis from this point of view.

The normal chain is

$$\dot{C}H_3 + CH_3OCH_3 \xrightarrow{1'} CH_4 + \dot{C}H_2OCH_3; \tag{4.129}$$

$$\dot{C}H_2OCH_3 \xrightarrow{2} CH_2O + \dot{C}H_3. $$

If no other reactions are important, the steady state ratio of $\cdot CH_2OCH_3$ to $\cdot CH_3$ is given by

$$\frac{(\dot{C}H_2OCH_3)}{(\dot{C}H_3)} = \frac{k_1'(Me_2O)}{k_2}. \tag{4.130}$$

The addition of HCl cannot affect the rate of the fission Step 2, but it can speed up the metathesis Step 1′. If it does, it effectively shifts the steady ratio in favor of higher $(\dot{C}H_2OCH)/(\dot{C}H_3)$ ratios by replacing $k_1'(Me_2O)$ in (4.130) by the much larger $k_1(HCl)$ (4.127). In the limit when this ratio is very large, there are relatively few $\dot{C}H_3$ radicals in the system, and termination is now predominantly by $\dot{C}H_2OCH_3$. Step 2 in the chain has now become the slow rate determining step. The time of the chain cycle is now effectively τ_2, whereas it was $\tau_1' + \tau_2$. The maximum acceleration in rate is

$$\frac{(\tau_1' + \tau_2)}{\tau_2} = 1 + \frac{\tau_1'}{\tau_2} \tag{4.131}$$

if we assume that termination rate constants are about the same for the two different radicals. Let us suppose that initially $\tau_1' \sim \tau_2$, implying that $(\dot{C}H_2OCH_3)/(\dot{C}H_3) \sim 1$. In such a case, the maximum acceleration we could observe would be a factor of 2.[27]

In the case of Me_2O small amounts of HCl produced ten-fold accelerations in the rate. This clearly signified that initially $\tau_1' \gg \tau_2$, so that $(\dot{C}H_2OCH_3) \ll (\dot{C}H_3)$, and consequently, $\dot{C}H_2OCH_3$ could be ignored in termination reactions. It also provided lower limits on a direct measure of the rate constant k_2, which was not otherwise measurable.

A similar study of the neopentane pyrolysis[28] showed that large accelerations in the initial rate could be produced by small amounts of HCl, again

[27] This clearly depends on CH_3OCH_3 concentration, by (4.128).
[28] S. W. Benson and K. C. Anderson, *J. Chem. Phys.*, **39**, 1677 (1963); **40**, 3747 (1964).

indicating that the pyrolytic step rate constant was much faster than the specific rate of the metathesis step. The mechanism is

Catalytic Transfer: Chain:

$$
\left\{
\begin{aligned}
&\cdot CH_3 + HCl \underset{}{\overset{1}{\rightleftharpoons}} CH_4 + Cl \\
&Cl + NpH \xrightarrow{2} HCl + N\dot{p} \\
&N\dot{p} \xrightarrow{3} (CH_3)_2C{=}CH_2 + \dot{C}H_3
\end{aligned}
\right.
\tag{4.132}
$$

and the conclusion was that $(N\dot{p}) \ll (\dot{C}H_3)$ and that $k_3 > k_1'(NpH)$ where k_1' is for the step

$$
CH_3 + NpH \xrightarrow{1'} CH_4 + N\dot{p}. \tag{4.133}
$$

A very substantial catalysis of many orders of magnitude is observed in the effect of HCl on the pyrolysis of peroxides. In the case of $t\text{-}Bu_2O_2$, very small amounts of HCl produce a catalytic effect independent of HCl and rapidly quenched by products.[29] The products are, in addition, altered:

$$
t\text{-}Bu_2O_2 \xrightarrow{i} 2t\text{-}Bu\dot{O},
$$

$$
t\text{-}Bu\dot{O} + HCl \xrightarrow{1} t\text{-}BuOH + Cl,
$$

$$
t\text{-}Bu\dot{O} \xrightarrow{2} CH_3COCH_3 + \dot{C}H_3,
$$

$$
Cl + t\text{-}Bu_2O_2 \xrightarrow{3} HCl + \dot{C}H_2C(CH_3)_2OO\text{-}t\text{-}Bu
$$

$$
\downarrow{\scriptstyle 4} \tag{4.134}
$$

$$
t\text{-}Bu\dot{O} + H_2C\overset{\displaystyle O}{\overbrace{\qquad}}C(Me)_2
$$

$$
\dot{C}H_3 + HCl \overset{5}{\rightleftharpoons} CH_4 + Cl,
$$

$$
Cl + CH_3COCH_3 \xrightarrow{t} HCl + \dot{C}H_2COCH_3,
$$

$$
2\dot{C}H_2COCH_3 \xrightarrow{t'} (CH_2COCH_3)_2.
$$

The $\dot{C}H_2COCH_3$ is essentially an inert radical in this system, incapable of reacting rapidly with HCl ($\Delta H_t^{\circ} \simeq 11$ kcal), and so can only terminate. In consequence Step t can be considered the virtual termination. The overall rate of pyrolysis becomes

$$
\frac{-d(t\text{-}Bu_2O_2)}{dt} = k_i(t\text{-}Bu_2O_2) + \frac{2k_3k_i(t\text{-}Bu_2O_2)^2}{k_t(CH_3COCH_3)}. \tag{4.135}
$$

Below 100°C only the second term in (4.135) is important. It is clearly an approximation that applies only after a few tenths of a percent of decomposition and above some small concentration of HCl, which can be $<10^{-3}$

[29] M. Flowers, L. Batt, and S. W. Benson, *J. Chem. Phys.*, **37**, 2662 (1962).

mole fraction. Because k_3 and k_t are comparable, the catalysis dies out very rapidly as CH_3COCH_3 approaches peroxide in concentration.

Equation (4.132) is also imprecise to the extent that it ignores contributions to "dead" radical production from the other products, isobutylene oxide and t-BuOH.

We can expect similar effects to those described above from HBr and H_2S for reactants that have weak C—H bonds. Thus HBr is a true catalyst for the gas phase oxidation of i-C_4H_{10}. The mechanism is[30]

$$t\text{-Bu}\cdot + O_2 \xrightarrow{\ 1\ } t\text{-BuO}_2\cdot,$$

$$t\text{-BuO}_2\cdot + HBr \underset{\longleftarrow}{\overset{2}{\rightleftharpoons}} t\text{-BuO}_2H + Br, \qquad (4.136)$$

$$Br + i\text{-}C_4H_{10} \underset{\longleftarrow}{\overset{3}{\rightleftharpoons}} t\text{-Bu} + HBr.$$

The rapid Reaction 1 keeps the t-Bu· concentration low and thereby inhibits the rapid back reaction, Step -3. Step 2 is exothermic by about 3 kcal, so that the equilibrium is well over toward t-BuO$_2$H at 150°C.

A similar behavior of H_2S has been explored in the case of Me_2O[31] and CH_3CHO.[32] The energetics of ·SH radical and Br· atom are very similar.

Species such as I_2 and HI, which were among the first catalysts to be investigated, operate essentially by altering the initiation mechanism and increasing the radical supply, as well as changing the chain. In the case of I_2 catalyzed decomposition of H_2CO, for example,[33] the I_2 is almost instantaneously consumed to form an I_2–HI mixture, and the remaining small concentration of I_2 reacts as follows:

$$I_2 \underset{\longleftarrow}{\overset{1}{\rightleftharpoons}} 2I \quad \text{(rapid, equilibrium)},$$

$$I + H_2CO \underset{\longleftarrow}{\overset{2}{\rightleftharpoons}} HI + H\dot{C}O,$$

$$H\dot{C}O + I_2 \xrightarrow{\ 3\ } HICO + I,$$

$$HICO \xrightarrow[\text{(wall?)}]{} HI + CO,$$

$$2HI \longrightarrow H_2 + I_2.$$

$$(4.137)$$

In this system catalysis can only occur if the temperature is sufficiently high ($>350°C$), so that the HI reaction can regenerate I_2. A similarly complex mechanism is found to be operative in the I_2-catalyzed pyrolysis of CH_3CHO.

---

[30] F. F. Rust and W. E. Vaughn, *Ind. Eng. Chem.*, **41**, 2595 (1949).
[31] N. Imai and O. Toyama, *Bull. Chem. Soc. Japan*, **34**, 328 (1961).
[32] N. Imai and O. Toyama, *Bull. Chem. Soc. Japan*, **33**, 1120, 1408 (1960).
[33] R. F. Faull and G. K. Rollefson, *J. Am. Chem. Soc.*, **58**, 1755 (1936); **59**, 625 (1937). See also R. Walsh and S. W. Benson, *J. Am. Chem. Soc.*, **88**, 4570 (1966).

4.17   HOMOGENEOUS CATALYTIC RECOMBINATION

An unusual instance of catalysis occurs in the recombination reactions involving atoms and small radicals. Reactions, such as $H + H \rightarrow H_2$ or $O + NO \rightarrow NO_2$, all require third bodies to remove the energy, and hence are termolecular. This makes them fairly slow reactions compared to recombinations of larger radicals, such as $2Me \rightarrow C_2H_6$. At 1 atm pressure the termolecular recombination rates are about one-twenty-fifth that of the bimolecular recombinations, and this factor increases proportionately with the reciprocal pressure. At 1 torr, the ratio is about $10^{-4.3}$.

Such termolecular recombination can be speeded up by suitable catalysts C, which can engage in the following cycle:

$$\text{Chain recombination:} \quad \left\{ \begin{array}{l} X + \dot{C} \underset{}{\overset{1}{\rightleftharpoons}} CX^* \\ CX^* + M \overset{2}{\longrightarrow} CX + M; \\ X + CX \overset{3}{\longrightarrow} X_2 + C \end{array} \right. \qquad (4.138)$$

Net reaction: $\qquad\qquad 2X \longrightarrow X_2.$

The requirements that such a catalyst be effective are that k_3, the metathesis step, be fast (that is, have a low activation energy) and that the lifetime of the hot species, CX^*, be sufficiently long under the ambient conditions that a reasonable fraction of them be stabilized by collisional deactivation (Step 2).

Analysis[34] has shown that above $1000°K$, $\dot{C}H_3$ can act as an extremely effective catalyst for H atom recombination. At room temperature almost any hydrocarbon, ketone, or aldehyde, can perform a similar role. Thus 0.1 mole percent of acetone in H atoms can increase the effective recombination rate at 1 torr total pressure by a factor of about 100-fold. Such effects suggest that impurities can be very important in systems containing H atoms.

NO_2 plays a similar, but less spectacular, role in catalyzing the recombination of O atoms via

$$O + NO_2 \rightarrow O_2 + NO,$$
$$O + NO + M \rightarrow NO_2 + M. \qquad (4.139)$$

O_2 appears to do something comparable in the recombination of Cl atoms, the mechanism being

$$Cl + O_2 + M \rightleftharpoons Cl\dot{O}O + M,$$
$$Cl + Cl\dot{O}O \rightarrow Cl_2 + O_2. \qquad (4.140)$$

[34] S. W. Benson, *J. Chem. Phys.*, **38**, 2285 (1963).

An interesting consequence of such catalysis as those described above is observed in the pyrolysis of N_2O. The initial step is the production of O atoms by direct split:

$$N_2O \xrightarrow{\ i\ } N_2 + O. \tag{4.141}$$

In the initial stages of the reaction, this is followed by secondary attack of the O on N_2O, leading to

$$
\begin{array}{c}
2NO \\[6pt]
N_2O + O \\[6pt]
N_2 + O_2
\end{array}
\tag{4.142}
$$

Both of these paths have about the same rate constants, and the initial stoichiometry is 2 moles of N_2O decomposed for each O atom produced.[35] However, both these secondary reactions are quickly arrested by the catalytic effect of NO in decreasing the O atom concentration (4.139), and the apparent rate of decomposition of N_2O falls by a factor of 2 as the stoichiometry changes to 1 mole N_2O per O atom produced. If NO is added initially, no further NO is produced, and the stoichiometry remains constant at unity, all the O atoms going to O_2 via $NO–NO_2$ catalysis.

4.18   ISOMERIZATION STEPS IN CHAINS

Radicals containing more than two polyvalent atoms may in principle isomerize by a unimolecular process. This can take the form of atom abstraction, cyclization, displacement, or our already discussed fission reaction. We may expect that our usual rules apply to these steps. For example, we do not expect to find displacements to occur at saturated C, N, or O atoms, except with very large activation energies, and we may expect to find the activation energies for atom abstraction to parallel those for the more usual bimolecular metatheses.

A new feature of these unimolecular processes is that they must go through a cyclic transition state and hence, should have low A factors, depending on the number of hindered internal rotations, which become inhibited by the ring formation. In addition, ring formation involves strain energy, and we should expect to see this reflected in correspondingly higher activation energies. As an example, we should expect those processes to be the fastest that involve the formation of strain-free, six-membered rings. Five- and

---

[35] F. Kaufman, *Progress in Reaction Kinetics*, **1**, 1 (1961).

seven-membered rings have about 7 kcal of strain, and these should be less favorable by this amount. Four- and three-membered rings have strain energies of about 27 kcal for atoms from the second row of the periodic table, and this should make such transition states extremely rare.

In line with such expectations as those presented above are the observations that internal H-atom abstraction occurs with facility between carbon atoms n and $n + 5$ in alkyl radicals, and more slowly between $n \leftrightarrow n + 4$ and $n \leftrightarrow n + 6$. n-butyl radicals can exchange D atoms via such a path:

$$
CD_3CH_2CH_2\dot{C}H_2 \quad\quad\quad\quad \dot{C}D_2CH_2CH_2CH_2D
$$

$$
CD_3\dot{C}H_2 + C_2H_4 \quad \left[\begin{array}{cc} \overset{\displaystyle D}{\underset{\displaystyle CH_2-CH_2}{CD_2}} & \overset{\displaystyle \cdot}{CH_2} \end{array} \right]^{\ddagger} \quad CD_2{=}CH_2 + \dot{C}H_2CH_2D.
$$

$$(4.143)$$

Such a 1-4 shift has been observed in n-pentyl radicals:[36]

$$
\begin{array}{l}
\dot{C}H_3 + C_2H_4 \rightarrow n\,\dot{C}_3H_7 \\
\dot{C}_3H_7 + C_2H_4 \rightarrow n\,\dot{C}_5H_{11} \rightleftharpoons
\end{array}
\left[\begin{array}{cc} & \overset{\displaystyle H}{} \\ \dot{C}H_2 & CH_2-CH_2 \\ \underset{\displaystyle CH_2-CH_2}{\searrow} & \nearrow \end{array} \right]^{\ddagger}
$$

$$(4.144)$$

$$
\dot{C}_2H_5 + C_3H_6 \leftarrow CH_3-CH_2-CH_2-\dot{C}H-CH_3
$$

No evidence exists for 1,2 or 1,3 H atom shifts in alkyl radicals.

The isomerization of i-propyl radical to i-propyl radical would have to take place via a three-membered ring:

$$
\dot{C}H_2-CH_2-CH_3 \rightleftharpoons \left[\overset{\displaystyle H}{\underset{\displaystyle CH_2-CH-CH_3}{}} \right]^{\ddagger} \rightleftharpoons CH_3-\dot{C}H-CH_3. \quad (4.145)
$$

If this ring has the same strain energy as cyclopropane or ethylene oxide, namely 27 kcal, and the normal activation energy for such abstraction is about 8 kcal (for example, $\cdot C_2H_5$ abstracting secondary H atoms), we might expect a net activation energy of about 35 kcal. The A factor should be about $10^{12.5}$ sec^{-1} because we are losing a low barrier, $\cdot CH_2$ hindered rotation. The competing steps could be external H-atom abstraction, recombination, or elimination of CH_3. This latter has an A factor of about $10^{13.8}$ sec^{-1} and an activation energy of 33 kcal; thus it would be about 30 to 100 times faster at most temperatures, and we would not expect to see such isomerizations.

[36] A. S. Gordon and J. R. McNesby, *J. Chem. Phys.*, **31**, 853 (1959); **33**, 1882 (1960); L. Endrenyi and D. L. LeRoy, *J. Phys. Chem.*, **70**, 4081 (1966).

The same analysis and conclusions made above should also extend to the n-butyl radical, which could only isomerize by a 1,2, or a 1,3 atom abstraction. The four-membered ring has only 1 kcal less strain than the three-membered ring, and the A factor should be lower by another factor of 5 because it involves loss of an additional hindered rotor.

It has been shown by isotope labeling experiments that the exothermic ($\Delta H^0 = -3.5$ kcal) isomerization of n-butyl radical to s-butyl radical must have an activation energy in excess of 36 kcal to account for the absence of s-butyl products.[37]

In surprising contrast to the result above, a considerable body of evidence has accumulated to indicate that Cl atoms can undergo 1,2 transfer in radicals. Thus the radical addition of Br_2 to trichloropropene leads to rearranged product[38]

$$Br + CH_2\!\!=\!\!CH\!-\!CCl_3 \rightleftarrows BrCH_2\!-\!\dot{C}H\!-\!CCl_3$$

$$CH_2Br\!-\!CHCl\!-\!CCl_2Br \xleftarrow{Br_2} BrCH_2\!-\!\dot{C}HCl\!-\!\dot{C}Cl_2$$

$$(4.146)$$

The C—Cl bond in these radicals is only about 16 kcal, so that it is not impossible that the abstraction takes place via dissociation in a solvent cage, followed by readdition of the Cl atom to the short-lived olefin. It would require an activation energy at least this small to account for the results. By way of partial explanation, however, it is observed that third row atoms, like S, have strain energies in three- and four-membered rings about 8 kcal lower than that for second row atoms.

Another piece of evidence on H atom internal abstraction comes from data on the biradicals produced in cyclopropane pyrolysis. Analysis of this data has shown that the 1,2 H-atom shift in the trimethylene radical, which produces C_3H_6 with $\Delta H^0 = -62$ kcal, has an activation energy of 11 kcal and the expected A factor of about 10^{13} sec^{-1}. The driving force for the reaction is the double bond formation, and it appears from the low activation energy as though it is about 40% developed in the transition state:

$$(4.147)$$

[37] A. S. Gordon and J. R. McNesby, *J. Chem. Phys.*, **33**, 1882 (1960).
[38] A. N. Nesmeyanov, R. K. Freidlina, and V. N. Kost, *Tetrahedron Letters*, **1**, 241 (1957).

Oxidation of hydrocarbons in the liquid state provides a very interesting example of internal H-atom abstraction. In the sensitized oxidation of 2,4-dimethyl pentane,[39] it is observed that very high yields of a di-OOH are formed. The mechanism is

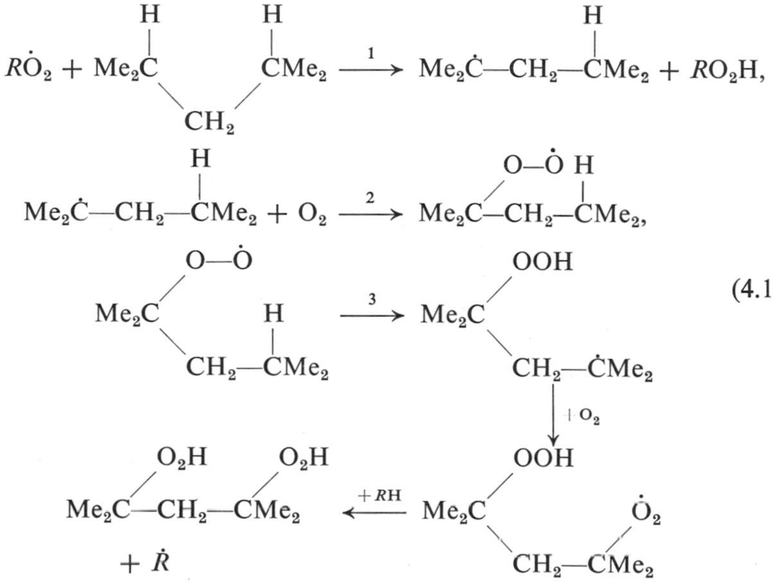

$$(4.148)$$

Here a six-membered ring is involved, so that the activation energies for internal and external abstraction should be equal. The A factor for internal abstraction involves tightening of three internal rotors and therefore should be about 10^{11} sec^{-1}, which is still larger than the expected $10^{8.5}$ (RH) for external abstraction even in pure liquid where $(RH) = 10$ M. If the isomer 2,3-dimethyl pentane is used, then only mono-hydroperoxide is produced in agreement with our simple expectation of an additional 7 kcal activation energy for H atom abstraction in the five-membered ring. A faster process would involve H-atom abstraction via a six-membered ring, but this is about 3 kcal endothermic, compared to tertiary H-atom abstraction, and might have an activation energy 4 kcal higher. This would make it about five-fold slower than external abstraction at 150°C, and there is some evidence for comparable amounts of such a product with the isomeric hydrocarbon.

It is interesting to consider, in the light of this analysis, a commonly assumed reaction of alkyl radicals with O_2:

$$R\dot{C}H_2 + O_2 \rightarrow RCHO + \dot{O}H. \qquad (4.149)$$

[39] F. F. Rust, *J. Am. Chem. Soc.*, **79**, 4000 (1957).

Such a reaction is about 57 kcal exothermic. However, it must proceed via the peroxy intermediate with liberation of about 29 kcal:

$$R\dot{C}H_2 + O_2 \rightleftarrows (RCH_2O\dot{O})^* + 29 \text{ kcal.} \qquad (4.150)$$

The peroxy radical would then rearrange to a hydroperoxyl radical via a four-membered ring:

$$RCH_2O\dot{O} \rightleftarrows \left[\begin{array}{c} RCH-O. \\ \cdot \quad \quad O \\ H \quad \cdot \end{array} \right]^{\ddagger} \rightleftarrows R\dot{C}HO_2H. \qquad (4.151)$$

This reaction is about 3.5 kcal endothermic and would have an estimated activation energy of about 26 (strain energy) + 7 (normal abstractions) + 3.5 (endothermicity) = 36.5 kcal. The initial excitation is insufficient to provide this, so the reaction rate should not be faster for the initially hot radical, which will instead be rapidly thermalized.

However, if the hydroperoxy radical is formed, we may expect a rapid, exothermic fission into $\dot{O}H + RCHO$ ($\Delta H^0 \sim -26$ kcal). This step should still have some small activation energy (~ 5 kcal). We thus see that despite the large exothermicity of the radical oxidation, the overall rate is expected to be negligibly slow, for it has to proceed as a bimolecular reaction with about 40 kcal of activation energy.[40] There is, in fact, very little experimental evidence for this step.

About the first investigators to suggest the importance of internal abstraction in hydrocarbon pyrolyses were Rice and Kossiakoff,[41] who showed that in the pyrolysis of long chain hydrocarbons, $C_{16}H_{34}$, etc., the product distribution was in reasonable accord with a statistical abstraction of secondary H atoms, followed by very rapid isomerization equilibrium via H-atom abstraction across mainly six-, but also five- and seven-membered rings. At pyrolysis temperatures of 700 to 1100°K, these isomerizations are indeed rapid, compared to competing bimolecular and fission steps.

There is one point worth emphasizing in regard to these internal rearrangements described above. Generally, only exothermic processes ($\Delta H_r < 0$) are important. The reason for this is that any endothermic process always has a reverse rate, which is exothermic, and hence, faster by the factor $10^{-\Delta H_r/\theta}$. Thus, if we consider the endothermic reaction

$$CH_3CH_2CH_2O\dot{O} \rightleftarrows \dot{C}H_2CH_2CH_2O_2H, \qquad (4.152)$$

the reverse reaction is exothermic by about 8 kcal and hence faster by about 10^3 at 600°K. The result is a negligible steady state concentration of the

---

[40] Note also that the competing step is redissociation back into $O_2 + R\dot{C}H_2$ with a lower activation energy and a higher A factor.

[41] A. Kossiakoff and F. O. Rice, *J. Am. Chem. Soc.*, **65**, 590 (1943).

endothermic species. We may make a general rule that we expect internal rearrangements to be significant only if the reaction is exothermic or nearly thermoneutral.

4.19 HOT MOLECULE REACTIONS

Many chain reactions are exothermic. This means that one or more of the chain propagation steps must reflect this exothermicity and hence produce radical or molecule species which jointly contain this heat of reaction. If the exothermic step had an activation energy in addition, this too must appear in the product species. The following are some representative, fairly exothermic steps:

$$H + Cl_2 \xrightarrow{1} HCl + Cl + 44 \text{ kcal},$$

$$H + F_2 \xrightarrow{2} HF + F + 96 \text{ kcal},$$

$$O + O_3 \xrightarrow{3} 2O_2 + 93 \text{ kcal},$$

$$H + C_2\dot{H}_4 \xrightarrow{4} C_2H_5 + 39 \text{ kcal},$$

$$\dot{C}H_2CH_2C\dot{H}_2 \xrightarrow{5} CH_3CH=CH_2 + 62 \text{ kcal}, \qquad (4.153)$$

$$2CH_3\dot{O} \xrightarrow{6} CH_2O + CH_3OH + 80 \text{ kcal},$$

$$O + NO_2 \xrightarrow{7} O_2 + NO + 46 \text{ kcal},$$

$$H + NO_2 \xrightarrow{8} OH + NO + 30 \text{ kcal},$$

$$H + O_3 \xrightarrow{9} OH + O_2 + 77 \text{ kcal}.$$

The energy of the reaction can be distributed among all of the degrees of freedom of the products, including translation, vibration, rotation, and electronic. Recent studies of excited HCl produced in Step 1, show that up to 90% of the heat of the reaction can appear in vibrational excitation.[42] This is, however, rare and typically most of the energy is in translation. The principle of detailed balancing then implies that in the reverse endothermic process, the maximum contribution to the reaction comes from translationally excited species. This is not an especially surprising result, for translational energy is rapidly partitioned among molecules, whereas vibrational energy exchanges only very slowly with translational and rotational modes.

[42] J. C. Polanyi, *J. Quant. Spec. Radiat. Trans.*, **3**, 471 (1963). Th HBr* case is discussed in J. R. Airey, P. D. Pacey, and J. C. Polanyi, *Eleventh Int. Symp. on Comb.*, **85**, Combustion Institute, Pittsburgh, 1967.

There is another way of appreciating the result described above, from a molecular point of view. If all of the activation energy of the Cl + HCl reaction ($\sim$46 kcal) were in the H–Cl vibration, conservation of momentum dictates that the H atom has $(1 - 1/35.5) \approx 97\%$ of it because of its light mass. However, the new bond to be formed is between the two Cl atoms, and if there is no relative kinetic energy in the Cl—Cl collision, it is hard to understand how they can approach closely enough to deform their electron shells and form the new bond.

On this basis, we expect translational energy to provide most of the activation energy source for bimolecular events. Even more rare will be the conversion of the energy into electronic energy which may then appear as chemiluminescence. This appears to happen in the case of the disproportionation of two $CH_3O \cdot$ radicals (Step 6), which can give rise to excited CH_2O and a blue luminescence. With electronic excitation, the reason for the low probability is (aside from the lack of availability of sufficiently low-lying electronic energy levels for most stable molecules), the low *a priori* probability for such a concentration of energy. The degeneracies of translation, vibration, and rotational energy states are quite large, relative to electronic states.

The translationally excited species produced in exothermic reactions can have abnormally high probabilities for bimolecular reaction and thus give rise to what can appear to be an abnormal rate constant. Such effects arise, typically, in photolysis reactions which fragment bonds. Thus, the H—I photolysis at 2537 Å gives rise to an H atom with 99.2% of the excess energy of the reaction, namely 41 kcal. It is abnormally reactive.

When the step reaction is an association or is a unimolecular isomerization, all of the excess energy is localized in the vibrational modes of the product. The unimolecular isomerization of cyclopropane to propylene is a good example. The reaction is 7.5 kcal exothermic and has an activation energy of 65 kcal. Hence the product C_3H_6 molecules are formed with an excess internal energy of 72.5 kcal.[43] This qualifies them as hot molecules. This energy will be dissipated in consecutive collisions, but it can also participate in other competitive internal reactions. As an example, the isomerization of methyl cyclopropane produces butene-2 molecules with virtually the same 72 kcal excess energy. Because the cis-trans isomerization of butene-2 requires only 63 kcal (Table 3.4) of activation energy, we might expect to obtain cis-trans equilibrium in this pyrolysis. This is not the case (Table 3.7). The cis is produced about twice as fast as the thermodynamically more stable trans. This implies that collisional deactivation is faster than reaction of the hot species.

[43] This is above the normal thermal energy that they already have at the reaction temperature, $E_v = \int_0^{T_c} C_{\text{vib.}} \, dT$.

We can use the RRK theory to make a rough estimate of the result described above. The rate of reaction of the hot cis species will be given by

$$k_{c \to t} = A \left(\frac{E - E^*}{E} \right)^{s-1} \tag{4.154}$$

$$= 10^{13.8} \left(\frac{E - 63}{E} \right)^{s-1} \sec^{-1}. \tag{4.155}$$

when the A factor and activation energy are for the high-pressure reaction parameters (Table 3.4). The thermal energy is estimated from

$$\int_0^{800} (C_p - 8) \, dt = E_{th.} = 10.5 \text{ kcal}$$

with C_p taken from our tables (Appendix A-1). The molecule C_4H_8 has thirty internal modes of which we can take $\frac{2}{3} = 20$, or more accurately use $S_{eff.} = (C_p - 8)/R = 15$ at $700°K$. Then, with $E = \Delta H^0 + E_{th.}$, we have

$$k_{c \to t} = 10^{13.8} (\tfrac{20}{83})^{14} \approx 10^{5.4} \sec^{-1}. \tag{4.156}$$

This is so very slow compared to collision frequencies even at 1 torr ($10^7 \sec^{-1}$) that we can conclude there is no significant effect of the excess energy.

An entirely different case is presented by the pyrolysis of ethylene oxide, isoelectronic with cyclopropane. We can expect a parallel mechanism of decomposition to acetaldehyde, which is in fact, observed:

$$\overset{\lceil \qquad \qquad \rceil}{CH_2 - CH_2 - O} \rightleftarrows \cdot CH_2 - CH_2 - O \cdot \rightarrow CH_3 - CHO^*. \tag{4.157}$$

The overall reaction has $\Delta H^0 = -28$ kcal/mole, and an observed activation energy of 57 kcal. The product CH_3CHO is thus excited by 85 kcal of excess energy, and because ΔH^0 for decomposition to $\cdot CH_3 + \dot{C}HO$ radicals is 82 kcal[44] at $700°K$, we can write

$$k(CH_3CHO^*) \simeq 10^{16} \left(\frac{10.5}{90} \right)^9 \sim 10^{7.5} \sec^{-1} \tag{4.158}$$

where $E_{th.} \sim 5$ kcal and $S_{eff.} \sim 10$, $S_{max} = 3n - 6 = 15$. Assuming a deactivation efficiency of $\frac{1}{3}$, we can estimate that half of the CH_3CHO^* will decompose at 10 torr and only 5% at 1 atmosphere, in good agreement with observation (Reference 12, Table 3.7). At 1 atmosphere, about 10% of the product species are dissociated into radicals.

Comparable types of reactions are seen in photochemical systems where recombinations can produce excited species with sufficient energy to undergo

---

[44] We actually use $\Delta E^0 - RT$ instead of ΔH^0 on the assumption that the mean rotational energy of RT is effectively utilized in bond breaking.

further reaction. The recombination of two $\cdot CH_2I$ radicals will be about 88 kcal exothermic and produce hot $C_2H_4I_2$, which requires only 36 kcal to split into I_2 and C_2H_4.

$$k(C_2H_4I_2^*) = 10^{13.5}(\tfrac{52}{88})^{13} \approx 10^{10.9} \text{ sec}^{-1} \qquad (4.159)$$

where we have neglected the very small amount of thermal energy. Decomposition is about 20 times faster than collision at 1 atmosphere, so we can anticipate almost nothing but $I_2 + C_2H_4$ as products of the recombination. Similar effects have been observed with the recombination of $\cdot CH_3 + \cdot CH_2Cl$, $2 \cdot CH_2Cl$, and $\cdot CHCl_2 + \cdot CH_3$, and the corresponding fluoro radicals, all of which have enough excess energy to split out $HF + \text{olefin}$ in the range $300°K$ to $500°K$.[45]

Even more energetic species are obtained from the carbenes (CH_2, etc.) and isoelectronic O-atom reactions. A typical CH_2 reaction is addition to a double bond. The reaction of CH_2 with C_2H_4 leads to hot trimethylene, or hot cyclopropane. The latter has 89 kcal of excess energy calculated for ground state (triplet) CH_2. Because only 65 kcal are required for chemical isomerization to propylene, we can write (at $300°K$)

$$k(c\text{-}C_3H_6^*) \simeq 10^{15.2}(\tfrac{24}{89})^{s-1} \text{ sec}^{-1}. \qquad (4.160)$$

To estimate $S_{\text{eff.}}$, we must calculate it for a temperature at which the internal energy would be 24 kcal. This is given approximately by the temperature T where

$$\int_0^T (C_p - 8)\, dT \sim 24 \text{ kcal.}$$

At $1500°K$

$$\int_0^T (C_p - 8)\, dT \simeq 18 \text{ kcal,} \qquad \text{and} \qquad (C_p - 8)/R \simeq 17.$$

Thus it seems reasonable to use $S_{\text{eff.}} = 3n - 6 = 21$.

$$k \sim 10^{15.2}\left(\frac{1}{3.65}\right)^{20} \approx 10^{3.6} \text{ sec}^{-1}. \qquad (4.161)$$

It is interesting to make a calculation similar to that made above for the cis-trans isomerization of dimethyl cyclopropane, produced by the addition of CH_2 to cis-butene-2. The reaction is about 89 kcal exothermic and the Arrhenius parameters from Table 3.7 give (using $S_{\text{eff.}} = \tfrac{2}{3}S_{\text{max.}} = 26$)

$$k(\Delta)^* = 10^{15.25}(\tfrac{30}{89})^{25}$$

$$\approx 10^{3.2} \text{ sec}^{-1}, \qquad (4.162)$$

[45] S. W. Benson and G. R. Haugen, *J. Phys. Chem.*, **69**, 3898 (1965).

so that isomerization should be almost negligibly small compared to quenching in either gas or liquid states. The implication of this calculation is that any observed isomerization in the system cannot come after the ring has formed. It has to come, instead, from an initially open biradical with 38 kcal of excess energy and with three competing paths open to it: rotation to produce geometric isomer, ring closing to form cyclopropane, and H migration to yield 2-methyl butenes-1 (or 2). The relative rates for rotation $R_{rot.}$, for example, relative to ring closure $R_{(c.)}$ is

$$\frac{R_{(c)}}{R_{(rot.)}} = \frac{10^{13.5}}{10^{11.5}}\left(\frac{38-10}{38-5}\right)^{38} \approx 10^{2.0-2.6} \approx \frac{1}{4},$$ (4.163)

so that, depending on the rate of quenching and the precise energy of the system, we get varying amounts of isomerization. These calculations militate very strongly against the initial formation of a ring compound. They do not rule out triplet state intervention, which would also lead only to biradical, however.

4.20 REACTIONS OF OZONE WITH OLEFINS

The amazing and not too stable compound O_3, undergoes very unusual reactions of addition to olefins, both at low temperatures ($-70°C$) in non-polar solvents and also at higher temperatures in the gas phase. Many of the adducts of such reactions are quite stable species, but show the unexpected structure

$$R \atop R' \Big\rangle C{=}C\Big\langle {R \atop R'} \quad + O_3 \quad \rightarrow \quad R \atop R' \Big\rangle C\underset{O-O}{\overset{O}{\diamond}} C\Big\langle {R \atop R'} .$$ (4.164)

The unusual finding is that there has been a scission of the $C{=}C$ double bond. Let us consider these reactions from an energetic point of view. For the simplest olefin, $C_2H_4 + O_3$, the production of the expected product would be 45 kcal exothermic:

$$O_3 + C_2H_4 \rightarrow \underset{O\quad\quad O}{\overset{O}{\diamond}}{CH_2{-}CH_2} + 45 \pm 6 \text{ kcal.}$$ (4.165)

This is a sufficiently energetic reaction to produce a consequently "hot" species. However, even if this initial hot adduct is stabilized, the energy to open the ring and form the peroxy biradical is only 13 ± 2 kcal. Even at $-70°$ with $\theta = 0.92$ kcal, the half-life for ring opening with an estimated A factor of $10^{14.5}$ sec^{-1} is ~0.1 sec:

$$
\underset{CH_2-CH_2}{\overset{\displaystyle O}{\diagup\diagdown}} \rightleftarrows \quad \underset{CH_2-CH_2\dot{O}}{\overset{\displaystyle \cdot O}{\diagdown}} \tag{4.166}
$$

A secondary split into two fragments has an enthalpy change ≤ 23 kcal, the upper limit being set by the assumption of no interaction energy aside from σ bonding in the biradical:

$$
\overset{\cdot O}{\underset{CH_2-CH_2\dot{O}}{\diagdown}} \rightarrow CH_2{=}O + \dot{C}H_2-O-\dot{O} \; (?). \tag{4.167}
$$

If the biradical has the structure of an aldehyde-oxide, the reaction above is actually more than 9 kcal exothermic:

$$
\overset{\cdot O}{\underset{CH_2-CH_2\dot{O}}{\diagdown}} \rightarrow CH_2-O + CH_2{=}O \rightarrow 0 + >9 \text{ kcal.} \tag{4.168}
$$

The formation of such a pair of species in a cage would now begin to make sense of the subsequent reactions of true ozonide formation and exchange of species with dissolved aldehydes or ketones.

$\dot{O}O-CH_2-CH_2\dot{O}$

$$
\begin{array}{c}
\overset{O}{\underset{\diagup}{\nearrow}} \\
O\diagdown\diagdown \\
\rightleftarrows CH_2 + CH_2{=}O \xrightarrow[\longleftarrow]{(+CH_3CHO)} CH_2O + CH_2 \quad \overset{O}{\diagup\diagdown}CHCH_3 \\
\underset{CH_2}{\overset{O}{\diagup}} \quad \underset{O-O}{CH_2} \leftarrow \dot{C}H_2-O-O-CH_2-\dot{O} \qquad O-O
\end{array} \tag{4.169}
$$

The overall rearrangement of initial trioxacyclopentane to true ozonide is exothermic by an estimated 61 kcal, so that the entire reaction starting with

$C_2H_4 + O_3$ is exothermic by 106 kcal/mole! The ozonide is now capable of a further ring opening to form biradicals with an estimated activation energy of $\sim$30 kcal. Such a reaction, however, leads to no net products without a further split into the dioxo biradicals:

$$\underset{\substack{CH_2 \\ \diagdown \\ O\!-\!O}}{\overset{\substack{O \\ \diagup\diagdown}}{\diagup}}\!\!CH_2 \rightleftarrows \underset{\substack{CH_2 \\ \diagdown \\ O\ \ O}}{\overset{\substack{O \\ \diagup\diagdown}}{\diagup}}\!\!CH_2 \rightleftarrows \underset{\substack{CH_2 \\ \diagdown \\ O\cdot}}{\overset{\substack{CH_2 \\ O\cdotO}}{\diagup}}\!\!\overset{O\ (\sim 0)}{\underset{}{}} + CH_2\!\!=\!\!O. \qquad (4.170)$$

At the moment we can only speculate about the existence of the aldehyde oxide species, but there is evidence from the chain oxidation of C_2F_4 to indicate that the active chain carrier is $CF_2\!\!=\!\!O \rightarrow O$; furthermore, recently a very stable diperoxide has been obtained from the photolysis of diphenyl ketene in O_2:[46]

$$\phi_2C\!\!=\!\!C\!\!=\!\!O + h\nu \rightarrow \phi_2C\!: + CO,$$

$$\phi_2C\!: + O_2 \rightarrow \phi_2C\!\!=\!\!O \rightarrow O,$$

$$2\phi_2C\!\!=\!\!O \rightarrow O \rightarrow \phi_2C\underset{\substack{\diagdown \\ O\!-\!O}}{\overset{\substack{O\!-\!O \\ \diagup}}{}}C\phi_2. \qquad (4.171)$$

Despite the weak peroxide linkage, this turns out to be a very stable peroxide, for a second, fairly energetic bond has to be ruptured before a net reaction can occur:

$$\phi_2C\underset{\substack{\diagdown \\ O\!-\!O}}{\overset{\substack{O\!-\!O \\ \diagup}}{}}C\phi_2 \rightleftarrows \phi_2C\underset{\substack{\diagdown \\ O\ \cdot O}}{\overset{\substack{O\!-\!O \\ \diagup}}{}}C\phi_2 \rightarrow \phi_2C\underset{\substack{\diagdown \\ O\!-\!\dot{O}}}{\overset{\substack{\dot{O} \\ \diagup}}{}} + O\!\!=\!\!C\phi_2.$$

$$\downarrow$$
$$\phi_2C\dot{O} + O_2$$

The overall activation energy can be in excess of 45 kcal/mole.

[46] P. D. Bartlett and T. G. Traylor, *J. Am. Chem. Soc.*, **84**, 3408 (1962).

Appendix: Tables

The following data all (unless otherwise noted) refer to standard states of ideal gas at 1 atmosphere and 25°C. Data sources will be found in the *A.P.I.* Tables, N.B.S. Circular 270-1, and *JANAF* Tables. Units are kcal/mole for ΔH_f° and gibbs/mole for S° and C_p°.

Further discussion of the sources of the data and limits of reliability will be found in S. W. Benson et. al., Chem. Rev. **68,** in press (1968).

Table A.1 Group Values for ΔH_f°, S°, and C_p°. Hydrocarbons

Group	ΔH_f° 298	S° 298	C_p°						
			300	400	500	600	800	1000	1500
C—(H)$_3$(C)	−10.08	30.41	6.19	7.84	9.40	10.79	13.02	14.77	17.58
C—(H)$_2$(C)$_2$	−4.95	9.42	5.50	6.95	8.25	9.35	11.07	12.34	14.25
C—(H)(C)$_3$	−1.90	−12.07	4.54	6.00	7.17	8.05	9.31	10.05	11.17
C—(C)$_4$	0.50	−35.10	4.37	6.13	7.36	8.12	8.77	8.76	8.12
C$_d$—(H)$_2$	6.26	27.61	5.10	6.36	7.51	8.50	10.07	11.27	13.19
C$_d$—(H)(C)	8.59	7.97	4.16	5.03	5.81	6.50	7.65	8.45	9.62
C$_d$—(C)$_2$	10.34	−12.70	4.10	4.61	4.99	5.26	5.80	6.08	6.36
C$_d$—(C$_d$)(H)	6.78	6.38	4.46	5.79	6.75	7.42	8.35	8.99	9.98
C$_d$—(C$_d$)(C)	8.88	−14.6	(4.40)	(5.37)	(5.93)	(6.18)	(6.50)	(6.62)	(6.72)
[C$_d$—(C$_B$)(H)]	6.78	6.38	4.46	5.79	6.75	7.42	8.35	8.99	9.98
C$_d$—(C$_B$)(C)	8.64	(−14.6)	(4.40)	(5.37)	(5.93)	(6.18)	(6.50)	(6.62)	(6.72)
[C$_d$—(C$_t$)(H)]	6.78	6.38	4.46	5.79	6.75	7.42	8.35	8.99	9.98
C—(C$_d$)(C)(H)$_2$	−4.76	9.80	5.12	6.86	8.32	9.49	11.22	12.48	14.36
C—(C$_d$)$_2$(H)$_2$	−4.29	(10.2)	(4.7)	(6.8)	(8.4)	(9.6)	(11.3)	(12.6)	(14.4)
C—(C$_d$)(C$_B$)(H)$_2$	−4.29	(10.2)	(4.7)	(6.8)	(8.4)	(9.6)	(11.3)	(12.6)	(14.4)
C—(C$_t$)(C)(H)$_2$	−4.73	10.30	4.95	6.56	7.93	9.08	10.86	12.19	14.20
C—(C$_B$)(C)(H)$_2$	−4.86	9.34	5.84	7.61	8.98	10.01	11.49	12.54	13.76
C—(C$_d$)(C)$_2$(H)	−1.48	(−11.69)	(4.16)	(5.91)	(7.34)	(8.19)	(9.46)	(10.19)	(11.28)
C—(C$_t$)(C)$_2$(H)	−1.72	(−11.19)	(3.99)	(5.61)	(6.85)	(7.78)	(9.10)	(9.90)	(11.12)
C—(C$_B$)(C)$_2$(H)	−0.98	(−12.15)	(4.88)	(6.66)	(7.90)	(8.75)	(9.73)	(10.25)	(10.68)
C—(C$_d$)(C)$_3$	1.68	(−34.72)	(3.99)	(6.04)	(7.43)	(8.26)	(8.92)	(8.96)	(8.23)
C—(C$_B$)(C)$_3$	2.81	(−35.18)	(4.37)	(6.79)	(8.09)	(8.78)	(9.19)	(8.96)	(7.63)
C$_t$—(H)	26.93	24.7	5.27	5.99	6.49	6.87	7.47	7.96	8.85
C$_t$—(C)	27.55	6.35	3.13	3.48	3.81	4.09	4.60	4.92	6.35
C$_t$—(C$_d$)	29.20	(6.43)	(2.57)	(3.54)	(3.50)	(4.92)	(5.34)	(5.50)	(5.80)
C$_t$—(C$_B$)	(29.20)	6.43	2.57	3.54	3.50	4.92	5.34	5.50	5.80
C$_B$—(H)	3.30	11.53	3.24	4.44	5.46	6.30	7.54	8.41	9.73
C$_B$—(C)	5.51	−7.69	2.67	3.14	3.68	4.15	4.96	5.44	5.98
C$_B$—(C$_d$)	5.68	−7.80	3.59	3.97	4.38	4.72	5.28	5.61	5.75
[C$_B$—(C$_t$)]	5.68	−7.80	3.59	3.97	4.38	4.72	5.28	5.61	5.75
C$_B$—(C$_B$)	4.96	−8.64	3.33	4.22	4.89	5.27	5.76	5.95	(6.05)
C$_a$	34.20	6.0	3.9	4.4	4.7	5.0	5.3	5.5	5.7

Table A.1 (Continued)

Next-nearest Neighbor Corrections

Group	ΔH_f° 298	S° 298	C_p°						
			300	400	500	600	800	1000	1500
Alkane gauche correction	0.80								
Alkene gauche correction	0.50								
cis correction	1.00[a]	(b)	−1.34	−1.09	−0.81	−0.61	−0.39	−0.26	0
ortho correction	0.57	−1.61	1.12	1.35	1.30	1.17	0.88	0.66	−0.05

[a] When one of the groups is t-butyl the cis correction = 4.00, when both are t-butyl, cis correction = ~10,00, and when there are two cis corrections around one double bond, the total correction is 3.00.

[b] +1.2 for but-2-ene, 0 for all other 2-enes, and −0.6 for 3-enes.

Corrections to be Applied to Ring Compound Estimates[a]

Ring (σ)	ΔH_f° 298	S° 298	C_p°						
			300	400	500	600	800	1000	1500
Cyclopropane (6)	27.6	32.1	−3.05	−2.53	−2.10	−1.90	−1.77	−1.62	(−1.52)
Cyclopropene (2)	53.7	33.6							
Cyclobutane (8)	26.2	29.8	−4.61	−3.89	−3.14	−2.64	−1.88	−1.38	−0.67
Cyclobutene (2)	29.8	29.0	−2.53	−2.19	−1.89	−1.68	−1.48	−1.33	−1.22
Cyclopentane (10)	6.3	27.3	−7.50	−6.49	−5.40	−4.37	−2.93	−1.93	−0.37
Cyclopentene (2)	5.9	25.8	−5.98	−5.35	−4.89	−4.14	−2.93	−2.26	−1.08
Cyclopentadiene	6.0								
Cyclohexane (6)	0	18.8	−6.40	−4.60	−3.30	−1.60	0.82	1.98	3.19
Cyclohexene (2)	1.4	21.5	−4.28	−3.04	−1.98	−1.43	−0.29	0.08	0.81
Cyclohexadiene 1,3	4.8								
Cyclohexadiene 1,4	0.5								
Cycloheptane (1)	6.4	15.9							
Cycloheptene	5.4								
Cycloheptadiene, 1,3	6.6								
Cycloheptatriene 1,3,5 (1)	4.7	23.7							
Cycloöctane (8)	9.9	16.5							
Cis-cycloöctene	6.0								
Trans-cycloöctene	15.3								
Cycloöctatriene 1,3,5	8.9								
Cycloöctatetraene	17.1								
Cyclononane	12.8								
Cis-cyclononene	9.9								
Trans-Cyclononene	12.8								
Spiropentane (4)	63.5	67.6							
Bicyclo-(1,1,0)-butane (2)	68.4	69.2							
Bicyclo-(2,1,0)-pentane	55.3								
Bicyclo-(3,1,0)-hexane	32.7								
Bicyclo-(4,1,0)-heptane	28.9								
Bicyclo-(5,1,0)-octane	29.6								
Bicyclo-(6,1,0)-nonane	31.1								

[a] Note that in most cases the ΔH_f° correction equals ring strain energy.

Table A.2 Oxygen-Containing Compounds

Group	ΔH_f°	S°	C_p° 300	400	500	600	800	1000	1500
CO—(CO)(C)	−29.2								
CO—(O)(C$_d$)	−33.5								
CO—(O)(C$_B$)	−46.0								
CO—(O)(C)	−33.4	14.78	5.97	6.70		8.02	8.87	9.36	
CO—(O)(H)[a]	−29.5	34.93	7.03	7.87	8.82	9.68	11.16	12.20	
CO—(C$_d$)(H)	−31.7								
CO—(C$_B$)$_2$	−39.1								
CO—(C$_B$)(C)	−37.6								
CO—(C$_B$)(H)[b]	−31.7								
CO—(C)$_2$	−31.5	15.01	5.59	6.32	7.09	7.76	8.89	9.61	
CO—(C)(H)	−29.6	34.93	7.03	7.87	8.82	9.68	11.16	12.20	
CO—(H)$_2$	−27.7	53.67	8.47	9.38	10.46	11.52	13.37	14.81	
CO—(CO)(C)	−29.2								
CO—(O)(C$_d$)	−33.5								
CO—(O)(C$_B$)	−46.0								
CO—(O)(C)	−33.4	14.78	5.97	6.70		8.02	8.87	9.36	
CO—(O)(H)[a]	−29.5	34.93	7.03	7.87	8.82	9.68	11.16	12.20	
CO—(C$_d$)(H)	−31.7								
CO—(C$_B$)$_2$	−39.1								
CO—(C$_B$)(C)	−37.6								
CO—(C$_B$)(H)[b]	−31.7								
CO—(C)$_2$	−31.5	15.01	5.59	6.32	7.09	7.76	8.89	9.61	
CO—(C)(H)	−29.6	34.93	7.03	7.87	8.82	9.68	11.16	12.20	
CO—(H)$_2$	−27.7	53.67	8.47	9.38	10.46	11.52	13.37	14.81	
O—(CO)$_2$	−50.9								
O—(CO)(O)	−19.0								
O—(CO)(C$_d$)[c]	−44.1								
O—(CO)(C)	−41.3	8.39							
O—(CO)(H)	−60.3	24.52	3.81	4.98	5.80	6.34	7.19	7.75	
O—(O)(C)	−4.5	[9.4]	3.7	3.7	3.7	3.7	4.2	4.2	4.8
O—(O)$_2$	(19.0)	(9.4)	(3.7)	(3.7)	(3.7)	(3.7)	(4.2)	(4.2)	(4.8)
O—(O)(H)	−16.27	27.85	5.17	5.79	6.28	6.66	7.15	7.51	8.17
O—(C$_d$)$_2$	−32.8	8.1							
O—(C$_d$)(C)	−31.3								
O—(C$_B$)$_2$	−19.3								
O—(C$_B$)(C)	−22.6								
O—(C$_B$)(H)[d]	−37.9	29.1	4.3	4.5	4.8	5.2	6.0	6.6	
O—(C)$_2$	−23.0	8.68	3.4	3.7	3.7	3.8	4.4	4.6	
O—(C)(H)	−37.88	29.07	4.33	4.45	4.82	5.23	6.02	6.61	
C$_d$—(CO)(O)	6.3								
C$_d$—(CO)(C)	9.4								
C$_d$—(CO)(H)[e]	7.68								
C$_d$—(O)(C$_d$)[f]	8.9								
C$_d$—(O)(C)[g]	10.3								
C$_d$—(O)(H)[h]	8.6	8.0	4.16	5.03	5.81	6.50	7.65	8.45	9.62
C$_B$—(CO)	9.7								
C$_B$—(O)	−1.8	10.2	3.9	5.3	6.2	6.6	6.9	6.9	

[a] CO—(O)(H)≡CO—(C)(H), assigned.
[b] CO—(C$_B$)(H)≡CO—(C$_d$)(H), assigned.
[c] O—(CO)(C$_d$)≡O—(CO)(C), assigned.
[d] O—(C$_B$)(H)≡O—(C)(H), assigned.

[e] C$_d$—(CO)(H)≡ mean of C$_d$—(C$_d$)(H) and C$_d$—(C)(H), assigned.
[f] C$_d$—(O)(C$_d$)≡C$_d$—(C$_d$)(C).
[g] C$_d$—(O)(C)≡C$_d$—C$_2$.
[h] C$_d$—(O)(H)≡C$_d$—(C)(H), assigned.

Table A.2 (Continued)

Group	ΔH_f°	S°	C_p°						
			300	400	500	600	800	1000	1500
C—(CO)$_2$(H)$_2$	−7.2								
C—(CO)(C)$_2$(H)^i	−1.8								
C—(CO)(C)(H)$_2$	−5.0	9.6	6.2	7.7	8.7	9.5	11.1	12.2	
C—(CO)(C)$_3$	1.6								
C—(CO)(H)$_3$^{j}	−10.08	30.41	6.19	7.84	9.40	10.79	13.02	14.77	17.58
C—(O)$_2$(C)$_2$	−18.1								
C—(O)$_2$(C)(H)	−17.2								
C—(O)$_2$(H)$_2$	−17.7								
C—(O)(C$_B$)(H)$_2$	−6.6	9.7							
C—(O)(C$_d$)(H)$_2$	−6.9								
C—(O)(C)$_3$	−6.60	−33.56	4.33	6.19	7.25	7.70	8.20	8.24	
C—(O)(C)$_2$(H)	−7.00	−11.0	4.80	6.64	8.10	8.73	9.81	10.40	
C—(O)(C)(H)$_2$	−8.5	10.3	4.99	6.85	8.30	9.43	11.11	12.33	
C—(O)(H)$_3$^{k}	−10.08	30.41	6.19	7.84	9.40	10.79	13.03	14.77	17.58

^{i} C—(CO)(C)$_2$(H), estimated.
^{j} C—(CO)(H)$_3$ ≡ C—(C)(H)$_3$, assigned.
^{k} C—(O)(H)$_3$ ≡ C—(C)(H)$_3$, assigned.

Strain	ΔH_f°	S°	C_p°						
			300	400	500	600	800	1000	1500
ether oxygen gauche	0.3								
Di-tertiary ethers	8.4								
(oxirane)	26.9	30.5	−2.0	−2.8	−3.0	−2.6	−2.3	−2.3	
(oxetane)	25.7	26.1	−4.6	−5.0	−4.2	−3.5	−2.6	+0.2	
(tetrahydrofuran)	6.0								
(tetrahydropyran)	1.5								
(1,3-dioxane)	4.2								
(1,4-dioxane)	4.0								
(1,3,5-trioxane)	1.3								

Table A.2 (Continued)

Strain	ΔH_f°	S°	C_p°						
			300	400	500	600	800	1000	1500
(structure)	−6.2								
(structure)	2.5								
(structure)	6.0								
(structure)	3.4								
(structure)	1.1								
(structure)	1.4								
(structure)	4.6								

Table A.3 Group Contributions to C_p°, S°, and ΔH_f° at 25°C and 1 atmosphere for Nitrogen Containing Compounds

Group	ΔH_f° (kcal/mole)	S° (eu)	C_p° (eu)						
			300	400	500	600	800	1000	1500
C—(N)(H)$_3$	−10.08	30.41	6.19	7.84	9.40	10.79	13.02	14.77	17.58
C—(N)(C)(H)$_2$	−6.6	9.8ᵃ	5.25ᵃ	6.90ᵃ	8.28ᵃ	9.39ᵃ	11.09ᵃ	12.34ᵃ	
C—(N)(C)$_2$(H)	−5.2	−11.7ᵃ	4.67ᵃ	6.32ᵃ	7.64ᵃ	8.39ᵃ	9.56ᵃ	10.23ᵃ	
C—(N)(C)$_3$	−3.2	−34.1ᵃ	4.35ᵃ	6.16ᵃ	7.31ᵃ	7.91ᵃ	8.49ᵃ	8.50ᵃ	
N—(C)(H)$_2$	4.8	29.71	5.72	6.51	7.32	8.07	9.41	10.47	12.28
N—(C)$_2$(H)	15.4	8.94	4.20	5.21	6.13	6.83	7.90	8.65	9.55
N—(C)$_3$	24.4	−13.46	3.48	4.56	5.43	5.97	6.56	6.67	6.50
N—(N)(H)$_2$	11.4	29.13	6.10	7.38	8.43	9.27	10.54	11.52	13.19
N—(N)(C)(H)	20.9	9.61	4.82	5.8	6.5	7.0	7.8	8.3	9.0
N—(N)(C)$_2$	29.2	−13.80							
N—(N)(C$_B$)(H)	22.1								
N$_I$—(H)									
N$_I$—(C)	21.3								
N$_I$—(C$_B$)ᵇ	16.7								
N$_A$—(H)	25.1	26.8	4.38	4.89	5.44	5.94	6.77	7.42	8.44
N$_A$—(C)	34.3								
N—(C$_B$)(H)$_2$	4.8	29.71	5.72	6.51	7.32	8.07	9.41	10.47	12.28
N—(C$_B$)(C)(H)	14.9								
N—(C$_B$)(C)$_2$	26.2								
N—(C$_B$)$_2$(H)	16.3								
C$_B$—(N)	−0.5	−9.69	3.95	5.21	5.94	6.32	6.53	6.56	
N$_A$—(N)	23.0								
CO—(N)(H)	−29.6	34.93	7.03	7.87	8.82	9.68	11.16	12.20	
CO—(N)(C)	−32.8	16.2	5.37	6.17	7.07	7.66	9.62	11.19	
N—(CO)(H)$_2$	−14.9	24.69	4.07	5.74	7.13	8.29	9.96	11.22	
N—(CO)(C)(H)	−4.4	3.9ᵃ							
N—(CO)(C)$_2$									
N—(CO)(C$_B$)(H)	+0.4								
N—(CO)$_2$(H)	−18.5								
N—(CO)$_2$(C)	−5.9								
N—(CO)$_2$(C$_B$)	−0.5								

Corrections to be Applied to Ring Compound Estimates

Group	ΔH_f° (kcal/mole)	S° (eu)	300	400	500	600	800	1000	1500
C—(CN)(C)(H)$_2$	22.5	40.20	11.10	13.40	15.50	17.20	19.7	21.30	
C—(CN)(C)$_2$(H)	25.8	19.80	11.00	12.70	14.10	15.40	17.30	18.60	
C—(CN)(C)$_3$		−2.80							
C—(CN)$_2$(C)$_2$		28.40							
C$_d$—(CN)(H)	37.4	36.58	9.80	11.70	13.30	14.50	16.30	17.30	
C$_d$—(CN)$_2$	34.1								
C$_d$—(NO$_2$)(H)		44.4	12.3	15.1	17.4	19.2	21.6	23.2	25.3
C$_B$—(CN)	35.8	20.50	9.8	11.2	12.3	13.1	14.2	14.9	
C$_T$—(CN)	63.8	35.40	10.30	11.30	12.10	12.70	13.60	14.30	15.30
C—(NO$_2$)(C)(H)$_2$	−15.1	48.4ᵃ							
C—(NO$_2$)(C)$_2$(H)	−15.8	26.9ᵃ							
C—(NO$_2$)(C)$_3$		3.9ᵃ							
C—(NO$_2$)$_2$(C)(H)	−14.9								
O—(NO)(C)	−5.9	41.9	9.10	10.30	11.2	12.0	13.3	13.9	14.5
O—(NO$_2$)(C)	−19.4	48.50							

ᵃ Estimates by authors.
ᵇ For ortho or para substitution in pyridine add −1.5 kcal/mole per group.

Group	ΔH_f° (kcal/mole)	S° (eu)	C_p° (eu)						
			300	400	500	600	800	1000	1500

Corrections to be Applied to Ring Compound Estimates

Group	ΔH_f° (kcal/mole)	S° (eu)	300	400	500	600	800	1000	1500
Ethyleneimine	27.7	31.6[a]							
Azetidine	26.2[a]	29.3[a]							
Pyrrolidine	6.8	26.7	−6.17	−5.58	−4.80	−4.00	−2.87	−2.17	
Piperidine	1.0								
	3.4								
	8.5								

Group	ΔH_f° 298	S° 298	C_p° 300	400	500	600	800	1000
C—(F)₃(C)	−158.4	42.5	12.7	15.0	16.4	17.9	19.3	20.0
C—(F)₂(H)(C)	(−102.3)	39.1	9.9	12.0		15.1		
C—(F)(H)₂(C)	−51.8	35.4	8.1	10.0	12.0	13.0	15.2	16.6
C—(F)₂(C)₂	−97.0	17.8	9.9	11.8	13.5			
C—(F)(H)(C)₂	−48.4	(14.0)						
C—(F)(C)₃	−43.9							
C—(F)₂(Cl)(C)	−106.3	40.5	13.7	16.1	17.5			
C—(Cl)₃(C)	−20.7	50.4	16.3	18.0	19.1	19.8	20.6	21.0
C—(Cl₂)(H)(C)	(−18.9)	43.7	12.1	14.0	15.4	16.5	17.9	18.7
C—(Cl)(H)₂(C)	−15.6	37.8	8.9	10.7	12.3	13.4	15.3	16.7
C—(Cl)₂(C)₂	(−19.5)							
C—(Cl)(H)(C)₂	−12.8	17.6	9.0	9.9	10.5	11.2		
C—(Cl)(C)₃	−12.8	−5.4	9.3	10.5	11.0	11.3		
C—(Br)₃(C)		55.7	16.7	18.0	18.8	19.4	19.9	20.3
C—(Br)(H)₂(C)	−5.4	40.8	9.1	11.0	12.6	13.7	15.5	16.8
C—(Br)(H)(C)₂	−3.4							
C—(Br)(C)₃	−0.4	−2.0	9.3	11.0				
C—(I)(H)₂(C)	7.95	42.5	9.2	11.0	12.9	13.9	15.8	17.2
C—(I)(H)(C)₂	10.7	22.2	(8.7)					
C—(I)(C)₃	13.0	(0.0)	(9.7)					
C—(Cl)(Br)(H)(C)		45.7	12.4	14.0	15.6	16.3	17.9	19.0
N—(F)₂(C)	−7.8							
C—(Cl)(C)(O)(H)	−20.2	19.5	(9.0)	(9.9)	(10.5)	(11.2)		

Table A.4 (Continued)

Group	ΔH_f° 298	S° 298	C_p°					
			300	400	500	600	800	1000
C_d—$(F)_2$	−77.5	37.3	9.7	11.0	12.0	12.7	13.8	14.5
C_d—$(Cl)_2$	−1.8	42.1	11.4	12.5	13.3	13.9	14.6	15.0
C_d—$(Br)_2$		47.6	12.3	13.2	13.9	14.3	14.9	15.2
C_d—(F)(Cl)		39.8	10.3	11.7	12.6	13.3	14.2	14.7
C_d—(F)(Br)		42.5	10.8	12.0	12.8	13.5	14.3	14.7
C_d—(Cl)(Br)		45.1	12.1	12.7	13.5	14.1	14.7	—
C_d—(F)(H)	−37.6	32.8	6.8	8.4	9.5	10.5	11.8	12.7
C_d—(Cl((H)	2.1	35.4	7.9	9.2	10.3	11.2	12.3	13.1
C_d—(Br)(H)	12.7	38.3	8.1	9.5	10.6	11.4	12.4	13.2
C_d—(I)(H)	24.5	40.5	8.8	10.0	10.9	11.6	12.6	13.3
C_T—(Cl)		33.4	7.9	8.4	8.7	9.0	9.4	9.6
C_T—(Br)		36.1	8.3	8.7	9.0	9.2	9.5	9.7
C_T—(I)		37.9	8.4	8.8	9.1	9.3	9.6	9.8

Arenes

Group	ΔH_f° 298	S° 298	300	400	500	600	800	1000
C_B—(F)	−42.8	16.1	6.3	7.6	8.5	9.1	9.8	10.2
C_B—(Cl)	−3.8	18.9	7.4	8.4	9.2	9.7	10.2	10.4
C_B—(Br)	10.7	21.6	7.8	8.7	9.4	9.9	10.3	10.5
C_B—(I)	24.0	23.7	8.0	8.9	9.6	9.9	10.3	10.5
C—$(C_B)(F)_3$	−162.7	42.8	12.5	15.3	17.2	18.5	20.1	21.0
C—$(C_B)(Br)(H)_2$	−6.9							
C—$(C_B)(I)(H)_2$	8.4							

Corrections for Next Nearest Neighbors

Group	ΔH_f° 298	S° 298	300	400	500	600	800	1000
Ortho (F)(F)	5.0	0	0	0	0	0	0	0
Ortho (Cl)(Cl)	2.2							
Ortho (Alk)(Halogen)[a]	0.6							
Cis (Halogen)(Halogen)	(0)							
Cis (Halogen)(Alk)	(0)							

[a] Halogen = Cl, Br, I only.

186

Table A.5 Organosulphur Groups

Group	ΔH_f° 298	S° 298	C_p° 300	400	500	600	800	1000
C—(H)$_3$(S)^a	−10.08	30.41	6.19	7.84	9.40	10.79	13.02	14.77
C—(C)(H)$_2$(S)	−5.65	9.88	5.38	7.08	8.60	9.97	12.26	14.15
C—(C)$_2$(H)(S)	−2.64	−11.32	4.85	6.51	7.78	8.69	9.90	10.57
C—(C)$_3$(S)	−0.55	−34.41	4.57	6.27	7.45	8.15	8.72	8.10
C—(C$_B$)(H)$_2$(S)	−4.73							
C—(C$_d$)(H)$_2$(S)	−6.45							
C$_B$—(S)^b	−1.8	10.20	3.90	5.30	6.20	6.60	6.90	6.90
C$_d$—(H)(S)^c	8.56	8.0	4.16	5.03	5.81	6.50	7.65	8.45
C$_d$—(C)(S)	10.93	−12.41	3.50	3.57	3.83	4.09	4.41	5.00
S—(C)(H)	4.62	32.73	5.86	6.20	6.51	6.78	7.30	7.71
S—(C$_B$)(H)	11.96	12.66	5.12	5.26	5.57	6.03	6.99	7.84
S—(C)$_2$	11.51	13.15	4.99	4.96	5.02	5.07	5.41	5.73
S—(C)(C$_d$)	9.97							
S—(C$_d$)$_2$	−4.54	16.48	4.79	5.58	5.53	6.29	7.94	9.73
S—(C$_B$)(C)	19.16							
S—(C$_B$)$_2$	25.90							
S—(S)(C)	7.05	12.37	5.23	5.42	5.51	5.51	5.38	5.12
S—(S)(C$_B$)	14.5							
S—(S)$_2$	3.01	13.4	4.7	5.0	5.1	5.2	5.3	5.4
C—(SO)(H)$_3$^{d}	−10.08	30.41	6.19	7.84	9.40	10.79	13.02	14.77
C—(C)(SO)(H)$_2$	−7.72							
C—(C)$_3$(SO)	−3.05							
C—(C$_d$)(SO)(H)$_2$	−7.35							
C$_B$—(SO)^e	2.3							
SO—(C)$_2$	−14.41	18.10	8.88	10.03	10.50	10.79	10.98	11.17
SO—(C$_B$)$_2$	−12.0							
C—(SO$_2$)(H)$_3$^{f}	−10.08	30.41	6.19	7.84	9.40	10.79	13.02	14.77
C—(C)(SO$_2$)(H)$_2$	−7.68							
C—(C)$_2$(SO$_2$)(H)	−2.62							
C—(C)$_3$(SO$_2$)	−0.61							
C—(C$_d$)(SO$_2$)(H)$_2$	−7.14							
C—(C$_B$)(SO$_2$)(H)$_2$	−5.54							
C$_B$—(SO$_2$)^g	2.3							
C$_d$—(H)(SO$_2$)	12.5							
C$_d$—(C)(SO$_2$)	14.5							
SO$_2$—(C$_d$)(C$_B$)	−68.6							
SO$_2$—(C$_d$)$_2$	−73.6							
SO$_2$—(C)$_2$	−69.74	20.90	11.52					
SO$_2$—(C)(C$_B$)	−72.29							
SO$_2$—(C$_B$)$_2$	−68.58							
SO$_2$—(SO$_2$)(C$_B$)	−76.25							
CO—(S)(C)^h	−31.56	15.43	5.59	6.32	7.09	7.76	8.89	9.61
S—(H)(CO)	−1.41	31.20	7.63	8.09	8.12	8.17	8.50	8.24
C—(S)(F)$_3$		38.9						
S—(C)(CN)	37.18	41.06	9.51	10.44	11.22	11.86	12.85	13.50
CS—(N)$_2$^{i}	−31.56	15.43	5.59	6.32	7.09	7.76	8.89	9.61
N—(CS)(H)$_2$	12.78	29.19	6.07	7.28	8.18	8.91	10.09	10.98
S—(S)(N)^j	−4.90							
N—(S)(C)$_2$	29.9							
SO—(N)$_2$^{k}	−31.56							
N—(SO)(C)$_2$	16.0							
SO$_2$—(N)$_2$^{l}	−31.56							
N—(SO$_2$)(C)$_2$	−20.4							

^{a} C—(S)(H)$_3$ ≡ C—(C)(H)$_3$, assigned.
^{b} C$_B$—(S) ≡ C$_B$—(O), assigned.
^{c} C$_d$—(S)(H) ≡ C$_d$—(O)(H), assigned.
^{d} C—(SO)(H)$_3$ ≡ C—(CO)(H)$_3$, assigned.
^{e} C$_B$—(SO) ≡ C$_B$—(CO), assigned.
^{f} C—(SO$_2$)(H)$_3$ ≡ C—(SO)(H)$_3$.

^{g} C$_B$—(SO$_2$) ≡ C$_B$—(CO), assigned.
^{h} CO—(S)(C) ≡ CO—(C)$_2$, assigned.
^{i} CS—(N)$_2$ ≡ CO—(C)$_2$, assigned.
^{j} S—(S)(N) ≡ O—(O)(C), assigned.
^{k} SO—(N)$_2$ ≡ CO—(C)$_2$, assigned.
^{l} SO$_2$—(N)$_2$ ≡ SO—(N)$_2$, assigned.

Table A.5 (Continued)
Corrections to be Applied to Organosulphur Ring Compounds

Ring (σ)	ΔH_f° 298	S° 298	C_p° 300	400	500	600	800	1000
(thiirane) (2)	19.72	29.47	−2.85	−2.59	−2.66	−3.02	−4.32	−5.82
(thietane) (2)	19.37	27.18	−4.59	−4.18	−3.91	−3.91	−4.60	−5.70
(thiolane) (2)	1.73	23.56	−4.90	−4.67	−3.68	−3.66	−4.41	−5.57
(thiane) (2)	0	17.46	−6.22	−4.26	−2.24	−0.69	0.86	1.29
(thiepane) (2)	3.89							
(2,3-dihydrothiophene) (2)	5.07							
(2,5-dihydrothiophene) (1)[m]	5.07							
(sulfolane, SO$_2$) (2)	5.74							
(thiophene) (2)[n]	1.73	23.56	−4.90	−4.67	−3.68	−3.66	−4.41	−5.57

[m] Assume ring corrections for (2,3-dihydrothiophene) and (2,5-dihydrothiophene) are the same.

[n] Assume ring corrections for (thiophene) and (thiolane) are the same.

188

Table A.6 Organometallic Compounds[a]

Metal	Groups	$\Delta H_f^\circ\,298$	Remarks
Tin	C—(Sn)(H)$_3$	−10.08	C—(Sn)(H)$_3$≡C—(C)(H)$_3$, assigned
	C—(Sn)(C)(H)$_2$	−2.18	
	C—(Sn)(C)$_2$(H)	3.38	
	C—(Sn)(C)$_3$	8.16	
	C—(Sn)(C$_B$)(H)$_2$	−7.77	
	C$_B$—(Sn)	5.51	C$_B$—(Sn)≡C$_B$—(C), assigned
	C$_d$—(Sn)(H)	8.77	C$_d$—(Sn)(H)≡C$_d$—(C)(H), assigned
	Sn—(C)$_4$	36.2	
	Sn—(C)$_3$(Cl)	−9.8	
	Sn—(C)$_2$(Cl)$_2$	−49.2	
	Sn—(C)(Cl)$_3$	−89.5	
	Sn—(C)$_3$(Br)	−1.8	
	Sn—(C)$_3$(I)	9.9	
	Sn—(C)$_3$(H)	34.8	
	Sn—(C$_d$)$_4$	36.2	Sn—(C$_d$)$_4$≡Sn—(C)$_4$, assigned
	Sn—(C$_d$)$_3$(Cl)	−8.2	
	Sn—(C$_d$)$_2$(Cl)$_2$	−50.7	
	Sn—(C$_d$)(Cl)$_3$	−82.2	
	Sn—(C)$_3$(C$_d$)	37.6	
	Sn—(C$_B$)$_4$	26.26	
	Sn—(C)$_3$(C$_B$)	34.93	
	Sn—(C)$_3$(Sn)	26.4	
Lead	C—(Pb)(H)$_3$	−10.08	C—(Pb)(H)$_3$≡C—(C)(H)$_3$, assigned
	C—(Pb)(C)(H$_2$)	−1.70	
	Pb—(C)$_4$	72.9	
Chromium	O—(Cr)(C)	−23.5	O—(Cr)(C)≡O—(Ti)(C), assigned
	Cr—(O)$_4$	−64.0	
Zinc	C—(Zn)(H)$_3$	−10.08	C—(Zn)(H)$_3$≡C—(C)(H)$_3$, assigned
	C—(Zn)(C)(H)$_2$	−1.78	
	Zn—(C)$_2$	33.3	
Titanium	O—(Ti)(C)	−23.5	O—(Ti)(C)≡O—(P)(C), assigned
	Ti—(O)$_4$	−157	
	N—(Ti)(C)$_2$	39.1	N—(Ti)(C)$_2$≡N—(P)(C)$_2$, assigned
	Ti—(N)$_4$	−123	
Vanadium	O—(V)(C)	−23.5	O—(V)(C)≡O—(Ti)(C), assigned
	V—(O)$_4$	−87.0	
Cadmium	C—(Cd)(H)$_3$	−10.08	C—(Cd)(H)$_3$≡C—(C)(H)$_3$, assigned
	C—(Cd)(C)(H)$_2$	−0.30	
	Cd—(C)$_2$	46.4	

[a] No gauche corrections across C—M bond.

Table A.6   (Continued)

Metal	Groups	ΔH_f° 298	Remarks
Aluminum	C—(Al)(H)$_3$	−10.08	C—(Al)(H)$_3$≡C—(C)(H)$_3$, assigned
	C—(Al)(C)(H)$_2$	0.70	
	Al—(C)$_3$	9.2	
Germanium	C—(Ge)(C)(H)$_2$	−7.7	
	Ge—(C)$_4$	36.2	Ge—(C)$_4$≡Sn—(C)$_4$, assigned
	Ge—(Ge)(C)$_3$	15.6	
Mercury	C—(Hg)(H)$_3$	−10.08	C—(Hg)(H)$_3$≡C—(C)(H)$_3$, assigned
	C—(Hg)(C)(H)$_2$	−2.68	
	C—(Hg)(C)$_2$(H)	3.62	
	C$_B$—(Hg)	−1.8	C$_B$—(Hg)≡C$_B$—(O), assigned
	Hg—(C)$_2$	42.5	
	Hg—(C)(Cl)	−2.82	
	Hg—(C)(Br)	4.88	
	Hg—(C)(I)	15.78	
	Hg—(C$_B$)$_2$	64.4	
	Hg—(C$_B$)(Cl)	9.9	
	Hg—(C$_B$)(Br)	18.1	
	Hg—(C$_B$)(I)	27.9	

Organophosphorus Groups[a]

Group	ΔH_f° 298	S° 298	Remarks
C—(P)(H)$_3$	−10.08	30.41	C—(P)(H)$_3$≡C—(C)(H)$_3$, assigned
C—(P)(C)(H)$_2$	−2.47		
C—(PO)(H)$_3$	−10.08	30.41	C—(PO)(H)$_3$≡C—(C)(H)$_3$, assigned
C—(PO)(C)(H)$_2$	−3.4		
C—(P:N)(H)$_3$	−10.08	30.41	C—(P:N)(H)$_3$≡C—(C)(H)$_3$, assigned
C—(N:P)(C)(H)$_2$	19.4		
C$_B$—(P)	−1.8		C$_B$—(P)≡C$_B$—(O), assigned
C$_B$—(PO)	2.3		C$_B$—(PO)≡C$_B$—(CO), assigned
C$_B$—(P:N)	2.3		C$_B$—(P:N)≡C$_B$—(CO), assigned
P—(C)$_3$	7.0		
P—(C)(Cl)$_2$	−50.1		
P—(C$_B$)$_3$	28.3		
P—(O)$_3$	−66.8		
P—(N)$_3$	−66.8		P—(N)$_3$≡P—(O)$_3$, assigned
PO—(C)$_3$	−72.8		
PO—(C)(F)$_2$		46.77	
PO—(C)(Cl)(F)		50.80	
PO—(C)(Cl)$_2$	−123.0	52.97	
PO—(C)(O)(Cl)	−112.6		
PO—(C)(O)$_2$	−99.5		
PO—(O)$_3$	−104.6		
PO—(O)$_2$(F)	−167.7		
PO—(C$_B$)$_3$	−52.9		

[a] No gauche corrections across the X—P, X—PO, and X—P:N bonds (X represents C, O, N).

190

Table A.6 (Continued)

Group	ΔH_f° 298	S° 298	Remarks
PO—(N)₃	−104.6		PO—(N)₃≡PO—(O)₃, assigned
O—(C)(P)	−23.5		O—(C)(P)≡O—(C)₂, assigned
O—(H)(P)	−58.7		
O—(C)(PO)	−40.7		O—(C)(PO)≡O—(C)(CO), assigned
O—(H)(PO)	−65.0		
O—(PO)₂	−54.5		
O—(P:N)(C)	−40.7		O—(P:N)(C)≡O—(C)(CO), assigned
N—(P)(C)₂	32.2		
N—(PO)(C)₂	17.8		
P:N—(C)₃(C)	0.50		P:N—(C)₃(C)≡C—(C)₄, assigned
P:N—(C_B)₃(C)	−25.7		
P:N—(N:P)(C)₂(P:N)	−15.5		
P:N—(N:P)(C_B)₂(P:N)	−22.9		
P:N—(N:P)(Cl)₂(P:N)	−58.2		
P:N—(N:P)(O)₂(P:N)	−43.4		

Organoboron Groups

Group	ΔH_f° 298	Remarks
C—(B)(H)₃	−10.08	C—(B)(H)₃≡C—(C)(H)₃, assigned
C—(B)(C)(H)₂	−2.22	
C—(B)(C)₂(H)	1.1	
C—(BO₃)(H)₃	−10.08	C—(BO₃)(H)₃≡C—(C)(H)₃, assigned
C—(BO₃)(C)(H)₂	−2.2	
C_d—(B)(H)	15.6	
B—(C)₃	0.9	
B—(C)(F)₂	−187.9	
B—(C)₂(Cl)	−42.7	
B—(C)₂(Br)	−26.9	
B—(C)₂(I)	−8.9	
B—(C)₂(O)	29.3	B—(C)₂(O)≡N—(C)₂(N), assigned
B—(C_d)(F)₂	−192.9	B—(C_d)(F)₂≡B—(C)(F)₂, assigned
B—(O)₃	24.4	B—(O)₃≡B—(N)₃, assigned
B—(O)₂(Cl)	−19.7	
B—(O)(Cl)₂	−61.2	
B—(O)₂(H)	19.9	
B—(N)₃	24.4	B—(N)₃≡N—(C)₃, assigned
B—(N)₂(Cl)	−23.8	
B—(N)(Cl)₂	−67.9	
BO₃—(C)₃	−208.7	
O—(B)(H)	−115.5	
O—(B)(C)	−69.43	
N—(B)(C)₂	−9.93	
B—(S)₃	24.4	
S—(B)(C)	−14.5	
S—(B)(C_B)	−7.8	

Gauche corrections across the C—B bond are +0.8 kcal/mole.

Table A.6 (Continued)

Thermodynamic Properties for Compounds Containing Unique Groups (Ideal Gas)

Compound	$\Delta H_f^\circ 298$	$S^\circ 298$	C_p°						Reference
			300	400	500	600	800	1000	
SOF		62.87	9.97	10.92	11.63	12.14	12.79	13.15	2
SOCl$_2$	−50.37	73.62	15.94	17.07	17.79	18.28	18.88	19.20	2
SOCl		66.17	10.88	11.62	12.15	12.54	13.03	13.31	2
S$_2$F$_2$	−54.5	69.30	15.33	16.83	17.74	18.31	18.94	19.26	2
SF$_2$	−51.8	60.92	10.44	11.50	12.18	12.63	13.14	13.40	2
SF		54.33	7.57	7.96	8.24	8.44	8.68	8.81	2
S$_2$Cl$_2$	−4.75	76.49	17.44	18.37	18.87	19.16	19.46	19.61	2
SCl$_2$	−5.15	67.20	12.19	12.83	13.18	13.39	13.61	13.71	2
SCl		57.25	8.20	8.51	8.69	8.81	8.95	9.04	2
CSCl$_2$		70.84	15.34	16.61	17.51	18.10	18.78	19.14	3, 4
H$_2$S$_2$	3.9								1
NSF$_3$		69.37	17.23	19.60	21.17	22.25	23.56	24.29	5
HNCS	30.0	59.15							14
P$_2$H$_4$	5.0								6
PBr$_3$	−28.9								6
PBr$_5$	−53.0								6
BO$_2$	−75.0	55.03	10.08	11.17	12.01	12.64	13.45	13.91	2
H$_2$BOH	−70.0								7
HB(OH)$_2$	−153.8								7
H$_3$SiBr		62.76	12.69	14.87			20.02		8
H$_3$SiI		64.54	12.86						8
H$_2$SiBr$_2$		73.92	15.68	17.71			21.73		8
SiBr$_4$	−98.0	90.22	23.21	24.2		25.1	25.4	25.5	8
ClSiBr$_3$		90.14	22.78	24.0		24.9	25.3	25.5	8
Cl$_2$SiBr$_2$		89.48	22.39	23.7		24.8	25.2	25.5	8
Cl$_3$SiBr		83.52	21.72	23.4		24.6	25.1	25.5	8
ISiBr$_3$		96.58	23.39	24.4	24.8	25.1	25.4	25.6	8
Si(CH$_3$)$_4$	(−26)	85.79	33.52	40.32	46.48	51.84	60.55	67.31	8
(CH$_3$)$_3$SiCl		85.56	31.36	36.94	41.63	45.71	52.15	57.08	13
(CH$_3$)$_2$SiCl$_2$	−106.0	86.02	26.17	36.81	34.61	37.72	42.54	46.13	8
(CH$_3$)$_3$SiF		83.81	29.42	35.09	40.14	44.40	51.30	56.58	12
(CH$_3$)$_2$SiF$_2$		80.21	25.26	30.01	33.97	37.17	42.16	45.87	12
CH$_3$SiF$_3$		75.07	22.73	26.15		30.54			8
[(CH$_3$)$_3$Si]$_2$O		127.85	57.22	68.40	78.16	86.48	99.95	110.33	8
H$_3$SiGeH$_3$	27.8								9
SiI$_4$	−28.0								8
(CH$_3$)$_3$SiH	(−21)	79.03	28.36	34.03	39.18	43.46	50.50	55.87	8, 12
(CH$_3$)$_2$SiH$_2$	(−17)	71.70	22.03	26.71	30.70	34.24	39.79	43.99	8, 12
CH$_3$SiH$_3$	(−12)								11
C$_2$H$_5$SiH$_3$	(−17)								8
(C$_2$H$_5$)$_2$SiH$_2$	(−27)								8
(C$_2$H$_5$)$_3$SiH	(−36)								8
(C$_2$H$_5$)$_4$Si	−44.0								8
C$_2$H$_3$SiH$_3$	−1.0								8
i-C$_4$H$_9$SiH$_3$	−31.0								8
n-C$_4$H$_9$SiH$_3$	(−27)								8
(CH$_3$)$_2$Si(i—C$_3$H$_7$)$_2$	−47.0								8
(C$_6$H$_5$)$_2$SiCl$_2$	−50.0								8

Table A.6 (Continued)

Compound	ΔH_f° 298	S° 298	C_p°						Reference
			300	400	500	600	800	1000	
$Si(OCH_3)_4$	-300 ± 3								8
$Si(OC_2H_5)_4$	-322.0								8
$Si(O—iC_3H_7)_4$	-346.0								8
$Si_2O(OCH_3)_6$	-540.0								8
$Si_3O_2(OCH_3)_8$	-803.0								8
$(CH_3)_2Si(OC_2H_5)_2$	-199.0								8
$(n\text{-}C_3H_7)_2Si(OC_2H_5)_2$	-215.0								8
$(CH_3)_2(SiOH)_2O$	-330.0								8
$(CH_3)_2Si(OH)_2$	-192.0								8
$(C_2H_5)_2Si(OH)_2$	-208.0								8
$(C_6H_5)_2Si(OH)_2$	-136.0								8
$Si_2O(CH_3)_6$	-203.0								8
$Si_3O_2(CH_3)_8$	-350.0								8
$Si_3O_2(CH_3)_8$	-351.0								8
$Si_4O_3(CH_3)_{10}$	-405.0								8
	-527.0								8
	-488.0								8
$Si_5O_4(CH_3)_{12}$	-667.0								8
$Si_2(OCH_3)_6$	-448.0								8
$HC{\equiv}CSiH_3$		64.27	17.31	20.56	23.05	25.05	28.14	30.35	10

1. H. Mackle and P. A. G. O'Hare, *Tetrahedron Letters*, **19**, 961 (1963).
2. B. J. McBride *et al.*, NASA SP-3001.
3. M. G. Krishna Dillai and F. F. Cleveland, *J. Mol. Spect.*, **6**, 465 (1961).
4. H. W. Thompson, *Trans. Faraday Soc.*, **37**, 251 (1941).
5. K. Ramaswamy, K. Sathianandan, and F. F. Cleveland, *J. Mol. Spect.*, **9**, 107 (1962).
6. S. B. Hartley *et al.*, *Quarterly Reviews*, **17**, 204 (1963).
7. R. F. Porter and S. K. Gupta, *J. Phys. Chem.*, **68**, 2732 (1964).
8. H. E. O'Neal and M. A. Ring, *Inorg. Chem.*, **5**, 435 (1966).
9. S. R. Gunn and J. H. Kindsvater, *J. Phys. Chem.*, **70**, 1750, (1960).
10. M. G. K. Pillai, K. Ramaswamy, and S. G. Gnanadesikan, *Czech. J. Phys. B.*, **16**, 150 (1966).
11. H. A. Skinner, *Advances in Organometallic Chemistry*, Academic Press, New York, 1964, Vol. **2**, p. 49.
12. H. J. Spangenberg and M. Pfeiffer, *Z. Physik. Chem.* (Leipzig) **232**, 343 (1966).
13. H. J. Spangenberg, *Z. Physik. Chem.* (Leipzig), **232**, 271 (1966).
14. J. T. Brandenburg, *Diss. Abst.*, **18**, 1994 (1958).

Table A.7 Values of C_p° for the Common Elements in Their Standard States at Different Temperatures

Element	Temperature °K							
	298	400	500	600	800	1000	1200	1500
$H_2(g)$	6.9	7.0	7.0	7.0	7.1	7.2	7.4	7.7
$O_2(g)$	7.0	7.2	7.4	7.7	8.1	8.3	8.5	8.7
B(cr)	2.7	3.7	4.5	5.0	5.6	6.0	6.3	6.7
C(cr)-graphite	2.0	2.9	3.5	4.0	4.7	5.1	5.4	5.7
$N_2(g)$	7.0	7.0	7.1	7.2	7.5	7.8	8.1	8.3
$F_2(g)$	7.5	7.9	8.2	8.4	8.7	8.9	9.0	9.1
$S(cr)(l)/(g)(S_2)$	5.4(cr)	7.7(l)	9.1(l)	8.21(l)	4.4[a]	4.4	4.5	4.5
Na(cr)/(l)/(g)	6.7(cr)	7.5(l)	7.3(l)	7.1(l)	6.9(l)	6.9(l)	5.0	5.0
Mg(cr)/(l)/(g)	6.0(cr)	6.3(cr)	6.6(cr)	6.8(cr)	7.4(cr)	7.9(l)	8.4(l)	5.0
Al(cr)/(l)	5.8(cr)	6.1(cr)	6.4(cr)	6.7(cr)	7.3(cr)	7.0(l)	7.0(l)	7.0(l)
Hg(l)/(g)	6.7(l)	6.6(l)	6.5(l)	6.5(l)	5.0	5.0	5.0	5.0
$Cl_2(g)$	8.1	8.4	8.6	8.7	8.9	9.0	9.0	9.1
$Br_2(l)(g)$	18.1(l)	8.8	8.9	8.9	9.0	9.0	9.0	9.1
$I_2(cr)/(l)$	13.0(cr)	19.3(l)	9.0	9.0	9.0	9.1	9.1	9.1
K(cr)-(l)(g)	7.1(cr)	7.5(l)	7.3(l)	7.2(l)	7.1(l)	7.3(l)	5.0	5.0
Pb(cr)/(l)	6.4	6.6	6.8	7.0	7.2(l)	7.0(l)	6.9(l)	6.9(l)
Si(cr)	4.8	5.3	5.6	5.8	6.1	6.3	6.4	6.5
Fe(cr)	6.0	6.5	7.0	7.6	9.2	13.6	8.2[a]	8.6[b]
W(cr)	5.8	6.0	6.1	6.2	6.4	6.5	6.7	6.9
Ti(cr)	6.0	6.4	6.6	6.8	7.2	7.5	7.7	8.1
Be(cr)	3.9	4.8	5.3	5.6	6.1	6.5	7.0	7.7
$P(cr)/P_2(g)$	5.1	5.5	5.9	6.2	4.3g[c]	4.4g	4.4g	4.5g

[a] corresponds to 1 mole P or S.
[b] α phase to 1184°K; γ phase to 1665°K.
 (cr) = crystal; (l) = liquid; (g) = gas

Table A.8 Thermochemical Data for Some Gas Phase Atomic Species

Substance (degeneracy)		ΔH_f°	S°	C_p°				
				300°K	500°K	800°K	1000°K	1500°K
Ag	(2)	68.4	41.3	5.0				5.0
Al	(6)	78.0	39.3	5.1				5.0
Ar	(1)	0	37.0	5.0				5.0
Au	(2)	87.3	43.1	5.0				5.0
B	(6)	32.8	36.6	5.0				5.0
Be	(1)	78.3	32.5	5.0				5.0
Br	(4)	26.7	41.8	5.0			5.1	5.3
C	(9)	170.9	37.8	5.0				5.0
Ca	(1)	42.2	37.0	5.0				5.0
Cd		26.8	40.1					
Cl	(4)	28.9	39.5	5.2	5.4		5.3	5.2
Co	(~8)	101.6	42.9					
Cr	(~9)	95	41.6					
Cs	(2)	18.7	41.9					
Cu	(2)	81.0	39.7	5.0				5.0
e	(2)	0	5.0	5.0				5.0
F	(6)	18.9	37.9	5.4	5.3	5.1	5.0	5.0
Fe	(9–25)	99.5	43.1	6.1	5.9	5.5	5.4	5.3
H^1	(2)	52.1	27.4	5.0				5.0
H^2(D)	(2)	53.0	29.5	5.0				5.0
He	(1)	0	30.1	5.0				5.0
Hg	(1)	14.7	41.8	5.0				5.0
I	(4)	25.5	43.2	5.0				5.0
K	(2)	21.3	38.3	5.0				5.0
Kr	(1)	0	39.2	5.0				5.0
Li	(2)	38.4	33.1	5.0				5.0
Mg	(1)	35.3	35.5	5.0				5.0
Mn	(5)	67.2	41.5					
N	(4)	113.0	36.6	5.0				5.0
Na	(2)	25.9	36.7	5.0				5.0
Ne	(1)	0	35.0	5.0				5.0
O	(~7)	59.6	38.5	5.2	5.1	5.0		5.0
P^a	(4)	78.8	39.0	5.0				5.0
Pb	(1)	46.7	41.9	5.0			5.0	5.2
S	(~7)	66.7	40.1	5.7	5.4	5.2	5.1	5.1
Se	(~5)	49.2	42.2	5.0				
Si	(~9)	107.7	40.1	5.3	5.1			5.1
Sn	(3)	72.2	40.2	5.1				
Ti	(~21)	113.0	43.1	5.8	5.3	5.1	5.1	5.3
W	(1)	203.4	41.5	5.1	6.3	9.0	9.9	9.0
Xe	(1)	0	40.5	5.0				5.0
Zn	(1)	31.2	38.5	5.0			5.0	

Table A.8 (Continued)
Thermochemical Data for Some Gas Phase Diatomic Species

Substance	ΔH_f°	S°	C_p°				
			300	500	800	1000	1500
O_2	0	49.0	7.0	7.4	8.1	8.3	8.7
H_2	0	31.2	6.9	7.0	7.1	7.2	7.7
D_2	0	34.6	7.0	7.1	7.2	7.3	7.8
HD	0.1	34.3	7.0	7.1	7.1	7.2	7.7
HO	9.4	43.9	7.2	7.1	7.2	7.3	7.9
DO	8.7	45.3	7.1				
F_2	0	48.4	7.5	8.2	8.7	8.9	9.1
HF	−64.8	41.5	7.0	7.0	7.1	7.2	7.7
FO	39 ± 3	51.8	7.3	8.0	8.6	8.8	9.0
Cl_2	0	53.3	8.1	8.6	8.9	9.0	9.1
HCl	−22.0	44.6	7.0	7.0	7.3	7.6	8.1
ClO	24.2	54.1	7.5	8.2	8.7	8.8	9.0
ClF	−12.1	52.1	7.7	8.3	8.7	8.9	9.0
Br_2	7.4	58.6	8.6	8.9	9.0	9.0	9.1
HBr	−8.7	47.5	7.0	7.0	7.4	7.7	8.3
BrF	−14.0	54.7	7.9	8.5	8.8	8.9	9.1
BrCl	3.5	57.3	8.4	8.7	8.9	9.0	9.1
BrO	30	56.8	7.7				
I_2	14.9	62.3	8.8	8.9	9.0	9.1	9.1
HI	6.3	49.4	7.0	7.1	7.6	7.9	8.5
IF	−22.7	56.4	8.0	8.6	8.9	9.0	9.2
ICl	4.2	59.1	8.5	8.8	9.0	9.0	9.1
IBr	9.8	61.8	8.7	8.9	9.0	9.1	9.2
S_2	30.7	54.5	7.8	8.4	8.7	8.8	9.0
HS	34	46.7	7.7	7.5	7.6	7.9	8.4
SO	1.5	53.0	7.2	7.8	8.4	8.6	8.8
N_2	0	45.8	7.0	7.0	7.5	7.8	8.3
NH	80 ± 3	43.3	7.0	7.0	7.2	7.5	8.1
NO	21.6	50.3	7.1	7.3	7.8	8.1	8.6
NF	60 ± 8	51.4	7.3	7.9	8.5	8.7	8.9
P_2	40.6	52.1	7.7	8.3	8.7	8.8	8.9
PH	58	46.9	7.0	7.1	7.6	7.9	8.4
PO	-2.5 ± 2	53.2	7.6	7.9	8.4	8.6	8.8
PN	24	50.4	7.1	7.6	8.3	8.5	8.8
C_2	199 ± 2	47.6	10.3	8.9	8.5	8.6	8.9
CH	142	43.7	7.0	7.0	7.4	7.7	8.3
CO	−26.4	47.2	7.0	7.1	7.6	7.9	8.4
CF	75 ± 10	50.9	7.2	7.7	8.3	8.5	8.8
CCl		53.8	7.7	8.3	8.7	8.8	8.9
CN	111	48.4	7.0	7.2	7.7	8.0	8.5
CS	55 ± 5	50.3	7.1	7.7	8.3	8.5	8.8

Table A.8 (Continued)

Substance	ΔH_f°	S°	C_p°				
			300	500	800	1000	1500
Si_2	131 ± 5	54.9	8.2	8.7	8.9	9.0	9.0
SiO	-24.2	50.5	7.1	7.7	8.3	8.5	8.8
SiH		47.4	7.0	7.2	8.0	8.1	8.7
Pb_2	80 ± 5	67.2	8.8	9.1	9.2	9.3	9.5
B_2	195 ± 6	48.3	7.3	8.0	8.5	8.7	8.9
BH	106 ± 2	41.0	7.0	7.1	7.6	7.9	8.5
BO	10 ± 10	48.6	7.0	7.2	7.8	8.1	8.5
BF	-28 ± 3	47.9	7.1	7.6	8.2	8.5	8.8
BCl	34 ± 4	50.9	7.6	8.2	8.7	8.8	9.0
BC	198 ± 10	49.8	7.1	7.6	8.3	8.5	8.8
AlH	62 ± 5	44.9	7.0	7.4	8.1	8.4	8.8
AlO	22 ± 5	52.2	7.4	8.1	8.6	8.7	8.9
AlF	-62.5	51.4	7.6	8.3	8.7	8.8	9.0
AlCl	-11.2	54.4	8.3	8.7	8.9	9.0	9.1
AlBr	3.6 ± 5	57.3	8.5	8.8	9.0	9.0	9.1
Ag_2	100 ± 3						
AgCl	23						
HgH	57 ± 4	52.5	7.2	7.9	8.6	8.9	9.4
HgCl	18.8 ± 3	62.1	8.7	8.9	9.1	9.1	9.2
Cu_2	116 ± 3	57.7	8.7	8.9	9.0	9.1	9.2
CuCl	21.8	56.7	8.4	8.8	8.9	9.0	9.1
BeF	-50 ± 2	49.2	7.1	7.7	8.3	8.6	8.8
BeCl	14.5 ± 3	52.0	7.6	8.2	8.7	8.8	9.0
BeO	31 ± 3	47.2	7.0	7.5	8.1	8.4	8.7
MgO		52.9	7.5	8.2	8.7	8.8	9.0
MgF	-53.1	52.8	7.8	8.4	8.8	8.9	9.0
MgCl	-10 ± 10	55.8	8.3	8.7	8.9	9.0	9.1
Li_2	50.4	47.1	8.6	8.9	9.1	9.2	9.4
LiF	-79.5 ± 2	47.8	7.5	8.2	8.7	8.8	9.0
LiCl	-47 ± 3	50.9	7.9	8.5	8.8	8.9	9.1
LiI	-21.8 ± 2	55.5	8.3	8.7	9.0	9.0	9.2
Na_2	32.9	55.0	9.0	9.1	9.2	9.3	9.5
NaH	30 ± 5	45.0	7.2	7.9	8.5	8.8	9.1
NaF	-70.1 ± 2	52.0	8.2	8.7	8.9	9.0	9.1
NaCl	-43.4	54.9	8.6	8.9	9.0	9.1	9.2
NaBr	$-34,4$	57.6	8.7	8.9	9.0	9.1	9.2
K_2	30.4	59.7	9.1	9.2	9.3	9.4	9.7
KH	29 ± 4	47.3	7.4	8.1	8.7	8.9	9.1
KF	-77.9	54.1	8.4	8.8	9.0	9.0	9.2
KCl	-51.3	57.1	8.7	8.9	9.0	9.1	9.2

[a] Standard State is white phosphorous. JANAF uses red phosphorous as standard.

197

Table A.9 Thermochemical Data for Some Gas Phase Triatomic Species

Substance	ΔH_f°	S°	C_p° 300	500	800	1000	1500
O_3	34.1	57.1	9.4	11.3	12.7	13.2	13.7
H_2O	-57.8	45.1	8.0	8.4	9.2	9.9	11.2
D_2O	-59.6	47.4	8.2				
HO_2	5.0	54.4	8.3	9.5	10.8	11.4	12.4
F_2O	-5 ± 2	59.1	10.4	12.1	13.1	13.3	13.7
F—O—O·	(12 ± 5)	61.9	10.6	11.8	12.8	13.1	13.5
Cl_2O	21.0	64.0	11.4	12.8	13.4	13.6	13.8
O—Cl—O	25 ± 2	61.5	10.0	11.7	13.0	13.3	13.8
ClOO·	23 ± 2	63	11.6				
HOCl	-22 ± 3	56.5	8.9	10.1	11.1	11.6	12.4
HOBr	-19 ± 2	59.2	9.0				
SO_2	-70.9	59.3	9.5	11.1	12.5	13.0	13.6
H_2S	-4.8	49.2	8.2	8.9	10.2	10.9	12.3
SCl_2	-5.2	67.2	12.1	13.1	13.6	13.7	
S_2O		63.8	10.5	12.0	13.0	13.3	13.6
NO_2	7.9	57.3	8.8	10.3	11.9	12.5	13.2
N_2O	19.6	52.5	9.2	11.0	12.5	13.1	14.0
·NH_2	42 ± 3	46.5	8.0	8.5	9.5	10.2	11.5
HNO	23.8	52.7	8.3	9.3	10.8	11.5	12.5
FNO	-15.7	59.3	9.9	11.2	12.4	12.8	13.3
ClNO	12.4	62.5	10.7	11.8	12.8	13.3	13.9
BrNO	19.6	65.3	10.9	11.8	12.6	13.0	13.4
INO	37.0 ± 2	67.6	11.2	11.9	12.7	13.0	13.5
·NF_2	8.5 ± 2	59.7	9.8	11.6	12.8	13.2	13.6
C_3	190 ± 3	56.8	10.2	11.8	13.3	13.6	14.2
CO_2	-94.05	51.1	8.9	10.7	12.3	13.0	14.0
HCN	32.3	48.2	8.6	10.0	11.4	12.2	13.5
FCN	-3 ± 10	53.9	10.1	11.6	12.8	13.3	14.1
ClCN	33.0	56.5	10.8	12.2	13.2	13.6	14.2
BrCN	43.3	59.3	11.2	12.4	13.2	13.6	14.2
ICN	54.6	61.4	11.5	12.5	13.3	13.7	14.3
:NCN		54.2	10.2	12.3	13.6	14.0	14.5
CS_2	28.0	56.8	10.9	12.5	13.6	14.0	14.5
COS	-33.1	55.3	9.9	11.7	13.0	13.6	14.4
·CNO		54.0	9.2				
SiO_2	-76 ± 2	54.7	10.7	12.4	13.7	14.1	14.5
$PbCl_2$	-40.6	76.6	13.4	13.7	13.8	13.9	13.9
·BF_2	-130 ± 10	59.0	9.6	11.1	12.8	12.9	13.4
BOF	-144 ± 3	53.7	9.8	11.5	13.4	13.3	14.2
AlOF	-140 ± 3	56.0	10.7	12.8	14.0	14.3	14.6
Al_2O	-31 ± 7	62.0	10.9	12.3	13.2	13.4	13.7
$HgCl_2$	-35 ± 2	70.4	13.9	14.5	14.8	14.8	14.9
$BeCl_2$	-86.1 ± 3	60.3	12.3	13.5	14.2	14.4	14.7
MgF_2	-173 ± 2	61.7	11.6	13.8	13.4	13.0	13.8
$MgCl_2$	-95.5 ± 2	64.9	12.4	13.3	13.6	13.7	13.8
Li_2O	-40 ± 3	54.7	11.9	13.3	14.2	14.4	14.7

Table A.10 Thermochemical Data for Some Gas Phase Tetratomic Species

Substance	ΔH_f°	S°	C_p°				
			300	500	800	1000	1500
H_2O_2	−32.6	56.6	10.3	12.6	14.3	15.0	16.3
HOOO·	±2						
F_2O_2	8 ± 5						
ClF_3	−38.0	67.3	15.3	17.8	19.0	19.3	19.6
Cl_2O_2	28 ± 6						
BrF_3	−61.1	69.9	15.9	18.1	19.1	19.4	19.7
$SOCl_2$	−50.8	74.0	15.9	17.8	18.9	19.2	
SO_3	−94.6	61.3	12.1	15.1	17.4	18.2	19.1
H_2S_2	3.9		12.3				
SOF_2	−97.1	66.6	13.6	16.4	18.2	18.7	
NO_3 (sym)	17.0	60.4	11.2	15.0	17.5	18.3	19.1
ON—OO·	14 ± 3	70	11				
NH_3	−11.0	46.0	8.5	10.0	12.2	13.5	15.9
N_2H_2 (cis)	50 ± 5	52.2	8.7	10.9	13.5	14.8	16.9
HNO_2 (cis)	−18.3	59.6	10.8	13.4	15.6	16.5	17.9
FNO_2	−26 ± 2	62.2	11.9	14.9	17.2	18.0	18.9
$ClNO_2$	2.9	65.0	12.7	15.4	17.5	18.2	19.1
NO_2—OF	2.5	70.0	15.6	19.7	22.7	23.6	24.8
N_2F_2 (cis)	17.9	62.1	11.9	15.3	17.6	18.3	19.1
NF_3	−31.4 ± 1	62.3	12.8	16.1	18.2	18.7	19.3
HN_3	70.3	57.1	10.4				
P_4	14.0	66.9	16.1	18.3	19.2	19.4	19.7
PCl_3	−68.6	74.5	17.2	18.8	19.4	19.6	19.7
PF_3	−220 ± 4	65.2	14.0	16.9	18.5	19.0	19.5
PH_3	1.3	50.2	8.9	11.1	14.0	15.4	17.4
CH_2O	−27.7	52.3	8.5	10.5	13.4	14.8	17.0
C_2H_2	54.2	48.0	10.5	13.1	15.2	16.3	18.3
HNCO		56.9	10.7	13.1	15.2	16.1	17.6
HOCN		57	10.7				
COF_2	−151.7 + 2	61.9	11.3	14.5	16.9	17.8	18.8
$COCl_2$	−52.6	67.8	13.8	16.3	17.9	18.5	19.2
C_2N_2	73.9	57.7	13.6	15.6	17.4	18.2	19.4
BH_3	22 ± 2	44.9	8.7	10.0	12.5	14.0	16.4
BF_3	−271.7	60.7	12.1	15.0	17.3	18.1	19.0
BCl_3	−96.3	69.3	14.9	17.3	18.7	19.1	19.5
OBOH	−134.0	57.3	10.1	12.5	14.9	15.9	17.5
AlF_3	−290 ± 2	66.2	15.0	17.4	18.7	19.1	19.5
$AlCl_3$	−139.7	74.6	17.0	18.6	19.4	19.5	19.7
Li_2F_2	−222 ± 4	63.6	16.1	18.3	19.2	19.4	19.7
Na_2F_2	−196 ± 4	72.1	18.3	19.3	19.6	19.7	19.8
Na_2Cl_2	−135 ± 2	77.8	18.8	19.5	19.7	19.8	19.8
Na_2Br_2	−116.2	83.4	19.2	19.6	19.8	19.8	19.8
K_2Cl_2	−147.6	84.3	19.3	19.7	19.8	19.8	19.8

Table A.11 Thermochemical Data for Some Polyatomic Species

Species	ΔH_f°	S°	C_p°				
			300	500	800	1000	1500
H_2O_3	[−13.5]	[67]					
H_2O_4	[+5.5]	[77]					
HO_4^-	[+43]	[78]					
$HClO_3$	11 ± 4	67					
$HClO_4$	4 ± 4	69					
Cl_2O_7	65.0						
ClO_3F	−5.1	66.7	15.5	20.0	23.0	23.9	24.9
BrF_5	−102.5	77.3	24.2	28.5	30.4	30.9	31.4
IF_5	−196.4	80.1	24.7	28.7	30.5	30.9	31.4
IF_7	−224 ± 2	83.1	32.4	38.8	41.7	42.4	43.1
Cyclo-S_6	24.5						
Cyclo-S_8	24.5	103.0	37.4				
H_2S_3	3.6						
H_2S_4	5.7						
H_2SO_4	−177 ± 2	69.1	19.3	25.5	30.0	31.6	34.1
SF_4	−185 ± 2	70.0	17.5	21.8	24.1	24.6	25.3
SF_6	−291.8	69.7	23.4	30.7	34.6	35.7	36.8
SO_2F_2	−205.0	67.7	15.8	20.1	23.0	23.9	24.9
SO_2Cl_2	−87.0	74.5	18.4				
N_2O_3	19.8	73.9	15.7	18.7	21.4	22.4	23.6
N_2O_4	2.2	72.7	18.5	23.2	27.1	28.5	30.2
N_2O_5	2.7	82.8	23.0	29.0	32.7	33.8	34.9
N_2H_4	22.8	57.1	12.2	16.9	21.1	23.0	26.4
NH_2OH	−9						
$HONO_2$	−32.1	63.7	12.7	16.9	20.3	21.6	23.4
N_2F_4	−5(±1)	72.0	18.9	25.0	28.7	29.7	30.8
P_2H_4	5.0						
PF_5	−377.2	70.7	20.1	25.9	29.1	30.0	31.0
POF_3	−290 ± 4	68.2	16.5	20.7	23.3	24.1	25.0
$POCl_3$	−133.5	77.8	20.3	23.0	24.5	24.9	25.4
PCl_5	−89.6	87.0	26.7	29.7	30.9	31.2	31.5
CH_4	−17.9	44.5	8.5	11.1	15.0	17.2	20.7
C_2H_4	12.5	52.4	10.3	14.9	20.0	22.4	26.3
C_2H_6	−20.2	54.9	12.7	18.7	25.8	29.3	34.9
C_3H_4 (allene)	45.9	58.3	14.2	19.8	25.4	28.0	32.1
C_3H_6	4.9	63.8	15.3	22.6	30.7	34.5	40.4
c-C_3H_4	66.6	58.4					
c-C_3H_6	12.7	56.8	13.3				

200

Table A.11 (Continued)

Species	ΔH_f°	S°	C_p°				
			300	500	800	1000	1500
c-C₄H₈	6.3	63.4	17.3				
c-C₅H₁₀	−18.5	70.0	20.0	35.9	52.4	59.8	70.9
Cyclopentene	8.6	69.2	18.0	31.6	45.8	51.9	61.1
Cyclopentadiene	32.4						
Cyclohexane	−29.3	71.3	25.6	45.5	66.8	75.8	88.6
Cyclohexene	−0.8	74.3	25.1	42.8	59.5	66.6	77.3
Cyclohexadiene-1,3	25.9						
Cyclohexadiene-1,4	26.3						
CH₃OH	−48.0	57.3	10.5	14.2	19.0	21.4	
C₂H₅OH	−56.2	67.5	15.7	22.8	30.3	33.8	
CH₃OCH₃	−44.0	63.7	15.8	22.5	30.4	34.1	
Ethylene oxide	−12.6	58.1	11.4	18.0	24.6	27.5	31.8
C₆H₅OH	−23.1	75.1	24.8	38.7	50.7	55.5	62.7
C₆H₅OCH₃	−18.0	[86.2]					
CH₃OOH	[−31.3]	[67.5]					
CH₃OOCH₃	−30.0	[74.1]					
CH₂CO	−14.6	57.8	12.4	15.7	18.8	20.3	22.6
CH₃CHO	−39.7	63.2	13.2	18.2	24.2	27.0	
CH₃COCH₃	−51.7	70.5	18.0	25.9	34.9	39.2	45.7
HCOOH	−90.5	59.4	10.8	14.6	18.3	19.9	
CH₃COOH	−104.8	67.5	16.0		29.1	31.9	36.5
(COOH)₂	[−184]	[82]					
C₃O₂	−23.4	66.0	16.0	19.3	22.1	23.3	25.0
(CH₃CO)₂	−78.6	[91.6]					
HCOOCH₃	−81.0	[72.3]					
CH₃COOCH₃	[−94.9]	79.8					
H₂C(OH)₂	−93.5	[70]					
H₂CO₃	[−132]	[70]					
C₆H₅CHO	−6.0	[86]					
CH₃NH₂	−5.5	57.9	11.9		22.4		
(CH₃)₂NH	−4.5	65.4	16.6		33.9		
(CH₃)₃N	−5.9	69.2	22.1		45.6		
CH₃NHNH₂	22.6	66.6	17.0		31.3		
Ethylene imine	0.0						
CH₃CN	[19.1]	58.7	12.5	16.6	21.3	23.5	

Table A.11 (Continued)

Species	ΔH_f°	S°	C_p°				
			300	500	800	1000	1500
$\overline{CH_2\!-\!N\!=\!N}$	79	56.9	10.2	14.3	18.4	20.0	
$CH_2\!=\!N\!=\!N$	71	58.0	12.6	15.6	18.7	20.2	
CH_3NC	35.9	59.1	12.8	16.7	21.3	23.6	
$HCONH_2$	-44.5	59.6	11.1		21.1		
CH_3NO	[16]	[64]					
C_2H_5NO	[9]	[74]					
CH_3NO_2	-17.9	65.8	13.8	19.6	25.6	28.2	
CH_3ONO	-15.6	70.1	15.4		26.3		
CH_3ONO_2	-28.6	76.0					
CH_3SH	-5.5	61.0	12.05		20.3		
$(CH_3)_2S$	-8.9	63.3	17.8		31.6		
$(CH_3)_2S_2$	-5.7	80.5	22.6		37.7		
$HN\!=\!CS$	$+30.0$	59.2					
$CO(NH_2)_2$	(-60 ± 4)						
$C(NO_2)_4$	(19.4)						
CH_3F	-55 ± 2	53.3	9.0	12.3	16.4	18.4	21.6
CH_3Cl	-20.7	56.0	9.7	13.2	17.0	18.9	21.8
CH_3Br	-9.5 ± 1	58.9	10.2	13.6	17.3	19.0	21.8
CH_3I	3.3	60.5	10.6	14.0	17.5	19.2	21.9
CH_2Cl_2	-22.4	64.6	12.2	16.0	19.4	20.8	22.9
CH_2F_2	-107.2	59.0	10.3	14.1	18.2	20.0	22.5
CH_2Br_2	$(+1 \pm 3)$	70.1	13.1	16.7	19.7	21.1	23.1
CH_2I_2	$+26 \pm 2$	74.0	13.9	17.3	20.1	21.3	23.2
CHF_3	-166.8	62.0	12.2	16.6	20.3	21.7	23.6
$CHCl_3$	-25 ± 1	70.7	15.7	19.4	21.9	22.9	24.2
CF_2Cl_2	-115 ± 2	71.9	17.3	21.3	23.7	24.4	25.2
CF_4	-222 ± 2	62.5	14.6	19.3	22.6	23.6	24.8
CCl_4	-26.0	74.2	19.9	23.0	24.6	25.0	25.5
C_2F_4	-155 ± 2	71.7	19.2	24.0	27.6	28.9	30.4
C_2Cl_4	-3.6	81.3	22.7	26.6	29.2	30.0	
C_2F_6	-317	79.4	25.4	33.3	38.3	39.8	41.4
C_2Cl_6	-35.3	94.8	32.7	38.3	41.3	42.1	
C_2H_5F	-61	63.3	14.1	20.5			
C_2H_5Cl	-26.7	66.1	15.1	21.7	27.4	31.5	
C_2H_5Br	-14.8	68.6	15.5	22.0	28.6	31.6	
C_2H_5I	-2.1	70.7	15.4	22.3	28.8	32.0	
$CH_2\!=\!CHF$	(-31.6)	60.4	11.9	17.0	21.9	24.0	
$CH_2\!=\!CHNO_2$		70.6	17.4	24.9	31.7	34.5	38.5
$CH_2\!=\!CHCl$	8.1	63.1	12.9	17.8	22.4	24.3	
CH_3COF	-104						
CH_3COCl	-58.9	70.5	16.3	21.2	26.3	28.6	

Table A.11 (Continued)

Species	ΔH_f°	S°	C_p°				
			300	500	800	1000	1500
CH₃COI	−30.3	76.0	17.5	20.9			
SiH₄	8.2	49.0	10.3	14.1	18.3	20.2	22.8
Si₂H₆	17.0	65.6	19.0	25.5	31.8	34.5	
SiF₄	−386.0	67.5	17.6	21.4	23.8	24.4	25.2
SiH₃CH₃	−4.0	61.3	15.7				
SiCl₄	−157 ± 2	79.2	21.7	24.0	25.1	25.3	25.6
B₂H₆	9 ± 4	55.7	13.9	21.2	29.1	32.6	37.7
B₅H₉	17.5 ± 2	65.9	22.6	38.6	54.3	60.8	69.6
B₂Cl₄	−116.9	85.8	22.7	26.6	28.9	29.5	30.2
B₃F₃O₃	−565.3	81.8	27.5	36.2	42.8	44.9	47.4
Borazole(H₆B₃N₃)	−122 ± 3	69.0	23.2	36.0	47.1	51.8	58.5
B(CH₃)₃	−29.3	75.3	21.2				
Al₂Cl₆	−309.2	113.8	37.9	41.3	42.7	43.1	43.4
Al₂(CH₃)₆	−62 ± 4	125.4					
Al(CH₃)₃	−21 ± 2						
Al(BH₄)₃	3	91					

Table A.12 Thermochemical Data for Some Gas Phase Organic Free Radicals

Radical	(σ, S)	ΔH_f°	S°	C_p° 300	500	800	1000	1500
$:CO_3$	$(6, 1)$	-48 ± 6	61.2	11.3	15.0	17.5	18.3	19.1
$H\dot{C}O$	$(1, \frac{1}{2})$	7.2	53.7	8.3	9.2	10.5	11.2	12.3
$HCOO\cdot$	$(2, \frac{1}{2})$	-36 ± 4	57.3	9.6	12.4	15.0	15.9	16.8
$:C{=}C{=}O$	$(1, 1)$	68 ± 15	55.7	10.3	11.7	13.1	13.7	14.6
$\cdot COOH$	$(1, \frac{1}{2})$	-51 ± 3	61.0	10.8	13.4	15.6	16.5	17.9
$:CH_2$	$(2, 1)$	88 ± 3	43.3	7.5	8.8	10.3	11.1	12.6
$:CF_2$	$(2, 0)$	-41 ± 4	57.5	9.3	11.1	12.5	13.0	13.5
$:CCl_2$	$(2, 0)$	45 ± 10	63.7	10.8	12.3	13.1	13.4	13.7
$\cdot C{\equiv}C{-}H$	$(1, \frac{1}{2})$	122 ± 5	49.6	8.9	10.2	11.5	12.2	13.3
$Cl\dot{C}O$	$(1, \frac{1}{2})$	-4.0	63.5	10.8	11.7	12.5	12.9	13.4
$\cdot CH_3$	$(6, \frac{1}{2})$	34.0	46.1	8.8	10.6	13.2	14.5	16.8
$\cdot C_2H_3$	$(1, \frac{1}{2})$	69 ± 2	56.3	9.7	13.1	16.8	18.7	21.8
$\cdot CF_3$	$(3, \frac{1}{2})$	-112.5	63.8	12.2	15.2	17.5	18.2	19.1
$\cdot CCl_3$	$(3, \frac{1}{2})$	18.5	70.8	14.9	17.3	18.7	19.1	19.5
$\cdot C_2H_5$	$(6, \frac{1}{2})$	26.0	59.8	11.1	16.3	22.8	25.7	30.4
$n\text{-}C_3H_7$	$(6, \frac{1}{2})$	21.0	68.5	17.1	25.2	33.7	38.1	44.7
$i\text{-}C_3H_7$	$(18, \frac{1}{2})$	17.6	66.7	17.0	24.9	33.2	37.9	44.6
$i\text{-}C_4H_9$	$(9, \frac{1}{2})$	13.7	75.2	22.7	33.8	45.1	50.6	59.1
$t\text{-}C_4H_9$	$(162, \frac{1}{2})$	6.7	74.6	19.1	30.5	43.0	49.0	58.3
Allyl	$(2, \frac{1}{2})$	40.6	63.4	14.1				
Cyclopropyl	$(2, \frac{1}{2})$	61 ± 3	60.4	12.9				
Cyclobutyl	$(2, \frac{1}{2})$	51 ± 2	67.3	16.8				
Phenyl	$(2, \frac{1}{2})$	80 ± 1	69.4	18.8				
Benzyl	$(2, \frac{1}{2})$	45	77.3	34.9				
Cyclohexyl	$(1, \frac{1}{2})$	[13]	[76]					
Cyclohexen-yl-3	$(2, \frac{1}{2})$	[30]	[75]					
Cyclohexadien, 1,3-yl-5	$(2, \frac{1}{2})$	[43]	[69]					
$CH_3\dot{O}$	$(3, \frac{1}{2})$	3.5	55	9.0				
$CH_3S\cdot$	$(3, \frac{1}{2})$	[32.5]	[59]	9.0				
$CH_3\dot{N}H$	$(3, \frac{1}{2})$	[34.5]	[57]	10.5				
$\dot{C}H_2CN$	$(2, \frac{1}{2})$	[16.9]	[58]	11.4				
$\dot{C}H_2NH_2$	$(2, \frac{1}{2})$	[36.5]	[57]	10.5				
$CH_3\dot{C}O$	$(3, \frac{1}{2})$	-5.4	63.5	11.3	15.7			
$\dot{C}H_2COCH_3$	$(3, \frac{1}{2})$	[93.7]	[71.5]	17.6				
$\dot{C}H_2OCH_3$	$(6, \frac{1}{2})$	[86.0]	[64.7]	15.5				
$C_2H_5\dot{O}$	$(3, \frac{1}{2})$	-4	[65.3]	14.2				
$i\text{-}C_3H_7\dot{O}$	$(9, \frac{1}{2})$	[-12.6]	[71.8]					
$t\text{-}Bu\dot{O}$	$(81, \frac{1}{2})$	-21.6	[75.7]					
$CH_3O\dot{O}$	$(3, \frac{1}{2})$	[$+6.7$]	[65.3]					
$C_2H_5O\dot{O}$	$(3, \frac{1}{2})$	[-1.8]	[75]					
$t\text{-}BuO_2$	$(81, \frac{1}{2})$	[-19.2]	[85]					

Table A.13 Frequencies Assigned to Normal and Partial Bond Bending and Stretching Motions

Bond Stretches	Frequency (ω cm^{-1})[a]	Bond Bends	Frequency (ω cm^{-1})
C=O	1700	H–C–H	1450
C$\overset{\cdot}{-}$C	1400	H–C $\cdots$ H (one bond partial)	1000
C—O ethers C—O acids, esters	1100 1200	(H–C–C) t, w[b]	1150
C·O	710	H $\cdots$ C–C	800
C=C	1650	H–O–C	1200
C$\overset{\cdot}{-}$C	1300	H $\cdots$ O–C	840
C—C	1000	H–C=C	1150
C·C	675	H $\cdots$ C–C	800
C—H, O—H; N—H	3100		
S—H	2600	C–C=C	420
C·H	2200	C $\cdots$ C=C	290
C—F	1100	C–C $\cdots$ C	420
C·F	820	O–C=O	420
C—Cl	650	O $\cdots$ C $\cdots$ O	420

205

Table A.13 (Continued)

Bond Stretches	Frequency (ω cm^{-1})[a]	Bond Bends	Frequency (ω cm^{-1})
C·Cl	490	C=C=C	850
C—I	500	C / C⋅⋅C	635
C·I	375	(H / C \ C) r[b]	700
C—Br	560	(H / C ⋅ C) r	700
C·Br	420	(H / C \\ C) o.p	700
		C / C \ Cl	400
		C / C ⋅ Cl	280
		C / C \ Br	360
		C / C ⋅ Br	250
		C / C \ I	320
		C / C ⋅ I	220
		C / C \ C	420
		C / C ⋅ C	300
		O / C \ C	400
		O / C ⋅ C	280

206

Table A.13   (Continued)

Bond Stretches	Frequency (ω cm^{-1})[a] Bond Bends	Frequency (ω cm^{-1})

The bond bends column shows three angle structures:

$$\overset{\text{C}}{\underset{\text{C}\quad\text{O}}{\diagup\diagdown}} \qquad 400$$

$$\overset{\text{C}}{\underset{\text{C}\quad\cdot\quad\text{O}}{\diagup\diagdown}} \qquad 280$$

$$\overset{\text{C}}{\underset{\text{O}\quad\text{O}}{\diagup\diagdown}} \qquad 400$$

[a] Note that bending frequencies are surprisingly consistent with the relation, $\omega_1/\omega_2 = (\mu_2/\mu_1)^{1/2}$. Deviations from this relation seldom exceed 50 cm^{-1}. Here the reduced mass

$$\mu = \left(\frac{M_A M_B}{M_A M_B}\right) \quad \text{for the bend } (\widehat{A\text{-}R\text{-}B}).$$

[b] Methyl and methylene wags and twists, whose frequencies range from 1000–1300 cm^{-1} have been equated with $\left(\overset{\text{C}}{\underset{\text{H}\quad\text{C}}{\diagup\diagdown}} \right)$ t, w bends and assigned a mean value of 1150 cm^{-1}. Methylene rocks have lower frequencies (that is ~700 cm^{-1}), which correspond closely to the out of plane $\left(\overset{\text{C}}{\underset{\text{H}\quad\text{C}}{\diagup\diagdown}} \right)$ bends in olefins.

[c] Single dots, as in C $\cdot$ C, are meant to represent one-electron bonds.

Table A.14 Some Average Covalent Radii, Bond Lengths[a]

Atom	Radius (Å)	Bond Lengths	
H	0.32	C—H	1.08 ± 0.03 (range)
C	0.77	O—H	0.96
C_d	0.67	N—H	1.01
C_t	0.60	S—H	1.34
N	0.74	B—H	1.18
N_d	0.62	C—C	1.54
N_t	0.55	C=C	1.34
O	0.74	C≡C	1.20
O_d	0.62	C—F	1.33
S	1.04	C—Cl	1.77
S_d	0.94	C—Br	1.94
P	1.10	C—I	2.13
P_d	1.00	C—N	1.47
B	0.81	C≡N	1.16
Hg	1.48	C—O	1.43
F	0.72	C=O	1.23
Cl	0.99	C—S	1.81
Br	1.11	C=S	1.17
I	1.28		
Si	1.17		
Si_d	1.07		
Sn	1.40		

[a] Subscripts refer to (d) double and (t) triple bonds.

Table A.15 Contributions of Harmonic Oscillator to C_p (gibbs/mole) as a Function of Frequency and Temperature

Frequency (cm^{-1})	Temperature (°K)						
	300	400	500	600	800	1000	1500
100	1.95	1.97	1.97	1.98	1.98	1.98	1.99
200	1.84	1.90	1.93	1.95	1.97	1.97	1.98
250	1.76	1.86	1.90	1.93	1.95	1.97	1.98
300	1.68	1.80	1.87	1.90	1.94	1.96	1.97
350	1.58	1.74	1.83	1.87	1.92	1.95	1.97
400	1.47	1.68	1.78	1.84	1.90	1.93	1.96
500	1.26	1.53	1.68	1.76	1.86	1.90	1.95
600	1.04	1.37	1.56	1.68	1.80	1.87	1.93
800	0.66	1.04	1.30	1.47	1.68	1.78	1.89
1000	0.38	0.74	1.04	1.26	1.53	1.68	1.84
1200	0.21	0.51	0.80	1.04	1.37	1.56	1.78
1500	0.08	0.26	0.51	0.74	1.12	1.37	1.68
2000	0.01	0.08	0.21	0.38	0.74	1.04	1.30
2500	0.00	0.02	0.08	0.18	0.46	0.74	1.26
3000	0.00	0.00	0.03	0.08	0.26	0.51	1.04

Table A.16 Molar Heat Capacity C_p° (gibbs/mole) as a Function of Barrier (V), Temperature, and Partition Function Q_f[a]

$\dfrac{V}{RT}$	$(1/Q_f)$				
	0.0	0.2	0.4	0.6	0.8
0.0	1.0	1.0	1.0	1.0	1.0
0.5	1.1	1.1	1.1	1.0	1.0
1.0	1.2	1.2	1.2	1.1	1.1
1.5	1.5	1.4	1.3	1.2	1.1
2.0	1.7	1.7	1.5	1.4	1.2
2.5	1.9	1.9	1.7	1.5	1.3
3.0	2.1	2.0	1.8	1.6	1.3
4.0	2.3	2.2	2.0	1.7	1.4
6.0	2.3	2.2	1.9	1.5	1.2
8.0	2.2	2.1	1.7	1.3	0.9
10.0	2.1	2.0	1.5	1.0	0.7
15.0	2.1	1.8	1.2	0.7	0.4
20.0	2.0	1.7	1.0	0.5	0.2

From G. N. Lewis and M. Randall, revised by K. S. Pitzer and L. Brewer, *Thermodynamics*, McGraw-Hill, New York (1961) 2nd Ed.

$$Q_f = \frac{3.6}{\sigma}\left(\frac{I_r T}{100}\right)^{1/2} \text{ with } I_r \text{ in amu-Å}^2 \text{ and } T \text{ in } {}^{\circ}\text{K.}$$

σ = symmetry of barrier (for example, 3 for $-CH_3$, 2 for $-CH_2$, etc.)

Table A.17 Absolute Entropy (gibbs/mole) of a Harmonic Oscillator as a Function of Frequency and Temperature[a]

Frequency (cm^{-1})	Temperature (°K)							
	300	400	500	600	800	1000	1200	1500
50	4.8	5.4	5.9	6.3	6.8	7.3	7.7	8.1
75	4.1	4.7	5.0	5.4	6.0	6.5	6.9	7.3
100	3.4	4.1	4.5	4.8	5.6	5.9	6.3	6.7
125	3.1	3.6	4.1	4.4	5.2	5.5	5.9	6.3
150	2.7	3.3	3.7	4.1	4.7	5.0	5.4	5.9
200	2.2	2.7	3.1	3.5	4.1	4.4	4.8	5.3
250	1.8	2.3	2.7	3.0	3.6	4.1	4.5	4.9
300	1.4	1.9	2.3	2.7	3.3	3.6	4.1	4.5
350	1.2	1.7	2.1	2.4	3.0	3.4	3.8	4.2
400	1.0	1.4	1.8	2.1	2.7	3.2	3.5	3.8
500	0.7	1.1	1.4	1.8	2.3	2.7	3.0	3.5
600	0.5	0.8	1.0	1.4	1.9	2.3	2.7	3.1
700	0.3	0.6	0.8	1.2	1.7	2.1	2.4	2.8
800	0.2	0.5	0.8	1.0	1.4	1.8	2.1	2.6
900	0.2	0.4	0.6	0.8	1.2	1.6	1.9	2.3
1000	0.1	0.3	0.5	0.7	1.1	1.4	1.8	2.1
1200	0.0	0.1	0.3	0.5	0.8	1.0	1.4	1.8
1500	0.0	0.1	0.2	0.3	0.5	0.8	1.1	1.4
2000	0.0	0.0	0.0	0.1	0.3	0.5	0.7	1.0
2500	0.0	0.0	0.0	0.0	0.1	0.3	0.5	0.7
3000	0.0	0.0	0.0	0.0	0.1	0.1	0.3	0.5
3500	0.0	0.0	0.0	0.0	0.0	0.1	0.2	0.3

[a] $x = 1.44\tilde{\nu}/T$ determines $S°$, so that value of $S°$ must be the same for similar ratios of $\tilde{\nu}/T$. For $x \ll 1$, $S° = R + R \ln x = 1.99 + 4.575 \log x$.

Table A.18 Approximate Moments of Inertia, Entropies, and Partition Functions Q_f at 600°K of Some Free Rotors

Rotor	$(\sigma)^a$	Moment of Inertia[b]	Q_f (600°K)	$S^\circ_{f(int.)}$ (gibbs/mole)[c]		
				300°K	600°K	1000°K
—CH$_3$	(3)	3.0	5.2	5.8	6.5	7.0
—CH$_2$	(2)	2.0	6.5	5.4	6.1	6.6
—C$_2$H$_5$	(1)	44.0	52.0	8.2	8.2	9.4
—i-Propyl	(1)	87.0	65.0	8.6	9.3	9.8
—t-butyl	(3)	130.0	24.0	8.8	9.5	10.0
—phenyl	(2)	88.0	32.0	8.6	9.3	9.8
—benzyl	(1)	~700.0	93.0	10.7	11.4	11.9
—OH	(1)	1.0	9.1	4.6	5.3	5.8

[a] The moment is taken along the —C axis, assuming tetrahedral angles for saturated bonds and 120° for angles about double bonded atoms. The value in parentheses is the symmetry number, σ.

[b] Units are given in amu-Å^2. It is assumed that the rotor is connected to an infinite mass.

[c] For units and equations, see Table A.16.

[d] $S^\circ_{f(int.)} = S^\circ_f + R \ln \sigma$.

Table A.19 Some Characteristic Torsion Barriers, V (kcal/mole) to Free Rotation about Single Bonds[a]

Bond		V	Bond	V
CH_3—CH_3		2.9	CH_3—OH	1.1
CH_3—C_2H_5		2.8	CH_3—OCH_3	2.7
CH_3—isopropyl		3.6	CH_3—NH_2	1.9
CH_3—t-butyl		4.7	CH_3—$NHCH_3$	3.3
CH_3—CH=CHCH$_3$	cis	0.75[b]	CH_3—$N(CH_3)_2$	4.4
	trans	1.95	CH_3—SiH_3	1.7
CH_3—vinyl		2.0	CH_3—$SiH_2(CH_3)$	1.7
CH_3—CH_2F		3.3	CH_3—PH_2	2.0
CH_3—CF_3		3.5	CH_3—SH	1.3
CF_3—CF_3		4.4	CH_3—SCH_3	2.1
CH_3—CH_2Cl		3.7	CH_3—CHO	1.2
CH_2Cl—CF_3		5.8	CH_3—$COCH_3$	0.8
CCl_3—CCl_3		10.8	CH_3—allene	1.6
CH_3—CH_2Br		3.6	CH_3—(isobutene)	2.2
CH_3—CH_2I		3.2	CH_3—CO(OH)	0.5
CH_3—phenyl		0	CH_3—(epoxide ring)	2.6
CH_3—CCCH$_3$		0	$(CH_3)_2N$—$COCH_3$	20.0
CH_3—NO_2		0	CH_3—OCHO	1.2
CH_3O—NO		9.0	CH_3—ONO_2	2.3
CH_3O—NO_2		9.0	CH_3—O-vinyl	3.4
CH_3O—$CO(CH_3)$		13		

[a] For a more complete compilation, see J. Dale, *Tetrahedron* **22**, 3373 (1966).
[b] There seems to be a quite general "cis effect," such that F, Cl, CH_3, and CN, cis to a CH_3, lower the CH_3 barrier by ~1.4 kcal.

Table A.20 Decrease in Entropy of Free Rotor as Functions of Barrier Height (V), Temperature (T, °K) and Partition Function, $Q_f{}^a$

$\dfrac{V}{RT}$	$1/Q_f$		
	0.0	0.2	0.4
0.0	0.0	0.0	0.0
1.0	0.1	0.1	0.1
2.0	0.4	0.4	0.4
3.0	0.8	0.8	0.7
4.0	1.1	1.1	1.0
5.0	1.4	1.4	1.2
6.0	1.7	1.6	1.4
8.0	2.0	2.0	1.7
10.0	2.3	2.2	1.9
15.0	2.7	2.6	2.2
20.0	3.1	2.9	2.4

[a] Values listed are $\Delta S = S_f^\circ - S_h^\circ$ in gibbs/mole. From G. N. Lewis and M. Randall, *Thermodynamics*, McGraw-Hill, New York (1961) 2nd ed. See Table A.16 and A.17 for definition and values.

Table A.21 Torsion Frequencies for Methyl Substituted Ethylenes

	ω cm^{-1} a	ω cm^{-1} (Three electron Torsions)	μ(amu)
Ethylene (C$_2$H$_4$)	1000		
(E)$_t$ = (CH$_2$=CH$_2$		500	1.0
Propylene (C$_3$H$_6$)	800		
(P)$_t$ = CH$_2$=CHCH$_3$		400	1.78
Isobutene (C$_4$H$_8$)	700		
(i-B)$_t$ = (CH$_3$)$_2$C=CH$_2$		350	1.88
cis-2-butene (C$_4$H$_8$)	400		

(C-2-B)$_t$ =

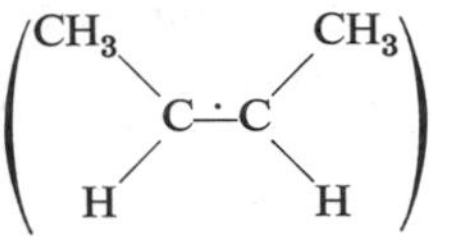

		200	8.0

| Trans-2-butene | 300 | | |

(t-2-B)$_t$ =

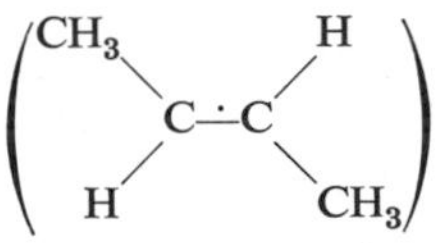

		150	8.0

2-Methyl but-2-ene	250		
(2-MB-2)$_t$ = (CH$_3$)$_2$C=CHCH$_3$		125	10.4
Tetramethyl ethylene	(210)		
(TME)$_t$ = (CH$_3$)$_2$C=C(CH$_3$)$_2$		105	15.0

a It should be noted that, to a reasonable approximation (that is, $\simeq \pm 50$ cm^{-1}), these torsional frequencies are consistent with the relation

$$\frac{\omega_1}{\omega_2} = \left(\frac{\mu_2}{\mu_1}\right)^{1/2}$$

where μ is given by the product of the sums of the oscillating masses on each end of the double bond, divided by the sum of the four masses. Thus, for

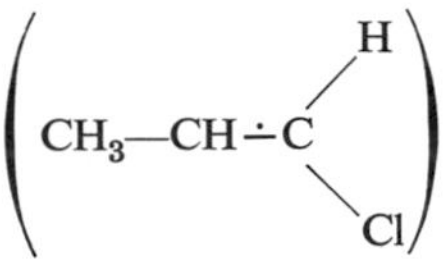

$$\mu = \frac{(16)(36.5)}{(52.5)}.$$

b The three electron torsion frequencies have been assigned a value of one half the corresponding double bond torsion.

Table A.22 Bond Dissociation Energies for Some Organic Molecules $R' - R''$[a]

	(52.1) H	(19.8) F	(28.9) Cl	(26.7) Br	(25.5) I	(9.3) OH	(40±2) NH$_2$	(3.5±1) OCH$_3$	(34±1) CH$_3$	(26±1) C$_2$H$_5$	(17.5±1) i-C$_3$H$_5$	(6.7±1) t-Bu	(80±1) C$_6$H$_5$
(34±1)[b] CH$_3$	104	108	83.5	70	56	91.5	79	81.5	88	85	84	80	102
(26±1) C$_2$H$_5$	98	106	81.5	69	53.5	91.5	78	81.5	85	82	80	77	99
(21±1) n-C$_3$H$_7$	98	106	81.5	69	53.5	91.5	78	81.5	85	82	80	77	99
(17.5±1) i-C$_3$H$_7$	94.5	105	81	68	53	92	(77)[c]	82	84	80	77.5	73	96.5
(6.7±1) t-Bu	91	—	78.5	63	49.5	90.5	(77)	79.5	80	77	73	67.5	93
(80±2) C$_6$H$_5$	112	125	—	80	65	112	100	101.5	102	98	96.5	93	118
(45±1) C$_6$H$_5$CH$_2$	85	—	—	—	40	77	—	70	72	69	67.5	64	78.5
(40.5±1) allyl	87.5	118	82.5	—	43.5	80	(95)	(68)	74.5	71.5	69.5	65.5	79.5
(−5) CH$_3$CO	86.5	—	—	—	51.6	108	—	97	81	78	80	—	97
(−5±1) CH$_3$CH$_2$O	103	—	—	—	—	44	—	(44)	81	81	82	81	101
(−1.5) CH$_3$CH$_2$O$_2$	90	—	—	—	—	(28)	—	(22)	72	72	(71)	(69)	93
(67.5±2) CH$_2$=CH	108	—	89	—	—	—	—	93	97	94	92	89	113

[a] All values are in kcal/mole.

[b] Values in parentheses near radicals and atom are ΔH_f.

[c] Values in parentheses are estimates by the author.

215

Index